Washington, D.C.

at its best

More praise for Robert S. Kane . . .

"The strength of Kane's books lies in their personal flavor and zestful writing style. He doesn't shy away from expressing opinion, is strong on culture, art, and history, along with dining and shopping."

—Jack Schnedler, *Chicago Sun-Times*

"Kane's books take the reader beyond the expected. His works are carefully researched, succinctly presented and opinionated."

—Jane Abrams, *New York Daily News*

"Kane is a man of perception and taste, with a knowledge of art, architecture and history. He doesn't spare the occasional sharp evaluation if something is less than the highest quality."

—Lois Fegan, *Jersey Journal*

"Anyone going should take one of Bob Kane's books."

—Paul Jackson, *New York Post*

"Kane's candor, conciseness and credibility have made his books among the top selling in the travel field—a must for travelers."

—Joel Sleed, *Newhouse News Service*

"Kane does not mince words. His choices, ranked according to price, service, location and ambience, are selective; he provides opinions."

—Ralph Gardner, *San Antonio Express-News*

"Kane wanders the globe, testing pillows, mattresses and, in some cases, abominable food in order to be a faithful guide, writing his own observations, and leaving nothing to ghost writers or a band of behind-the-scenes reporters; Kane's unafraid to recommend some places and condemn others."

—Maria Lisella, *The Travel Agent*

Robert S. Kane

Washington, D.C.
at its best

PASSPORT BOOKS
a division of *NTC Publishing Group*
Lincolnwood, Illinois USA

BY ROBERT S. KANE

The World at Its Best Travel Series
BRITAIN AT ITS BEST
FRANCE AT ITS BEST
GERMANY AT ITS BEST
HAWAII AT ITS BEST
HOLLAND AT ITS BEST
ITALY AT ITS BEST
LONDON AT ITS BEST
NEW YORK AT ITS BEST
PARIS AT ITS BEST
SPAIN AT ITS BEST
SWITZERLAND AT ITS BEST
WASHINGTON, D.C. AT ITS BEST

A to Z World Travel Guides
GRAND TOUR A TO Z: THE CAPITALS OF EUROPE
EASTERN EUROPE A TO Z
SOUTH PACIFIC A TO Z
CANADA A TO Z
ASIA A TO Z
SOUTH AMERICA A TO Z
AFRICA A TO Z

Published by Passport Books, a division of NTC Publishing Group.
4255 West Touhy Avenue
Lincolnwood (Chicago), Illinois 60646-1975 U.S.A.
© 1991 by Robert S. Kane. All rights reserved. No part of this book may be reproduced, stored in a retrieval system, or transmitted in any form or by any means, electronic, mechanical, photocopying, or otherwise, without the prior written permission of NTC Publishing Group.
Manufactured in the United States of America.
Library of Congress Catalog Card Number: 90-63158

1 2 3 4 5 6 7 8 9 ML 9 8 7 6 5 4 3 2 1

For Edward O. Douglas

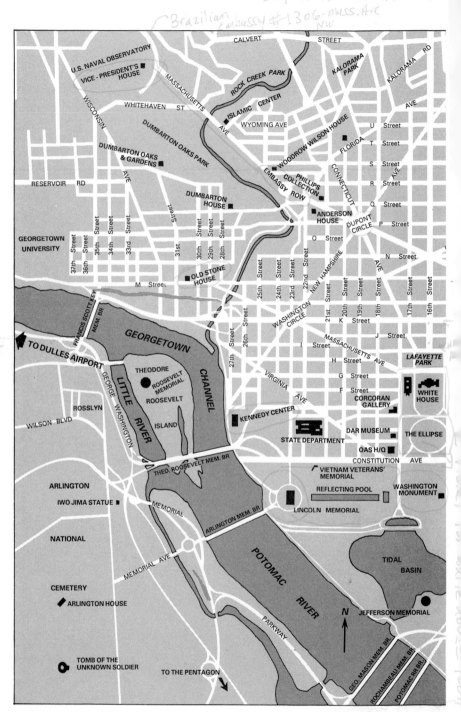

Dupont Cr = Downtown
Brazilian Embassy #1306 - Mass. Ave NW

Washington, D.C.

HOWARD
UNIVERSITY

W Street
V Street
U Street
T Street
S Street
R Street
Q Street
P Street
O Street
N Street
M Street
L Street
K Street

VERMONT AVE

FLORIDA AVE

RHODE ISLAND
LOGAN CIRCLE

THOMAS CIRCLE

NEW JERSEY AVE

NEW YORK AVE

15th Street
14th Street
13th Street
12th Street
11th Street
10th Street
9th Street
8th Street
7th Street

NORTH CAPITOL ST
1st Street

CONVENTION CENTER

MASSACHUSETTS AVE

I Street
H Street
G Street
F Street
E Street
D Street

CHINATOWN

6th Street
5th Street
4th Street
3rd Street
2nd Street

GOVERNMENT PRINTING OFFICE

UNION STATION

NATIONAL PORTRAIT GALLERY &
MUSEUM of AMERICAN ART

FORD'S THEATER /
LINCOLN MUSEUM

VISITOR INFO.
CENTER

FBI

POST OFFICE DEPT.

PENNSYLVANIA AVE

LOUISIANA AVE

SENATE OFFICE BUILDINGS

MARYLAND AVE

MUSEUM of
AFRICAN ART

AQUARIUM

NATIONAL GALLERY OF ART

CAPITOL

SUPREME COURT

MUSEUM OF
AMERICAN HISTORY

NATURAL HISTORY
MUSEUM

EAST CAPITOL ST

SMITHSONIAN

AIR & SPACE MUSEUM

FOLGER SHAKESPEARE
LIBRARY

FREER GALLERY

DEPT. OF AGRICULTURE

ARTS & INDUSTRIES BLDG.

HIRSHHORN MUSEUM

INDEPENDENCE AVE

VOICE OF
AMERICA

LIBRARY OF
CONGRESS

TO RFK STADIUM

SEWARD SQUARE

HOUSE OFFICE BUILDINGS

BUREAU OF
ENGRAVING
& PRINTING

L'ENFANT PLAZA

FOOD & DRUG
ADMIN.

CAROLINA AVE

EASTERN MARKET

NORTH CAROLINA AVE

SOUTH CAPITOL ST

GARFIELD PARK

SOUTH CAROLINA AVE

WASHINGTON CHANNEL

DELAWARE AVE

POTOMAC AVE

WASHINGTON NAVY YARD

Contents

Foreword

America's Capital Enters Its Third Century

When you consider that the United States turned 200 as long ago as 1976, it should come as no surprise that the national capital began its third century in 1990. Still, Washington's relatively advanced age—it was created as a compromise when Northerners led by Alexander Hamilton and Southerners under Thomas Jefferson agreed on its Potomac River situation at midpoint along the Atlantic Seaboard—can come as a surprise to the first-timer intent on exploring it.

What I attempt in these pages—as in the dozen companion volumes of my *World at Its Best* series—is to delineate its distinguishing characteristics. Believe me, I have learned, in the course of considerable D.C. and other wanderings, that this city is neither London (dating to the Romans who named it *Londinium*) nor Paris (conquered by Caesar and called after the *Parisii*, a resident tribal group), nor has it any semblance to other global capitals.

Not a few Americans get hooked on the seat of their government on a first visit—often with a high-school class group—and make return trips at the least provocation. Combined with visitors from abroad (an increasingly substantial group, given constantly expanding transatlantic air routes), Washington welcomes 20 million visitors each year. And we're spenders: tourism, a major industry after the business of operating the U.S. government, generates revenues of more than $2.5 billion per year in this sixteenth-largest of U.S. cities, the core of the ninth largest of American metropolitan areas.

The trick, in the case of absorbing Washington, is to go beyond the broad stretch of green—the Mall, surrounded by museums, with the dome of the Capitol to its east and the pinnacle-like Washington Monument to its west—and to take in the rest of what turns out to be a fabulous, too-often-underexplored city.

As in the other books of this series, I lead off *Washington at Its Best* with absolute requisites. These include not only the White House and the home of the first president—nearby Mount Vernon in Virginia—but the Capitol, the neighboring Supreme Court, National Gallery of Art, but also National Portrait Gallery and National Museum of American Art (between them sharing an impressively colonnaded nineteenth-century building), memorable memorials like the Lincoln and Vietnam Veterans, the unique-on-the-planet Air and Space Museum, and the National Museum of American History, wherein the Smithsonian Institution, its operator, allows itself a rarely encountered light touch.

You go on then—perhaps in the course of succeeding visits— to more than a score of museums from, say, D.A.R. through Navy and Marine. You watch paper money being manufactured at the Bureau of Engraving and Printing; stroll past facades of Embassy Row; have a look at originals of the Declaration of Independence and the Constitution of the United States in the National Archives; become acquainted with the three-building Library of Congress (the world's largest); tour the antique-furnished Diplomatic Reception Rooms at the State Department, as well as the refurbished Treasury and Old Executive Office Building; say hello to the pair of pandas at the zoo; observe piranhas at lunch in the National Aquarium; look over historic houses not only of Washington (including Woodrow Wilson's and the Octagon—which was, for a while, Madison's White House) but of Old Town Alexandria in Virginia; and have a good time in the evening at a play or musical or performances of the Washington Opera and National Symphony at the Kennedy Center.

Rest assured that you will be very comfortable in what originally was called the Federal City. In pages following, I evaluate half-a-hundred-plus hotels (not only some of the world's most celebrated in the Luxury Group, but First Class and Moderate hostelries, as well) and more than a hundred restaurants—again Luxury, First Class, and Moderate—embracing a score-plus categories, with emphasis on the most popular types: American, French, and Italian. The city's penchant for natural beauty is not overlooked from, say, the serene U.S. Botanic Garden at the foot of the Capitol steps to the nature trails of Theodore Roosevelt Island. Allow time for shopping: I evaluate not only in-town department stores and shopping areas, but modern malls in the Virginia and Maryland suburbs easily accessible on the Metro, Washington's modern, air-conditioned subway.

Withal, this city that Americans, once arrived, consider their second home (we appreciate that our tax dollars built and continue to operate much of it), is no less trend-prone than other cities. There is an obsession (not, of course, without foundation) about security, and guards can be arrogant. Chiefs of staff have become a status symbol. (Of course, the president has one—but so does his wife.) And once you leave familiar landmarks like the Washington Monument and the Capitol, geography in this uniformly low-slung city can confuse. Still, with two governments in charge—70-percent-black Washington has for some time had black mayors and black-dominated city councils, but Congress controls D.C. purse strings—the capital city of the United States remains one of the most beautiful in America. In this last decade of the twentieth century, it has become world-class.

ROBERT S. KANE

1

Washington to Note

ADDRESSES: *Washington Convention and Visitors Association* operates an excellent *Visitor Information Center*, knowledgeably and
courteously staffed, housing gratis maps and other giveaway
material, heart of town, at 1455 Pennsylvania Avenue NW, a hop
and a skip from the White House, in the Willard Collection shops
cluster adjacent to the Willard Inter-Continental Hotel. Traditionally it's open Monday through Saturday, 9 A.M. to 5 P.M.,
closed Sunday and Monday and major holidays. (The association's executive offices are at 1212 New York Avenue NW.)
Visitors speaking foreign languages will find the *International
Visitors Information Service* (733 15th Street NW) helpful. And the
National Park Service, which operates many of the places you'll visit
in Washington, maintains information booths at the park known
as the Ellipse, just south of the White House, between it and the
Washington Monument, and near the Vietnam Veterans Memorial (see "The Essential Washington," chapter 2).

AIRLINES AND AMTRAK: Easily a score of airlines, domestic
and international, link the Washington area's airports with the
world—*Air Canada* and *Air France, Air Jamaica* and *American Airlines, British Airways* and *Japan Airlines, Lufthansa* and *United*—to
give you an idea. There are three airports. Closest to town (three
and a half miles south in adjacent Arlington, Virginia) is *Washington National Airport*, which is for domestic flights exclusively,

including shuttle air service linking Washington and New York. It's a reasonably priced, quarter-hour taxi ride from central hotels, and if you've little or no baggage, consider taking the subway to or from National Airport Metro Station. *Dulles International Airport* is farther—26 miles, a half-hour drive—near Chantilly, Virginia, to the west. And *Baltimore–Washington International Airport* (called BWI locally) is the most distant of the trio, just over 30 miles to the northeast. Buses, limos, and of course taxis link the airports with the city. *Amtrak,* America's coast-to-coast rail system, serves Washington's Union Station. (I write about the station's superb restoration on later pages of this chapter, about its restaurants in chapter 5, and about its shops in chapter 6.) Amtrak trains travel north, south, and west, as part of its service to more than 500 destinations on some 24,000 miles of track, Colorado Rockies through New England villages, midtown Manhattan through Wyoming national parks, state of Washington to southern California. Foreign visitors touring the U.S., often accustomed to rail travel in their home countries, are avid Amtrak fans; so, increasingly, are Americans. Choose moderately tabbed coach service (trains invariably are café- or restaurant-equipped) or first class, which includes wide-seat club cars with complimentary drinks and meals, sleeping accommodations in deluxe bedrooms (which include private lavatory, toilet, and shower—for two), family bedrooms for as many as two adults and two kids, and one- and two-person roomettes. Many Amtrak trains retain romantic names—Southwest Chief and St. Louis Mule, California Zephyr and Empire State Express, Lake Shore Limited and City of New Orleans, Père Marquette and Metroliner. This last-mentioned is a premium-fare, all-seats-reserved, extra speedy service that links Washington with New York and Boston, offering both coach and first-class service.

ALCOHOL: Open hours, with respect to bars, are extremely liberal, prelunch through wee-hours closings, and if you're staying at a First Class or Luxury hotel, drinks may be ordered from room service, which operates round the clock in top hostelries. Spirits are sold by the bottle only in licensed liquor stores, but beer as well as wine are available in supermarkets and groceries.

BEGGARS have become a feature of Downtown—and other business areas—of Washington as in other big American cities. Social workers, psychologists, and other experts advise ignoring beggars rather than encouraging multiplication of their numbers by giving to them. Contribute instead to social service organizations whose function is to work with the homeless.

BUREAUCRACY: If Washington did not invent the term, it has perfected the practice. There are close to 300,000 in the federal government's Washington work force. Besides officialdom—president and vice president, 18 execs of cabinet rank, an additional score of major-agency directors, 435 members of the House of Representatives, an even hundred senators, and, as well, ambassadors of some 140 countries (to whose gala receptions not a few host-country bureaucrats vie avidly for invitations)—there are, too, Hugh Sidney has pointed out in *Time,* 55,000 lawyers, 700 lobbyists (you see the plush headquarters of organizations they represent—often in stylishly refurbished mansions and townhouses—dotted about town), 20,000 congressional staff members, and, to chronicle the daily goings-on of this motley mass, some 10,000 journalists.

The term "Chief of Staff," not heard, to my recollection, out of the armed services until General Dwight Eisenhower became president and borrowed the term for his No. 1 assistant—is now coin of the realm. Everybody who is anybody has a chief of staff, and for that matter a deputy chief of staff. That includes cabinet members, the vice president, and the president's wife.

Perks might well be the name of the bureaucrats' game. It started with the official residence of the president—to the government's great credit, open to the public five mornings of every week—and in more recent years has expanded to exclusive restaurants: the White House Mess for top brass and their guests, as well as Senate and House members' restaurants. Add congressional fitness centers; an official house (a one-time commandant's residence at the U.S. Naval Observatory in northwest Washington) and offices in the White House, Old Executive Office Building, and Capitol for the vice president; an entire floor of antique-filled rooms (open to visitors, chapter 2) where the secretary of state entertains; reception room for the secretary of the treasury's ranking visitors (also open to the public, chapter 2); official cars (with chauffeurs for higher-ups); and oft-arrogant guards (see "Security," below) at sensitive entrances, and chains of command on organization charts that, with "lieutenant commander" substituted for "deputy assistant secretary," could be in the military; even clerical people—secretaries and the like—are part of rigid pecking orders. And, given the strength of the Civil Service and enormous quantities of employees, efficiency is not always easily come by.

(It took five weeks, spurred by a phone call from me at the end of that period, to a secretary to the secretary of the treasury, before I received a reply from an underling to a letter I had written the treasury secretary, about the intimidation I experienced at the hands of security guards en route to a scheduled appointment at Treasury. And it took two months-plus—with phone calls midpoint to half a dozen members of his Washington and New York staffs—until one of my two senators, Daniel Moynihan—for whom I had voted term after term but never before disturbed—replied to a letter about my being treated like a thug by a rude guard because I was taking notes—on the appearance of the Senate Chamber, for the pages of this book—while in the Senate visitors' gallery. Against Senate rules—I was ultimately told—dating to the last century when lobbyists scribbling in the balcony disturbed senators on the floor.)

Visitors from large-population states, if my experience is typical, fare better with their representatives than with their senators—mine, Bill Green, for example, represents the 15th—one of 34 congressional districts in New York state, with many fewer constituents than each of the two New York senators.

BUSES: D.C. buses—Metrobus is the term—are aligned with the Metrorail, or subway, system (below); free transfers are available between one system and the other. Bus routes are many, indeed: Phone Metro information (202) 687-7000 for details and bus stop locations, bearing in mind that if you're a short-term visitor, the subway—though it doesn't go to nearly as many points—is easier to master.

THE BUSINESS TRAVELER: Like leading hotels in other major cities, Washington's Luxury hotels (and some First Class hotels, as well) cater to the business traveler, with business centers (including fax, computers, and secretarial and messenger services), two-line phones (usually several) with hold capability in rooms, spaces for meetings and group meals, and, increasingly, top-of-the-line fitness centers with elaborate exercise equipment and lap pools. Inquire when booking.

CABINET: Government departments headed by cabinet members increased by one (Veterans Affairs) during the Reagan presidency, with the total now 14 (Energy, Transportation, Housing, and Urban Development are relatively recent, too), to wit, alphabetically, with principal addresses: *Agriculture* (Independence Avenue between 12th and 14th streets SW); *Commerce* (14th Street between E Street and Constitution Avenue NW); *Defense,* with the secretary of defense boss of the secretaries of air force, army, and navy at the Pentagon in Arlington, Virginia (the site also of offices of the joint chiefs of staff, including the chairman and military heads of the air force, army, marines, and navy), open to visitors on tours (chapter 2); *Education* (400 Maryland Avenue SW); *Energy* (1000 Independence Avenue SW); *Health and Human Services* (200 Independence Avenue SW); *Housing and Urban Development* (451 7th Street SW); *Interior* (18th and C streets NW), with its museum open to visitors (chapter 2); *Justice* (Constitution Avenue between 9th and 10th streets NW), with a division at another address, the FBI, open to the public on tours (chapter 2); *Labor* (200 Constitution Avenue NW); *State* (2201 C Street NW); *Transportation* (400 7th Street SW); *Treasury* (Pennsylvania Avenue at 15th Street NW), open to the public on tours (chapter 2); and *Veterans Affairs* (810 Vermont Avenue NW). Also with cabinet rank are the *U.S. representative to the United Nations* (based at the U.S. Mission to the UN, opposite UN headquarters in New York, with the representative's official residence a suite in the Waldorf-Astoria Towers), the heads of the *Office of Management and Budget* and the *National Security Council* and the *U.S. Trade Representative.*

CALENDAR OF EVENTS: Washington is, to understate, busy; no city its size anywhere in America is as event-packed. Each year brings special celebrations and observances peculiar to that year. But what follows is a sampling of major annual activities:

January—Martin Luther King's Birthday, usually a theater event; Washington Antiques Show, Omni Shoreham Hotel; Chinese New Year's Parade, Chinatown. *February*—Black History Month—museum exhibits, cultural programs; Lincoln's Birthday—wreath-laying and reading of the Gettysburg Address, Lincoln Memorial; Washington's Birthday parade; Washington Boat Show, Washington Convention Center. *March*—St. Patrick's Day parades in Washington and Alexandria's Old Town; U.S. Army Band Anniversary Concert, Kennedy Center; Flower Show—through April, U.S. Botanic Garden; Ringling Brothers and Barnum & Bailey Circus, D.C. Armory, into April. *April*—National Cherry Blossom Festival; Washington International Film Festival, into May; White House Easter Egg Roll; Georgetown Gardens Tours; Old Town Tour; and, on different dates with different sponsorship, Georgetown houses tour. *May*—Goodwill Embassies Tour, an opportunity to see interiors of a number of embassies; Memorial Day Weekend Concert by the National Symphony, U.S. Capitol; Memorial Day wreath-laying ceremony, Vietnam Veterans Memorial and also at Tomb of the Unknown Soldier, Arlington, Virginia. *June*—Smithsonian Institution-sponsored Festival of American Folklife, on the Mall, into July—see chapter 3. *July*—Independence Day parade, day-long entertainment at Sylvan Theater on Washington Monument grounds; evening National Symphony Orchestra concert, U.S. Capitol; fireworks over Washington Monument. *August*—Arlington County Fair, Thomas Jefferson Center, Arlington, Virginia; D.C. Blues Festival, Anacostia Park. *September*—Adams-Morgan Day, ethnic entertainment, music, foods, arts, crafts; Old Town Alexandria historic houses tour; *October*—U.S. Navy Birthday Concert, Constitution Hall; Capital City Jazz Festival; Washington International Horse Show—a week long, at Capital Center, Largo, Maryland. *November*—Marine Corps Marathon, starting at Iwo Jima Marine Corps Memorial, Arlington, Virginia; Veterans' Day ceremony at Memorial Amphitheater, Arlington National Cemetery, with wreath-laying (by the president or other high-ranking official) at the Tomb of the Unknown Soldier, Arlington. *December*—Trees of Christmas exhibition,

National Museum of American History, mid-December through early January; People's Christmas Tree Lighting, with military bands in joint concert, U.S. Capitol; National Christmas Tree Lighting with a giant tree traditionally lit by the president on opening night, mid-December through January 1; Poinsettia Show, U.S. Botanic Garden, mid-December–January; "A Christmas Carol," the Charles Dickens play, second half of December, Ford's Theatre; White House Christmas Candlelight Tours of the Executive Mansion's Christmas decorations, two evenings in late December, traditionally starting at 6 P.M.; New Year's Eve at the Old Post Office Building, with the Postal Service's giant "Love"-theme stamp lowered in the atrium at midnight to ring in the New Year.

CLIMATE: You're in a four-season temperate-zone city, whose relatively southern situation means frequently high summer humidity (along with correspondingly steep summer temperatures), but with winters warmer than in the north, albeit with occasional snow; oft-lovely autumns and springs. Indeed, spring is the season (usually beginning of April, if not earlier) for cherry blossoms on the Tidal Basin, but April and May are the rainiest months. Average temperatures (Fahrenheit, the way we still gauge temperatures in the United States, comes first, followed by Celsius, the system employed by most of the rest of the planet):

	°F	°C		°F	°C
January	35	3	July	76	26
February	36	3	August	75	25
March	44	7	September	70	21
April	54	13	October	58	15
May	64	19	November	46	9
June	73	23	December	37	3

CLOTHES: On a business trip, regardless of season, gents will want a jacket and tie day and evening on weekdays; more casual duds for weekends; and business women will be correspondingly well dressed. Late spring through September, when it can be very warm and, as I indicate above, very humid, especially June through August, pleasure (as distinguished from business) visitors are comfortable when lightly dressed—walking shorts and (preferably) sport shirts rather than tank tops or tees for men; any kind of shorts and tops for kids; shorts as well for women. That said, let me make clear that for a good-category restaurant—even in summer—men want trousers, leather footwear (and in some instances jackets, if not ties); women, skirts or slacks even at midday, and most certainly for dinner. Casual eateries welcome casual clothes in Washington as everywhere; ditto al fresco summer concerts, although it's still considered good form—and in my view, good taste—to consider attendance at performing arts centers, theaters, and concert halls, especially in the non-summer months, as festive occasions, and dress accordingly. Take swimsuits in summer; many hotels have pools. Take umbrellas for use at any time of the year; raincoats for early spring and late autumn; heavier clothing, as well as gloves and scarves, for winter.

CONGRESS: We read about in the press, and watch on TV, disproportionately more about female, black, and Hispanic members of Congress than is actually the case. The Congress of the United States, make no mistake, is dominantly white male. All told, in this last decade of the twentieth century, that meant under 30 females, two dozen blacks, and about half that many Hispanics out of 435 members in the House of Representatives, whose size is based on each state's population, and includes a quartet of delegates from the District of Columbia, Guam, the American Virgin Islands, and American Samoa, with representation also from Puerto Rico in the person of a resident commissioner. This group of five may not vote at sessions of the House proper, but they do vote at meetings of House committees on which they serve. And only 2 of the 100 white senators (a pair from each state) are women, at the time of writing. I suggest, in chapter 2, that you watch a session of the House and of the Senate from their visitors' galleries, picking up gratis tickets from representatives' and/or senators' offices or by writing in advance—preferably to your representative; your two senators represent an entire state and are not so apt to be cordial, prompt, or efficient if my experience with Daniel Moynihan's office (see "Bureaucracy," above) is at all typical. Request tickets for visitors' galleries of *both* houses (each is valid for an entire months-long session of each house) and also, if you like, a ticket (each member of Congress receives a limited number each month) for so-called VIP tours of the White House, as distinct from the regular public tours. (See "The White House," the first entry in "The Essential Washington,"chapter 2.) This letter to your representative for tickets should be sent to him or her, by name, c/o House of Representatives, Washington, DC 20515. And hope that you'll be able to shake hands and have a chat with your representative when you fetch your tickets. Check *The Washington Post* for each day's congressional committee meeting schedules; these can be considerably more absorbing than sessions of Senate or House, especially when there are but a handful of members present. You're welcome to sit in as a spectator at many committee meetings; they're often very important. Bear in mind that it's only the legislation first approved in committee that goes to the floors of Congress for yea or nay decisions.

CONVENTION CENTER: Washington Convention Center (H Street through to New York Avenue, between 9th and 11th streets NW) is not going to win a beauty contest, but it's big (cost was $100 million), quite modern (it opened in 1982), and central, in the heart of Downtown, surrounded by a number of leading hotels, all with restaurants (chapters 4 and 5). The convention center lures about twenty-five major meetings annually and, each year, Washington also hosts approximately a thousand smaller conferences.

CREDIT CARDS: Top ones—*American Express, MasterCard, Visa,* and (to a lesser extent than in Europe, especially) *Diners Club*— are accepted in hotels, department stores, and virtually all better shops and restaurants, as well as by airlines and Amtrak (above), the long-distance railroad.

CURRENCY EXCHANGES: Foreign visitors entering the United States via any of the three area airports (see "Airlines and

Amtrak," above) will find currency exchange counters, to obtain dollars upon entry and dispose of them upon departure. Additionally, a number of Washington banks have currency-exchange departments (but not at all of their branches); these include *American Security Bank, First American Bank, National Bank of Washington, Crestar Bank,* and *Riggs National Bank.* Note, too, that *Deak International,* a currency exchange firm, has offices at 1800 K Street NW, and in the Georgetown Park shopping mall at 3222 M Street NW.

ELECTRIC CURRENT: 110 volts; if you're bringing appliances like hair dryers or shavers from abroad, you'll no doubt need converters to use them in Washington hotels, many of which, incidentally, provide hair dryers in their bathrooms (or on loan from reception counters).

EMBASSIES are the subject of a section in chapter 2; at this point, let me indicate that this capital has more than any other, and is in a select group, including Beijing, London, Moscow, Paris, Rome, and Tokyo. The envoy with the longest continuous tenure in Washington is accorded the honor of being identified as dean of the diplomatic corps. The dean represents his or her 139 fellow ambassadors when questions of privilege or immunity arise. At ceremonial events, he or she is officially first among diplomats present and is invariably invited to all major receptions and to official White House welcomes for visiting heads of state. Because of Washington's importance as the seat of a major power, the diplomatic corps is significant. To become ambassador to the United States is an honor of no little consequence; and because Washington's prime enterprise is government (unlike many capitals, where commerce, industry, and other endeavors may be dominant), diplomats—their names, their embassies, their politics, their dinners—often constitute news of consequence.

FLAG OF THE DISTRICT: If you suspect that the flag you see flying all around town, in conjunction with the Stars and Stripes, is the District of Columbia flag, well, you're right. It's good-looking and it stands out: two red stripes alternating with three white stripes and—atop the stripes—three red stars.

GEOGRAPHY IN A NUTSHELL: Carved originally from parts of bordering Maryland and Virginia (the latter area, constituting Alexandria [see "Old Town Alexandria," chapter 2] went back to Virginia in 1846), Washington borders the Potomac River (at its confluence with the Anacostia River) on its south and west, embraces 69 square miles, and, since it absorbed the older Georgetown in 1878, became coextensive with the District of Columbia. In other words, when you say D.C. you mean Washington, and vice versa.

Frenchman Pierre L'Enfant's design of the city is a distinctive mix of horizontal east-west streets named for letters of the alphabet, and numbered north-south streets, cut through diagonally by avenues called after American states, themselves punctuated by circles, with the entire municipal area divided into four sections or quadrants—designated NW, NE, SW, and SE, whose focal point is not the center of town, but rather, to confuse matters, the southeastern part of the city, near the U.S. Capitol (Capitol Street and the Mall are the dividing lines). There are, therefore, addresses with "NW" appended to them even when you would expect they would be "SE." Always notice—and use in writing, as well as when giving directions to cabbies—the directional designations of each thoroughfare, because many are in more than one quadrant. Although its population is but approximately 630,000 (15 U.S. cities have larger populations), this is a *very* spread-out city, bigger than many visitors expect. Bear in mind that the Metro, or subway (detailed on a later page), is an excellent and inexpensive means of transport. Before setting off, see "Lay of the Land," chapter 2.

HISTORY CAPSULIZED: Washington is a city whose formative and modern eras are in many respects more absorbing than its oft-difficult middle period. The manner in which its site was selected—a remarkably successful compromise—and its name determined manifest the logic of the nation's early leaders. As the eighteenth century reached its final decade, it was time to choose a permanent seat for the federal government, but even then, when the United States comprised but a baker's dozen sparsely populated, underdeveloped Atlantic Seaboard states, there was North–South rivalry. A settlement came when Thomas Jefferson and his supporters agreed to go along with a proposal of Alexander Hamilton for federal assumption of state debts in exchange for accepting a site for the capital along the Potomac River, a point midway, geographically, between north and south. And coincidentally only a little more than a dozen miles from the Virginia home of the first president (see Mount Vernon, chapter 2), who himself selected the precise location of the Federal City, as it was then called. A trio of commissioners created to spur actual development of the capital named it in the first president's honor. But it was George Washington himself who hired the French architect-engineer Pierre L'Enfant (alas, later fired and fated to die a poor man) to design the city, at the same time ordering Andrew Ellicott and his assistant, Benjamin Banneker (who remains oddly unheralded, although he was obviously the first black man to hold a position of importance in the nation's early years), to survey the city's original 100-mile area—larger then than today. As I indicate in "The Essential Washington" (chapter 2), the White House and Capitol were the first official buildings to rise. Jefferson was the first president to be inaugurated at the Capitol (to which Congress had moved in 1800 from Philadelphia), and John Adams the first president to inhabit the White House. Both of those buildings, and much else of the early city, were rebuilt after a severe British burning in the course of the War of 1812. (President and Mrs. Madison took up residence in the Octagon—chapter 2—where Madison signed the Treaty of Ghent, ending the war.) Charles Dickens, unimpressed on a visit from England in 1842, described the nation's capital as comprising "spacious avenues that begin in nothing and lead nowhere; streets a mile long that only want houses and inhabitants; public buildings that need but a public to be complete."

L'Enfant's grand and gracious city was a long time in coming. A canal that ran from the Capitol past the White House to the Potomac attracted bugs to the swampy terrain flanking it. Streets were largely unpaved. Still, the 1850s saw parks—Lafayette, the Ellipse, the Mall—take shape. The city, termed "equatorial" by early foreign ambassadors—who collected "hardship" pay from their governments while accredited to Washington—began to develop. Civil War activity spurred a population increase, both black and white; horsecar lines provided public transportation; Lincoln insisted on completing the dome of the Capitol as a symbol of unity. ("If the people see the Capitol going on, it's a sign we intend the Union shall go on," were his words.)

The 1870s saw the unsanitary central canal filled in. Congress, while Grant was president, granted the District territorial status, with a presidentially appointed governor, city council, and boards of health and public works. Also in the 1870s, by which time sewers and sidewalks had been introduced, and more streets paved, the same Frederick Law Olmsted who created New York's Central Park designed a park—planted with species from throughout the Americas—surrounding the Capitol. And the Smithsonian Institution's first two buildings (both still in use) went up. Three and a half decades after it was begun, the Washington Monument was completed—in 1884. (Its first steam-driven elevator carried men—and men only—to the top in 20 minutes. The expedition was considered too dangerous for women and children—who climbed the 897 steps if they insisted on ascending—until the current elevator was installed; it makes the trip in 70 seconds.)

As the nineteenth century became the twentieth, Washington became a substantial city, with its middle class—whites in the still largely (but not entirely) white northwest quadrant and around Capitol Hill, blacks largely in the southeast, professional whites and blacks north of Logan Circle—setting racial residential patterns.

Impressive mansions—now constituting the core of Embassy Row—were built north of Dupont Circle. Important structures like the Treasury Building (first such built to house a government department), Patent Office (now housing a pair of art museums), Library of Congress, and the Corcoran Gallery of Art became landmarks, to be followed by early twentieth-century structures of consequence: Union Station, the Episcopalians' Washington Cathedral (completed as recently as 1990), the Smithsonian's Natural History Museum and Freer Gallery, and the memorable Lincoln Memorial.

Starting with FDR in the early 1930s, and continuing through Harry Truman post–World War II, Washington burgeoned. Roosevelt's myriad Depression-era government agencies attracted thousands of professionals and their families. The government departments of the Federal Triangle complex, heart of town, were completed, along with the Andrew Mellon–contributed National Gallery of Art, the gloriously domed Jefferson Memorial, and the sprawling Pentagon.

In 1961, President Kennedy appointed the District of Columbia's first black commissioner. In 1964, a Constitutional Amendment at long last gave D.C. residents the right to vote for president. An elected school board was created in 1968. In 1970, the first nonvoting delegate representing D.C. in the House of Representatives was elected, and in 1974, District voters gained the opportunity to elect a mayor and city council. Nevertheless, it must be emphasized that the federal government retains control over District purse strings; Congress approves the D.C. budget.

The 1970s also saw the opening of the John F. Kennedy Center for the Performing Arts, the Metro or subway system, and additions to the Smithsonian Institution's museums and to the National Gallery of Art. In the 1980s came new hotels with all-U.S. leaders among them, and increasingly sophisticated restaurants in quantity (chapters 4 and 5). Political progress has coincided with other improvements. Though it still is not the 51st state (and only if you live in D.C. do you realize what it's like to be surrounded by states with voting representatives in both houses of Congress, when you have none yourself), it is—as indeed it should be with a black population of approximately 70 percent—dominantly black-governed, having elected black mayors for some years and a black-dominated city council, with many black civil servants and—visitors soons observe—a substantial black middle class. Indeed, black presence in the nation's capital, especially in positions of importance—such as heading the District government (as mayor), dominating membership of the City Council, occupying Cabinet and other federal executive posts, not to mention heading firms like the phone company—is a significant feature of the capital, which, with Howard University, is the site of the nation's most important dominantly black institution of higher learning. Today's Washington is—to understate—quite different from that of less than seven decades back when, in 1925, the Ku Klux Klan paraded through the city, concluding with a ceremony at the Washington Monument.

HOSPITALS: Washington is well equipped with hospitals. The one visitors pass by most often is *George Washington University Hospital* (901 23rd Street NW), adjacent to the Foggy Bottom Metro Station. Also worth noting—among a number—are *Georgetown University Hospital* (3800 Reservoir Road NW), *Howard University Hospital* (2041 Georgia Avenue NW), and *Sibley Hospital* (5255 Loughboro Road NW).

METRO—the subway system—has changed the face of tourism in Washington since its first stations opened in 1976. Visitors familiar with subways in larger cities—Paris, London, and New York, for example—can criticize D.C.'s Metro on several justifiable counts: It doesn't go to nearly enough places (Georgetown, for example, upper Massachusetts Avenue, other northern sections of town); certain stations are poorly illuminated; signposting is inadequate (there are not enough signs identifying each station so that you know where you're arriving when the train pulls in, and they can be difficult to read); street-level pylons identifying stations are often placed some distance away from actual entrances, so you find yourself wondering precisely where to descend. Withal, pluses outweigh minuses. Trains are spotless, graffiti-free, air-conditioned, and comfortable; stations, below high and dramatic honeycombed arches, are spacious and attractive (although you wish, at times, for advertising placards and billboards to liven things up, and you become nostalgic for the ads that flank and brighten the London Underground's escalators, in contrast to the unembellished escalators in D.C.—which, incidentally, are among the highest such of any subway escalators in the world).

There are 97 stations punctuating 103 miles of track, divided into four lines—Red, Orange, Blue, and Yellow. All four lines pass through aptly named Metro Center station, core of Downtown, and again, all four lines terminate beyond the District, in either Maryland or Virginia, so that you can get all around the area on the subway. The Metro operates 5:30 A.M. to midnight weekdays, 8 A.M. to midnight Saturday, 10 A.M. to midnight Sunday, with varying holiday schedules. Trickiest part for last: You use *tickets only,* no coins, no tokens. Note that tickets are purchased not from human cashiers at booths but *only* from machines in each station. Note, too, that fares are based on distance traveled and, to further complicate the system, the time of day when you make your purchases; they're pricier during rush hours. Near the ticket-purchasing machinery at every station you'll find a list of fares, destination by destination. The machines change bills into coins for you, and if you don't deposit the exact amount, you'll receive change with your ticket. What I suggest is that if your stay in Washington will extend over several days or longer, you buy a ticket with a five-dollar bill (or two tickets with two fives), rather than a single-fare ticket, which necessitates your making purchases for each ride, often having to queue up at busy periods. You insert your ticket in a turnstile *twice,* first upon entering, and second upon exiting. It's when you depart that the automated machinery stamps the amount of fare you have expended, noting the balance remaining. If your trip cost, say, $1.10, after inserting the $5 ticket in a departure turnstile, it will note a balance of $3.90 worth of fare. Take another ride for, say, a dollar, and you'll have $2.90 remaining, and so on. Should you get down to an amount that is less than the minimum fare—a quarter, say—you won't lose that 25 cents *if* you deposit the ticket in a special "add-on" slot at the machines, adding whatever amount you like to your 25 cents; if it's $2, you then have $2.25 worth of Metro fare. Read the ticket-machine instructions carefully, watching experienced riders make their purchases until you get the hang of it. Which, I guarantee, will be after, say, your second ride. If not sooner.

NEWSPAPERS AND MAGAZINES: Of the two dailies, *The Washington Post*—one of a relative handful of America's top-ranking papers—is indicated, hands down. The free weekly, *City Paper* by name, is commendable, too; pick it up at Metro stations and certain stores. And three locally published magazines, *The Wash-*

ingtonian, The Washington Monthly, and *Regardie's,* are worth becoming acquainted with.

PERSONAL SECURITY AND SECURITY GUARDS: Take care as you move about. All Metro cars are in radio contact with the Metro Transit Police through its Operators Control Center, and each Metro kiosk booth (where station managers are quartered) has a phone. Metro travel is among the safest such in the U.S., but it's wise to conceal neck chains and rings (turning stones to the palm side of your hand), keep a firm grip on your handbag, and cluster with other passengers on the platform while awaiting your train, rather than standing alone. If you find yourself alone in a Metro car, move to a car with other passengers. If you're a man with a wallet, carry it in an inside coat or side trouser pocket—*not*—I repeat, not—in a rear trouser pocket. If your hotel is some distance from a Metro station, invest in evening taxis, traveling with companions after dark, if possible. Carry the bulk of your funds in travelers' checks, keeping with you only those credit cards you think you may actually use. *Security guards*—not easily fired in a bureaucracy as massive as Washington's—can be disagreeable and are all over the place; if you've a business appointment in a government building, you'll come across them. The nastiest, in my experience, are at the Department of the Treasury. Have your passport or a driver's license ready to show, and be cognizant of the room number and phone extension of the person with whom you have an appointment.

PHONE NUMBERS: Police/fire emergencies: 911. *How to get there: Metrorail* (subway) and *Metrobus:* (202) 637-7000; *Washington Convention and Visitors Association:* (202) 789-7000; *International Visitors Information Service,* for visitors speaking foreign languages: (202) 789-6540; *National Park Service, Washington Region:* (202) 357-2020; *Weather:* (202) 936-1212; *Main Post Office:* (202) 682-9595.

POST OFFICES: In the city with the headquarters of the much— and often justifiably—maligned and overpriced Postal Service, you are, let it be said, never far from a post office. Centrally situated POs include those at 819 14th Street NW, 1125 19th Street NW, 1215 31st Street NW, and 458 L'Enfant Plaza SW.

PRESIDENTS: Who preceded Coolidge? Who followed Truman? And when was Millard Fillmore—or Rutherford B. Hayes—in the White House? Washington is so associated with the presidents that I offer this rundown of the order in which they served and their terms of office, followed in parentheses by years of birth and, where appropriate, death:

1	*George Washington*	1789–1797	(1732–1799)
2	*John Adams*	1797–1801	(1735–1826)
3	*Thomas Jefferson*	1801–1809	(1743–1826)
4	*James Madison*	1809–1817	(1751–1836)
5	*James Monroe*	1817–1825	(1758–1831)
6	*John Quincy Adams*	1825–1829	(1767–1848)
7	*Andrew Jackson*	1829–1837	(1767–1845)
8	*Martin Van Buren*	1837–1841	(1782–1862)
9	*William Henry Harrison*	1841	(1773–1841)
10	*John Tyler*	1841–1845	(1790–1862)
11	*James K. Polk*	1845–1849	(1795–1849)
12	*Zachary Taylor*	1849–1850	(1784–1850)
13	*Millard Fillmore*	1850–1853	(1800–1874)
14	*Franklin Pierce*	1853–1857	(1804–1869)
15	*James Buchanan*	1857–1861	(1791–1868)
16	*Abraham Lincoln*	1861–1865	(1809–1865)
17	*Andrew Johnson*	1865–1869	(1808–1875)
18	*Ulysses S. Grant*	1869–1877	(1822–1885)
19	*Rutherford B. Hayes*	1877–1881	(1822–1893)
20	*James A. Garfield*	1881	(1831–1881)
21	*Chester A. Arthur*	1881–1885	(1830–1886)
22,24	*Grover Cleveland*	1885–1889 and 1893–1897	(1837–1908)
23	*Benjamin Harrison*	1889–1893	(1833–1901)
25	*William McKinley*	1897–1901	(1843–1901)
26	*Theodore Roosevelt*	1901–1909	(1858–1919)
27	*William Howard Taft*	1909–1913	(1857–1930)
28	*Woodrow Wilson*	1913–1921	(1856–1924)
29	*Warren G. Harding*	1921–1923	(1865–1923)
30	*Calvin Coolidge*	1923–1929	(1872–1933)
31	*Herbert Hoover*	1929–1933	(1874–1964)

32	Franklin D. Roosevelt	1933–1945	(1882–1945)
33	Harry Truman	1945–1953	(1884–1972)
34	Dwight D. Eisenhower	1953–1961	(1890–1969)
35	John F. Kennedy	1961–1963	(1917–1963)
36	Lyndon B. Johnson	1963–1969	(1908–1973)
37	Richard M. Nixon	1969–1974	(1913–)
38	Gerald R. Ford	1974–1977	(1913–)
39	Jimmy Carter	1977–1981	(1924–)
40	Ronald Reagan	1981–1989	(1911–)
41	George Bush	1989–	(1924–)

RESERVATIONS FROM OUT OF TOWN: Even if you live outside the Washington area, consider phoning long-distance well in advance, if you have specific dates, for reservations at better restaurants included among those in chapter 5 and theaters (chapter 3).

RESTROOMS: Downtown department stores, *Woodward & Lothrop* (11th and F Streets NW) and *Hechts* (12th and G streets NW) are convenient, in this respect, as are hotels throughout town. There are, of course, public restrooms in places you'll visit (excepting the White House, but including the Lincoln and Jefferson memorials and the Washington Monument). Standout restrooms include those of the *National Gallery of Art, Arthur M. Sackler Gallery, Hirshorn Museum and Sculpture Garden*, and *National Museum of African Art*—all on the Mall; *Library of Congress, United States Supreme Court*, and *Senate and House office buildings*—on Capitol Hill.

SALES TAXES: You'll pay 6 percent on purchases in stores, 9 percent in restaurants, and 11 percent in hotels in the District of Columbia, but less over the borders: 5 percent is the sales tax in Virginia, 4 percent in Maryland.

TAXIS: D.C. taxis are unusual in that they are not metered but charge for the number of specially delineated taxi zones you pass through in the course of your journey. There are eight zones and subzones. Note too—this is unusual, too—that the tab goes up for additional passengers. There's a fee tacked on for phoned cabs and waiting rates, but there's no extra charge for baggage, unless you're lugging a trunk. As with the Metro, you pay more at rush hours—between 4 and 6 P.M. Settle rates in advance for trips to Dulles and Baltimore-Washington International airports. Many drivers are from Africa, and drivers' dispositions, as in every city, vary tremendously. They can be charming or otherwise, but mostly they're nice. Note that drivers are allowed to take more than one party at a time, and are entitled to full fare from *each* party. (Virginia and Maryland cabs are metered.)

TIPPING: Bellmen in better hotels expect easily a buck a bag. Tip 15 percent in restaurants, 20 percent in fancier eateries if you're flush—and in either case base your tip on the amount of the bill *before* the whopping 9 percent tax has been added to it. Tip 10 percent to cordial cabbies and minimal amounts in attended public restrooms and to checkroom attendants.

2

Washington to See

LAY OF THE LAND

Don't let statistics—69 square miles, population still considerably under three-quarters of a million—fool you. Washington, which is, of course, coextensive with the District of Colombia (a.k.a. The District, or simply D.C.), is big. By that I mean spread out, geographically capacious, well deserving of its modern Metro, or subway, system (chapter 1). You do well to position yourself at a hotel near a Metro station (the majority of the hotels I evaluate in this book are near the Metro) and, important this, you should enjoy walking. This is a city made for strolls. But you can't walk everywhere. Settle for promenades in your part of town, using the Metro or other motorized transport for other areas.

Washington is divided into four sections, or quadrants: Northwest (most important for visitors, in many, but not all respects), Northeast (the area of the U.S. Capitol), Southeast, and Southwest. Because a street or avenue can have similarly numbered buildings in more than one of the quadrants, it's important to signify the quadrant in the case of every address (and, important this, in indicating your destination to taxi drivers: 1100 Pennsylvania Avenue NW). It's worth pondering, too, that the District's central point for quadrants is not all that central. It's considerably east, in the neighborhood of the Capitol, with North and South Capitol streets dividing East from West and the southerly Mall

separating North from South. My point is: Don't be surprised at
"NW" and "SW" addresses considerably farther east than you
might expect.
   The city is largely but not entirely grid-shaped. Streets running north and south are numbered, beginning at the center,
with First Street NW and SW west of the dividing line (North
and South Capitol streets) and First Street NE and SE—a completely separate detached thoroughfare—to the east of the dividing line.
   East–west streets are lettered, starting alphabetically from the
center; D Street NW and NE north of the Mall and unconnected
D Street SW and SE south of the Mall. (There are no J, S, X, Y, or
Z streets.) As you near the end of the alphabet—at W—lettered
streets take two-syllable names (Belmont, Chapin), again alphabetically, and, later, three-syllable names, until, in the nethermost
neighborhoods, streets become botanical, called after trees and
plants.
   Relatively simple, and well planned, you say. Indeed. But there
are two hindrances. First is the lack of easily identifiable landmarks, once you leave the Mall with the Capitol dome and the
Washington Monument at its extremities. Indeed, it's the Washington Monument that's to blame; no building is supposed to be
higher, so that as a consequence Washington is without the
skyscrapers of many cities, where distinctive contours double as
directional markers. Once you leave the Mall, White House, and
Capitol Hill, the occasional church steeple excepted, there's a
sameness to the center of the District that's not only aesthetically
monotonous, but keeps you on your toes checking street signs.
   Second handicap, with respect to municipal layout, is capsulized in three words: avenues and circles. The L'Enfant design
may have been a beauty in the eighteenth century, but in the late
twentieth, diagonal thoroughfares—named for American states
(Massachusetts Avenue, New Jersey Avenue)—converging on
arbitrarily situated circles (Logan Circle, Washington Circle) can
lead to utter geographical confusion for pedestrians as well
as motorists. And, rest assured, not only newcomers. Long-
resident Washingtonians themselves often admit to bewilder-
ment. Everybody gets lost, or at least goes astray, upon occasion.
   Heart of the city is *Downtown*, with Dupont Circle—where
Connecticut, New Hampshire, and Massachusetts avenues and P

and 19th streets NW converge—as its northern terminus, the
body of water called Rock Creek to its west, and 6th Street NW
(through which small but restaurant-dotted *Chinatown* passes) as
its eastern frontier. (Chinatown's sole monument is the immense
and vivid *Chinese Friendship Archway.*) A hop and skip distant, core
of Downtown, is the massive albeit architecturally undistinguished *Washington Convention Center* extending from H Street
NW to New York Avenue NW, between 9th and 13th streets NW.
What I term *Downtown North,* between H and N streets and 21st
and 17th streets NW, more or less encloses the city's biggest
concentration of upscale restaurants, many in its office buildings. The Convention Center and the Downtown area lying
between it and the Mall to the south are served by the principal
station of the subway system, *Metro Center,* through which all four
subway lines (Red, Blue, Yellow, Orange) pass. There are a
number of hotels south of the Convention Center as far as (and
including) *Pennsylvania Avenue* and to the center's north, Dupont
Circle and beyond. But Downtown's greatest monument is the
White House, with Pennsylvania Avenue at its front door, *Lafayette
Park* to its rear, the *Treasury,* oldest of the Cabinet buildings, next
door to its west, and the *Old Executive Office Building* next door to
its east. Pennsylvania and Constitution avenues delineate the
core of the oddly named *Federal Triangle,* in which are situated a
cluster of pre–World War II federal government departments,
including Commerce (with the National Aquarium) and FBI
headquarters as well as National Archives, District Building
(Washington's City Hall), and the nicely restored, turn-of-
century Old Post Office Building, a standout, thanks to its 315-
foot tower.

North of Downtown, the earlier-mentioned *Dupont Circle*
anchors a substantial number of hotels, with good restaurants
and buzzy cafés dotted about. The Circle is the southern terminus of *Embassy Row,* whose nucleus, Massachusetts Avenue
NW, is the site of glossy mansion after glossy mansion, mostly
embassies with bronze nameplates of the nations whose ambassadors represent them, and often with national flags. *Georgetown,*
an organized municipality that predates the District of Columbia
but is now a part of it, lies west of Downtown, on the far side of
Rock Creek, and is at once an area of quiet streets lined by

eighteenth- and nineteenth-century houses of no little charm and of a main thoroughfare—M Street NW on either side of its intersection with Wisconsin Avenue NW—one of the liveliest after-dark areas in the city.

Due south of Downtown is a great oblong of a green enclosed by northerly Independence and southerly Constitution avenues—the *Mall*. The towering *Washington Monument* edges its western flank, with the *U.S. Capitol* to its east. In between lie a clutch of estimable museums (below). Seats of Establishment (albeit nongovernmental) organizations like the *American Red Cross* and the *Daughters of the American Revolution* edge the Ellipse behind the Mall, on 17th Street NW, just south of the *Corcoran Gallery of Art*.

Newer Cabinet departments—*Health and Human Services, Housing and Urban Development, Transportation*—are south of the Mall. To its east is *Capitol Hill*, its centerpiece the great domed *Capitol*, whose architecture has been adapted by many statehouses coast to coast, with the several office buildings for members of the House of Representatives to its south, and for members of the Senate to its north. The *Supreme Court of the United States* and the three-building *Library of Congress* complex are just east of the Capitol while relatively recently—and brilliantly—restored *Union Station*—now a shopping mall and restaurant complex, as well as the Amtrak terminal—is some blocks north, with its main entrance on Massachusetts Avenue NE. Memorials honoring two presidents are south of the Mall—the *Lincoln Memorial* (Reflecting Pool at 23rd Street NW, with the *Vietnam Veterans Memorial* a near neighbor, just south of Constitution Avenue NW) and the *Jefferson Memorial*, edging the *Tidal Basin*, an offshoot of the Potomac, to the south and the *Japanese cherry trees*, a gift to America from Japan in 1912, celebrated for the brilliance of their spring (March and/or April) blossoms. Due northwest are the modern *State Department Building* (23rd and C streets NW) and the *John F. Kennedy Performing Arts Center* edging the *Potomac River*. The *Washington Navy Yard* (site of both Navy and Marine museums) straddles the shore of the Anacostia River, a tributary of the Potomac, in southeast D.C. Just across the Potomac are Arlington and Alexandria, two Virginia cities linked with Washington by subway, and both requisite visitor lures (below). *Mount*

Vernon, but 16 miles from the capital, is the Virginia mansion that was the home of the first presidential couple, Martha and George Washington.

THE ESSENTIAL WASHINGTON

The White House (1600 Pennsylvania Avenue NW—opposite Lafayette Park to the north, extending south to E Street NW [a.k.a. Pennsylvania Avenue South], which separates it from the park known as the Ellipse; with the visitors' entrance on East Executive Avenue, a north–south thoroughfare running between the White House and the Treasury): Visitors to Washington are fortunate, with respect to the ease with which it is possible to inspect the White House. President in and president out, the official residence of the head of state/head of government of the world's most important country is open 10 A.M. to noon Tuesday through Saturday, except in the case of a state event of especial magnitude.

In my experience, the White House is the only residence of a world figure located in a capital city with regular visitor hours. In Britain (see *London at Its Best*), Buckingham Palace is never open to the public; you must head out of town to Windsor Palace, which welcomes visitors only when the Royal Family is not in residence. Élysée Palace, home of France's president (see *Paris at Its Best*), is not open to the public either (indeed, in recent years, pedestrians are directed by police to cross Rue du Faubourg St.-Honoré when passing by, so as not to walk on the sidewalk directly in front of the palace's gate). Rome's Palazzo Quirinale, now home to presidents of Italy, once a royal and a papal palace, is off limits, too. The vast garden of Tokyo's Imperial Palace is open upon rare occasions, but not the interior—at least to the public. I don't believe the precise address of the Soviet president is generally known, not to mention premises being available for public inspection. You can, to be sure, visit royal palaces in Brussels, Madrid, Stockholm, and Monaco, but these are not situated in capitals with the stature of Washington. In the case of Brussels and Madrid, the big palaces are for ceremonial purposes only: the kings and queens in question actually live elsewhere. When you consider its intense use—as a residence and office of the president—I think it's pretty nice that anyone can have a look at the White House five days out of seven, and for free, at that.

Forty of the forty-one presidents and their families (all but the first—Washington) have lived in this extraordinarily beautiful, Palladian-influenced Georgian mansion, which is the oldest building in town; its cornerstone was laid in 1792, almost a year before that of the next oldest building, the U.S. Capitol (below). The multitalented second occupant of the house, Thomas Jefferson, did not win the competition for its design (he submitted an entry using a fictitious name). Rather, an Irish-born immigrant architect, James Hoban, came out the victor, receiving $500 and a gold medal for his plan, obviously based on Dublin's Leinster House, the handsome eighteenth-century building now serving as the Parliament of Ireland, albeit sans the porticos that make the White House facade so distinctive. The curved south portico was appended in 1824; that at the north entrance, with its classical pediment, dates to 1829. Considerably earlier, President Jefferson engaged British-born architect Benjamin Latrobe to design modifications and additions, both exterior and interior. In 1814, the White House was burned by the British in the War of 1812, with virtually nothing but its walls remaining. While President Madison lived in the historic house called the Octagon (below), architect Hoban supervised a rebuilding of the sandstone structure—which came to be called after the white paint with which it was surfaced.

Theodore Roosevelt was in office when the West Wing—now the site of the president's and his staff's offices—was built. The Truman rebuilding (1949–52) came about after experts revealed that the building was falling apart. Its interior was replaced with substantial constructed-to-last steel frames, the while old paneling, ceiling, and other decorations were removed and meticulously replaced.

Every house's tenants make changes. The White House, which had tenants in residence for as long as a dozen years (the Franklin Roosevelts) and many for eight years, has been no exception. Redecoration has been recurrent, if not necessarily felicitous. The period from, say, John Tyler through to the early years of this century saw an essentially Victorian-look White

House, appreciably more heavy-handed than the elegant Federal style of early occupants. Remnants of the Lincoln years remain, although you would not know today that President and Mrs. Arthur's decorator was Louis Comfort Tiffany, famed for his stained glass and other Art Nouveau designs. (The Arthurs had an entire wall of Tiffany glass in the Entrance Hall.)

It was during the relatively brief period that John Kennedy was president (1961–63) that the White House public rooms, as we see them today, were set on a course that returned them to early nineteenth-century brilliance. Sensibly taking advantage of an education that exposed her to architecture and interiors of earlier periods, the then Mrs. Kennedy exposed America to the glory of the presidential residence with a network TV tour of the White House, herself the guide. She formed a Fine Arts Committee for the White House, gathering art historians and interior designers to work with the committee and its curator. She appealed—with success that continued in succeeding administrations—for gifts of appropriate antique furniture and paintings, and, in the early 1970s under Pat Nixon's aegis, the White House was treated to major renovation. Rosalyn Carter sought out—with considerable success—paintings by leading American artists. Nancy Reagan spearheaded redecoration of the presidential family quarters. Every First Family has played a role in the look of the president's house, but it's to Jackie Kennedy Onassis that we owe its authenticity of style.

How much you see of this house on a tour depends on the type of tour you choose. Most of the one and a half million yearly visitors get in by means of a ticket obtained the day of their visit. During the warm-weather months, between Memorial Day and Labor Day, there's a special procedure. You go not to the White House for your ducat, but to a special office operated by the National Park Service's Office of White House Visitors at the edge of the Ellipse. Arrive before 9 A.M., to preclude a long wait, and you'll be handed a ticket—for use on the day of issue—indicating the time that you will leave with a group from the Ellipse's covered grandstands. Tours are numbered ("Tour 17" for instance), and departures from the Ellipse are approximately quarter-hourly, and begin as much as two hours after you apply for your ticket. You may spend the waiting time as you like, but you want to be back at the Ellipse in advance of the scheduled departure time, when a Park Service ranger leads you to the White House visitors' entrance. From that point you're off on a self-conducted tour, with a knowledgeable staffer in each room en route to explain its furnishings and historical significance. In winter, crowds are down, and you go directly to the White House's East Gate for a walk-through.

Alternatively, if you're planning your Washington trip some weeks or months in advance, and you live in the United States and have representatives in the Congress, write or phone one of your two U.S. senators or your representative to request so-called VIP passes from among the limited number each legislator is allotted monthly by the White House. (They bear signatures of the president and his wife, and make a nice souvenir.) These congressional passes (which may be requested as much as six months in advance) are useful in summer, eliminating the Ellipse part of the procedure. Whereas the Park Service Ellipse procedure may easily involve a couple of hours' wait, with the congressional pass you queue in advance of the time on the ticket. (I warn you, in summer it's *very* hot under the broiling sun, and waits are as long as an hour, at least in my experience, to pass through the gate.) VIP tours are different from general tours, inside as well as out. VIP visits are guided—you must go at the speed of the guide, which can be *very* rapid—while regular tours allow you to go as slowly or quickly as you like, pausing to look for as long as you choose at whatever seems of special interest, and being able to ask questions of the attendant on duty in each room, for which there's no time in the case of the fast-paced VIP visit (on which, however, you see two more rooms than do the general tourists—a total of eight).

Observe the White House's south facade and you note its oval-shaped center. Architect Hoban created three rooms in this space, one above the other. Lowest is the ground floor's Diplomatic Reception Room, with symbols of the 50 states on its specially woven rug; yellow-upholstered Hepplewhite chairs comprise its furnishings, but its principal interest is a wallpaper mural encircling the room with early-nineteenth-century scenes of America. Next door's China Room is dominated by a Howard Chandler Christy portrait of a lady in red—Mrs. Calvin Coolidge—and is chockablock with china services, the first assembled by Mrs. Woodrow Wilson, from a number of administrations, including the extravagant red-bordered service ordered by Nancy Reagan, which set Americans' tongues tut-tutting. The adjacent Vermeil Room's shelves drip vermeil—gold-over-silver decorated dinnerware that's employed on gala occasions.

Up you go then to the State, or main, floor. Each of the salons named after a color is special. The Green Room is American Federal—early-nineteenth-century pieces by New York's noted cabinetmaker, Duncan Phyfe. Not surprisingly, the watered silk walls are green, and there are a couple of original pieces—silver candlesticks from the Madison years and a John Adams coffeepot. The Red Room is indeed vivid—but successfully so, with furniture and walls covered in the same scarlet fabric, and superb Empire furniture, some of it American, some French. The Blue Room is the State floor's oval-shaped room, and where the president receives guests at receptions and dinners. Seven of its chairs remain from those purchased by President Monroe, and the room's name comes from the dominant hue of its mid-nineteenth-century Chinese rug and the upholstery of its chairs.

The East Room, which you've no doubt seen on TV (it's used for press conferences, but it is also where seven presidents have lain in state, John Kennedy among them, in 1963). Gold-color fabric drapes its windows; walls are ivory, chandeliers splendid, and four bronze candelabra are examples of President Monroe's sophisticated taste. In the other big space, the State Dining Room, a long mahogany dining table and Queen Anne chairs are used for smallish dinners, with a network of circular tables of ten, gilt chairs before them, used for large dinners, at which 140 can be seated.

From the White House Historical Association's book, *The White House*, sold on the premises, you learn about the upstairs rooms not shown on tours. Most important are the Lincoln Bedroom, furnished in American Victorian out of the mid nineteenth century, with a huge rosewood bed its centerpiece; the Treaty Room, which was where the cabinet met, Presidents Andrew Johnson through Taft, where Presidents Kennedy and Nixon signed significant treaties, and with décor as it might have been during the administration of President Grant; the Yellow Oval

Room, with unusual-for-the-White-House Louis XVI furnishings, and the topmost of the oval-shaped rooms; the Queens'
Bedroom, in pink and white with a canopied bed of the Federal
period, American Sheraton chairs, and a name suggesting royal
occupants, including Britain's Queen Elizabeth II, her mother
(Queen Elizabeth the Queen Mother), and her daughter Anne,
the Princess Royal.

The West Wing's Oval Office is easily the White House's best-
known room (invariably redecorated by each occupant) and is
recognizable by the two flags—one U.S., the other the presidential standard—behind the chief executive's desk. Often pho-
tographed, too, is the Cabinet Room, illuminated by brass chandeliers, with each cabinet member's leather chair identified by a
brass nameplate.

I save paintings for last. Each president alters their arrangement as he will, but you will recognize familiar faces as you
move around—look sharp in corridors and halls, as well as in
each State room: Washington by Gilbert Stuart, Teddy Roosevelt
by Sargent, Kennedy by Aaron Shikler, Eisenhower by Anthony
Willis, Andrew Johnson by John Vanderlyn, Monroe by the
inventor-painter Samuel F. B. Morse, Jefferson by Rembrandt
Peale, Lincoln by George Healy. First ladies, too: Jacqueline
Kennedy Onassis by the same Aaron Shikler who painted her
husband; Lady Bird Johnson by Elizabeth Shoumatoff, who
depicted Lady Bird's husband; Betty Ford by Felix de Cossio;
Eleanor Roosevelt by Douglas Chandor; all the way back to
Martha Washington by E. F. Andrews. But there's nonpresiden-
tial art as well—Benjamin Franklin by David Martin, a Fra-
gonard drawing commemorating Franklin's visit to the Louvre in
Paris, an Epstein bust of Churchill, a Severin Rosen still life,
Asher Durand's *Last of the Mohicans,* Monet's *Morning on the Seine,*
Whistler's *Nocturne.*

The point to remember about a White House tour is that you
may not have cast your ballot for the occupant of the mansion at
the moment. (I have made visits during the terms of Nixon,
Reagan, and Bush, none of whom I voted for.) Still, you feel
welcome as you stroll about, proud that the United States puts its
best foot forward where it counts—in the official residence of its
chief executive. Indeed, if you're an American, your interest in
the White House is almost proprietary.

U.S. Capitol: The United States Capitol (atop Capitol Hill, at the eastern terminus of Pennsylvania Avenue, between Constitution Avenue on its northern flank and Independence Avenue to the south) is at its best in its 258-foot-high dome, which is in a class with only two others—that of St. Peter's Basilica in the Vatican, designed in the sixteenth century by Michelangelo (see *Italy at Its Best*) and that of St. Paul's Cathedral in London, designed by Sir Christopher Wren in the seventeenth century (see *Britain at Its Best*). It is, along with the White House and the Washington and Lincoln monuments, the District of Columbia's most universally recognized landmark. Even though the first president, George Washington, laid its cornerstone as long ago as 1793, most of the Capitol is nineteenth-century, and mid-nineteenth-century at that, its décor and art more a case of money than of taste, for which you move west on Pennsylvania Avenue (to No. 1600—the White House). Original designs of architects William Thornton and (somewhat later) Benjamin Latrobe have, to understate, been embellished. There is no denying the grandeur of its exterior porticos and pediments and the massive steps. The interior is something else again, a case, by and large (recently redecorated chambers of the Senate and House of Representatives as well as the old restored Senate and Supreme Court chambers are exceptions) of lavish reception rooms, committee rooms, leaders' "ceremonial" (in addition to "working") offices, even corridors. Make no mistake, the men and women we elect to the Congress, whose salaries and facilities come out of our taxes, are very comfortable indeed, not only in the Capitol, but in the buildings where their offices are located (below).

The original Capitol building (actually a wing) was ready for Congress in 1800, and was restored in 1814 after burning by the British during the War of 1812. Not much later, in 1826, the Capitol's central portion was completed, and topped with a low dome. Just before the Civil War, original House of Representatives and Senate chambers were replaced by larger spaces, and the first dome gave way, during Lincoln's presidency, to the giant dome we see today.

Early-nineteenth-century spaces, long used by the Senate and Supreme Court (below), were restored in time for the U.S. Bicentennial in 1976, a decade and a half after an extension was appended to the Capitol's East Front, from which many (but not all) presidents have taken the oath of office. More recently, the West Front has seen restoration activity too. The Capitol's most important areas, the houses of Congress, may be observed while in session from visitors' galleries; the office of your representative or of one of your senators will give you free passes for both houses. (If you're a foreigner—without representation in the Congress—ask a guard to direct you to each house's ticket counter.)

The House, in my experience, is the easier chamber to observe, with less security en route to the balcony, and considerably politer guards than on the Senate side. You'll be lucky if, during your visit, there are many members on the floor; most work gets done in committee. Still, you want to have an idea of what deliberations in this chamber are like, and you want to note seals of the 50 states, four territories, and D.C. bordering the ceiling, centered by a glass-carved eagle picked out in bronze. Paintings on either side of the Speaker's rostrum are of President Washington—the easier to recognize—and of the Marquis de Lafayette, a staunch French friend of the Colonies during the Revolution. In emulation of Britain's House of Commons, the House displays a ceremonial mace (to the Speaker's right) when in session. There are, as of course you know, 435 members and five nonvoting delegates (from the territories and D.C.). House members sit wherever they choose (there are, oddly enough, no assigned seats) as long as they stay on the left of the center aisle (as you're looking down from the gallery) if they're Democrats, and to the right if they're Republicans.

The smaller Senate chamber (there are but a hundred members—two from each state) might seem easier to observe in action than its much larger counterpart, but in my experience Senate security has been bothersome (it resembles that at air terminals, en route to a flight) and Senate guards unpleasant. Unlike the House, the Senate *does* assign its members seats, according to seniority within the ranks of their party. The busts in niches around the Chamber are of a score of vice presidents. The vice president of the United States doubles as president of the Senate, but is customarily present only for important votes when, in case of a tie, he can cast the determining ballot.

(Although the vice president has but one constitutional duty, to preside over the Senate, taxpayers support three separate vice presidential offices—one in the Capitol, another in the Old Executive Office Building [below], and another in the White House.) Not unlike the House ceiling, ceiling decoration—in the Senate's case, the Great Seal of the Republic—is in glass and bronze. Most of the original mahogany desks dating back to 1819 are still in use by contemporary senators, with newer desks designed along the lines of the originals. As in the House, Democrats are on the left as you look down from the Visitors' Gallery, Republicans on the right.

The Capitol's first-floor crypt is the circular chamber that was originally intended for the graves of Martha and George Washington, whose descendants preferred that they be buried at Mount Vernon (below). Up a flight—on the second floor—is the resplendent Rotunda, like the crypt directly below it a remnant of the 1820s, and the site of state ceremonies, presidential funerals (nine all told) especially. The Rotunda, in that part of the Capitol designed by the same Charles Bulfinch responsible for the gold-domed Massachusetts Statehouse in Boston, is the site of four paintings (alas, not his best) by the ranking late-eighteenth-, early-nineteenth-century American artist John Trumbull—*Signing of the Declaration of Independence, Surrender of Burgoyne at Saratoga, Surrender of Cornwallis at Yorktown, Resignation of Washington.* Much of the other painting in the Capitol—largely "official" and undistinguished—is by a mid-nineteenth-century Italian, Constantino Brumidi, who spent many years in the building, much of the time on scaffolding beneath high ceilings. (He died of shock several months after slipping from his perch, dangling 60 feet above the floor until rescued, while painting the Rotunda's frieze.) Statuary Hall, for long the meeting place of the House of Representatives, had been the site, since Congress asked for sculptures of two leading citizens of each state, of many but not all of the sculptures sent by the states. A good number are in adjacent areas.

Caveat: Even though they're free, it's not worth waiting in line for guided Capitol tours. They consist mainly of quick treks through the Rotunda and Statuary Hall, which you can undertake just as well by yourself, ideally with a gratis map of each floor of the Capitol, which your representative's or senator's office should be able to provide at the same time you pick up tickets for the House and Senate galleries.

Legislators' offices are in half a dozen detached Capitol Hill buildings. Senators are to the north of the Capitol, in *Russell Senate Office Building, Dirksen Senate Office Building,* and *Hart Senate Office Building*—edging Constitution Avenue. Representatives are in a trio of buildings to the Capitol's south—*Rayburn House Office Building, Longworth House Office Building,* and *Cannon House Office Building,* between Independence Avenue and C Street. Most of these buildings are linked to the Capitol by subways or tunnels, which may be used by all of us—unlike certain of the elevators in legislators' office buildings specifically restricted to members' use—and so labeled. Amenities like gyms and fitness centers for legislators are situated in their office buildings. There are, in addition, restaurants for members of each house and their personal guests. Additionally, though, there are Capitol coffee shops (chapter 5) for the rest of us.

Especially important are meetings of committees of both houses—where the nitty-gritty is accomplished. *The Washington Post* obligingly publishes a daily column, "Today In Congress," which indicates not only meeting times, if any, for the two houses, but all of the day's Senate and House committee seances, their subjects, and in certain cases invited witnesses, location, and whether they're open to the public. Attendance at, say, a meeting of the Senate Foreign Relations Committee, the House Energy and Commerce Committee, or the Joint Economic Committee (a unit with members from both houses) can be considerably more revealing of how the Congress operates than attendance at any number of the sessions of either entire body, where but a handful of members might drone away, often on incomprehensible-appearing subjects.

Supreme Court of the United States (1st Street between East Capitol Street and Maryland Avenue NE): Every American schoolchild learns that the federal government is divided into three co-equal branches—executive, legislative, and judicial. Since the founding of the republic, the first two branches have had impressive seats—the White House for the executive branch ever since the presidency of John Adams in 1800; Capitol Building of one sort or another (with the first in New York) for the legislative branch. But the third branch—the powerful law court at the very apex of the American judicial system—has been quartered in a building of its own only since 1935, which was its 146th year.

As if to compensate for long years without its own detached quarters, nothing was spared when the court's first home of its own was built during the Great Depression. Chief Justice Charles Evans Hughes laid the cornerstone in 1932. In 1934, the nine justices, their powerful clerks, and their staffs moved from space in the Capitol (where the court had met since 1860) into what has come to be known as the Marble Palace, with a sculpted portico supported by a Corinthian colonnade that is one of the city's architectural treasures. Architects were the same Cass Gilbert responsible for New York's Beaux Arts–style Custom House and other major American structures, in collaboration with John Rockart. We are in their debt. Still, partly because of its location—to the east of (and behind) the Capitol (so much bigger and with the much-visited United States Congress)—and its function—significant albeit hardly spectacular or publicity-seeking—a court visit is too often at the bottom of Washington visitors' lists. If that's the case with you, move it up into the Top Ten as I have, ideally observing the court in session, but settling, if you must, for an inspection of the building, supplemented by a lecture and/or film about the court.

What makes the court quite literally supreme is its status as the highest tribunal in the republic for—to quote one of its own publications—"all cases and controversies arising under the Constitution or the laws of the United States." We read about the court in the press—by and large, at least—only when controversial cases are being argued before it, or a new justice has been nominated. What is worth noting, in advance of your visit, is that the court's power derives from its constitutional authority to invalidate legislation or executive actions that in its judgment conflict with the United States Constitution. Of some 5000 cases on its docket each year, it hears, argued by attorneys authorized to plead before it, some 200 cases each term, from which it delivers written opinions on between 150 and 170 cases.

The nine justices are appointed by the president but must be approved by the Senate. Between 1790, when the court was founded, and 1990 there have been only 16 chief justices (whose title, incidentally, is Chief Justice of the United States—not Chief Justice of the Supreme Court), and 94 associate justices—all appointed for life, with 15 years the average time in office. Not all presidents have the opportunity to appoint justices (Franklin D. Roosevelt chose eight, Ronald Reagan three, but Jimmy Carter none). The justices do not always reflect the political spectrum of the president who named them.

Liberal Justice William Brennan was appointed by conservative President Dwight D. Eisenhower, for example, while conservative Justice Byron White was appointed by liberal President John F. Kennedy. Withal, the court approaches the twenty-first century as a highly conservative body. Although the justices heeded the admonition of President Jefferson, who pleaded with them not to emulate the wearing of white wigs, still prevalent in British courts, they adhere to other traditions. The practice of the "conference handshake" continues. All members of the court shake each others' hands at the start of each session and at their private conferences, as a reminder that whatever their judicial differences on individual cases, they are bound together as a major federal body.

And other venerable customs continue. They range from quill pens—a new batch is placed on desks used by attorneys arguing cases each day—to lawyers' attire. Those attached to government departments appear before the justices in morning suits, while most private lawyers show their respect by wearing dark-shaded suits. And for as long as anyone can remember, every morning session opens with the pounding of a gavel by the marshal of the court, as the black-robed justices file into their seats (allotted by seniority, with the chief justice in the center and the oldest-in-service justices at places closest to him) and those in the courtroom rise, resuming seats only after the marshal intones these words: "The Honorable the Chief Justice and the Associate Justices of the Supreme Court of the United States. Oyez! Oyez! Oyez! All persons having business before the Honorable the Supreme Court of the United States are admonished to draw near and give their attention for the Court is now sitting. God save the United States and this Honorable Court."

Some classic-style buildings are handsomer without than within. The Supreme Court—with 16 marble columns supporting the sculpted pediment of its portico at the main west entrance, and still another colonnaded portico at the east entrance—dazzles also after you pass through its bronze west doors (each weighs six and a half tons) to the Great Hall, a fitting passageway to the Court Chamber. No one can deny that the justices deliberate in dignity. The courtroom's walls are set off by Ionic columns backed by maroon draperies, under a 44-foot-high blue-and-maroon coffered ceiling, with marble—from Italy, Spain, and Africa—throughout the building, often as the material for sculpted friezes. (The court's paneled and chandeliered library is not seen by visitors, nor is the justices' dining room, but the building's unique pair of elliptical, self-supporting five-story staircases are easily inspected.) Those seated directly behind the justices in the courtroom are their clerks. Count on their being honors graduates of cream-of-the-crop law schools; they remain for a year and often go on to ultimately fabulous jobs, including, for example, chief justice of the United States (William Rehnquist clerked in the early 1950s, was appointed to the court by President Nixon in 1972, and tapped as chief justice by President Reagan in 1986).

The court, traditionally, is open 9 A.M. to 4:30 P.M. Monday through Friday. Check newspapers for when it is in actual session; on such days, getting in to watch is a matter of first come, first served; arrive by, say, 9 A.M., for the 10 A.M. session. When the court is *not* in session, lectures about its operation are given in the courtroom, customarily every hour on the half hour the day long. And regularly each day, there's a film about the court and its activities on the ground floor—the location also of a pair of open-to-visitors restaurants (chapter 5) and a shop (chapter 6).

Lincoln Memorial (23rd Street NW, in West Potomac Park, south of Constitution Avenue and at the west edge of the long reflecting pool in Constitution Gardens): Of the four great Washington memorials—memorials without utilitarian functions, as for example the performing arts center that is an official memorial to President John F. Kennedy—Lincoln is like no other. At the

Jefferson Memorial we walk about, dazzled by architectural brilliance that puts us in mind of buildings Jefferson himself designed. The Washington Monument recalls the first president only fleetingly; it is more a symbol of the city bearing his name. At the Vietnam Veterans Memorial, we weep—or come close to it.

But at the Lincoln we stand in awe. No memorial associates us more movingly to the person it honors. And how could it be otherwise? The setting is a transatlantic variation on the theme of the Parthenon of Athens, its 36 outer columns (with Doric capitals) representing the states of the Union at the time of Lincoln's death by an assassin's bullet in 1865. Higher up are inscribed names of the 48 states extant in 1922, when Chief Justice William Howard Taft, chairman of the commission responsible for construction, presented the memorial to the people of the United States, through President Warren Harding, at an on-site ceremony.

Inscribed on the marble north wall is Lincoln's Second Inaugural Address, while the south wall contains his even more celebrated Gettysburg Address, from which is so often quoted the enduring phrase: "That this nation under God shall have a new birth of freedom—and that government of the people, by the people, for the people shall not perish from the earth." There's a pair of 60-foot-long allegorical murals related to Lincoln's principles. But it is Daniel Chester French's statue of a seated Lincoln—as high (19 feet) as it is wide, executed in New York by a pair of marble carvers who spent four years on the project—that draws us to the memorial on a first Washington visit and lures us back on succeeding visits. We approach the statue of the 16th president—the president who symbolizes not only the Civil War but the freeing of the slaves—with awe and pride.

Vietnam Veterans Memorial (Henry Bacon Drive NW, leading south from Constitution Avenue, in Constitution Gardens, just northeast of the Lincoln Memorial, above): You might call it the sleeper of the major Washington memorials. Within less than a year after its boldly unconventional design was accepted in May 1981 by a national jury of eight artists and designers, bureaucrats ordered a prosaic sculpture to supplement the memorial proper, for visitors who might be dissatisfied with it.

Dissatisfied? There need not have been any concern. Long queues come to pay their respects, many unrelated or not even having known any of the 58,000 members of the U.S. armed forces who lost their lives in the Vietnam War—the nation's longest, most unpopular, and most controversial conflict, extending over the administrations of five presidents, until a peace treaty was signed in 1973.

Constructed entirely with private funds—corporate as well as from many individuals—raised by the vet-founded Vietnam Veterans Memorial Fund, albeit with congressional authorization—the memorial proper embraces a complex of polished black granite walls pointing to the Lincoln Memorial and Washington Monument, so as to link the Vietnam War to the historical context of the United States. What fascinates viewers are the names of the deceased carved into 140 joined panels, with the arrangement by year and month (started with July 1959) under this carved-in-granite introductory text: "In Honor Of The Men And Women Of The Armed Forces Of The United States Who Served In The Vietnam War. The Names Of Those Who Gave Their Lives And Of Those Who Remain Missing Are Inscribed In The Order They Were Taken From Us. This Memorial Was Built With Private Contributions From The American People. November 11, 1982."

President Reagan, at a 1984 ceremony, accepted the memorial on behalf of the nation. We are in debt not only to veterans who organized the campaign for the monument, but to its designer, Maya Ying Lin, an Ohioan studying at the time at Yale. The sculpture adjacent—of a trio of servicemen in fatigues and with weapons, one black, two white—though undistinguished as art, is probably comforting to some. But it bears little relation to the Lin monument, itself nothing less than a modern masterwork.

It is no wonder that so many visitors are so affected by it, leaving vases of flowers, a single rose or carnation, or tiny flags near the granite-inscribed names of companions in arms and loved ones. Many visitors go simply to pay their respects—often, in the process, being moved to tears. But if you're seeking out a specific name or names, bear in mind that all 58,000 are arranged alphabetically in a directory at the memorial, with panel and line location indicated for each name. The National Park Service, which operates the memorial, has rangers present the day and evening long, customarily until midnight.

National Gallery of Art (on the Mall, 4th to 6th Streets between Constitution Avenue and Madison Drive NW)—a snooty cousin of the Smithsonian Institution, with its own board of trustees, administration, and open-hours that are just different enough from those of neighboring Smithsonian museums to let you know the National is a distinct entity—is arguably the most extraordinary of the world's great art museums in that it started in the big time—without having to build considerably from a nucleus of a relative handful of royally contributed Old Masters, or the limited collection of a local bigwig, in modest quarters and but a tiny band of early visitors. Unlike counterparts that started off with cheers from supporters and, say, an undoubtedly valuable Corot to lure initial viewers in the loft of a nondescript nineteenth-century structure, the National Gallery—young as world-class museums go—opened as recently as 1941 in a building designed by the same architect, John Russell Pope, responsible for the Jefferson Memorial and other important buildings.

By the time it welcomed its first visitors, it had amassed some 600 paintings and sculptures. And within a relatively short period, the National became home to four magnificent private collections. The first and most spectacular was that of the founder, Andrew Mellon, a Pittsburgh banker and steel tycoon who became secretary of the treasury and started buying art with the encouragement of a fellow Pittsburgher, Henry Clay Frick (himself a museum organizer; see *New York at Its Best*). Mellon began with Baroque Dutch painters (9 of the gallery's 24 Rembrandts were his, as were 6 of the 8 Hals works, and 3 paintings by the unprolific Vermeer). Mellon took a liking to the eighteenth- and early-nineteenth-century British, too, gathering as a consequence half a dozen Gainsboroughs, a trio each of Reynolds and Raeburn, and a Turner.

The Mellon nucleus was supplemented by the treasures of a Philadelphian who was at once a banker and a railway exec, Peter A. B. Widener, and his son Joseph—a collection ravishingly rich in Italian Renaissance masters, painters as well as sculptors,

Rococo-era French bronzes, Raeburn and Romney, Hoppner and Lawrence, Constable and Turner, to supplement Mellon masterworks from that era. Samuel H. Kress contributed paintings—many from the Italian Renaissance—bought on the advice of Kress's mentor, the Florence-based art authority Bernard Berenson, but paintings and sculpture with other origins as well. (Kress, whose wealth came from a chain of variety stores, amassed so many works that they're not only in the National, but in a score-plus museums throughout the U.S.)

The collection of New York financier Chester Dale rounds out the quartet of the National Gallery's majors. Dale's contribution embraces some 250 French Impressionists and Post-Impressionists, the range Renoir and Cézanne, Degas and Monet, Boudin and Manet, Van Gogh and Gauguin, through later painters like Bonnard and Vuillard, Modigliani and Matisse.

This is a museum abounding in superlatives. A severely narrowed-down group of don't-miss works might run to beautiful curly-headed *Ginevra de' Benci*, the only work of Leonardo da Vinci on display in the United States; Raphael's *Alba Madonna* (one of several Raphael *Madonnas* in the collection), Van Dyck's *Marchesa Balbi*, El Greco's *Laocoön*, *The Feast of the Gods*, believed to have been painted partly by Giovanni Bellini (the foreground) and partly by Titian (the background), Vermeer's *A Lady Writing*, and Picasso's *Family of Saltimbanques*—one of a dozen-plus paintings by that modern master in the gallery.

But you'll determine your own favorites from the hundreds of paintings hung on either side of the fountain-centered, colonnaded rotunda centering the main floor of the classic-style West Building. Consider Giotto's *Madonna and Child* against a gilded background, Lippi's portrait of a haughty youth, Dürer's incisive *Clergyman*, Holbein's scarlet-clad *Edward VI As a Child*, Lorrain's *The Judgment of Paris*, Largillière's black-robed nun, *Elizabeth Throckmorton*, Fragonard's lovely *A Young Girl Reading*, Gilbert Stuart's black-garbed *The Skater*, arms folded as he glides on the ice; Goya's lace-mantled *Bookseller's Wife*, Ingres's elegant *Madame Moitessier*, Donatello's *David of the Casa Martelli*, this last mentioned to call your attention to the Gallery's exceptional sculptures. To be noted, as well: The too-often-bypassed ground floor of the West Building celebrating decorative arts, from, say, *The Triumph of Christ*, a 1500 Brussels tapestry, through Italian Renaissance chests, medieval enamels, Chinese porcelains, and—special, these—four rooms of French eighteenth-century furniture, Louis XV and Louis XVI, a writing table of Queen Marie-Antoinette included.

The Gallery's East Building, designed by the architect I. M. Pei, opened in 1978 to virtually universal acclaim, certainly deserved in my view (unlike the same Pei's enormous pyramidal entrance to Paris's Louvre Museum, criticized by many, myself certainly included—see *France at Its Best*—as inappropriate to the venerable Louvre's setting in the formal Tuileries Gardens).

The East Building—daringly trapezoid-shaped and divided into a pair of triangles—could do with escalators linking all levels. Otherwise, it works well as a venue for modern works from the permanent collection, Matisse through Robert Mother-well, and for a never-ending succession of special exhibitions, too often viewed by visitors at the expense of masterworks in the adjacent West Building. Still, there is no denying the aesthetic excitement of the East Building, a mix of marble walls, glass skylights, bridges, and balconies creating interest in a high central Court, whose embellishment is minimal—an immense Calder mobile, a black-and-white Miró, a bold Moore sculpture—but marvelous.

Withal, I repeat, don't let the aptly titled "blockbuster" short-term shows keep you from masterworks of the original West Building, linked with its newer counterpart by an underground passage sheltering the largest of the gallery's eateries (chapter 5) and an enormous shop (chapter 6). Note too that the National Gallery operates its very own, critically well-regarded chamber orchestra (there are free Sunday evening concerts, usually October through June), screens free movies (both feature and art films) in the East Building's auditorium, offers free daily tours of both buildings' collections. (Alas, these can be high school level if the one I joined was typical, with as many pointless questions from the lecturer to participants as simple declarative statements by the lecturer about the paintings.) And every day, the gallery zeroes in on a single work of art from the permanent collection as the subject of a brief presentation, with the text printed and distributed without charge to listeners. The National Gallery is a frequent repeat destination for Washingtonians, as well as visitors, in the manner of New York's Metropolitan, the Art Institute of Chicago, the Los Angeles County Museum of Art, and the fine arts museums of Boston and Philadelphia. You will want to return.

National Portrait Gallery/National Museum of American Art—both outposts of the Mall-centered Smithsonian Institution—have, since 1968, shared a splendid Greek Revival building that opened in 1840 as the U.S. Patent Office and narrowly escaped being razed to become the site of a gargantuan garage in the 1950s. The portrait gallery entrance is on one side—at 8th and F streets NW; and the American art museum is on the other, at 8th and G streets NW.

I open *London at Its Best* with the British capital's National Portrait Gallery—similar to and possibly the inspiration for Washington's—as the ideal introduction for visiting Yanks to British monarchs and leaders in other fields, and I do likewise in *Britain at Its Best*, in the case of the Scottish National Portrait Gallery in Edinburgh, for Americans just arrived in Scotland. Although Americans usually are more familiar with our own country's leaders than might be the case with those of a foreign land, Washington's *National Portrait Gallery* is a wonderful way to reacquaint ourselves not only with presidents but other outstanding Americans—painters and poets, scientists and savants.

The portrait gallery's special standout—an all-Washington standout, in my view—is its second floor Hall of Presidents. Every visitor spends time before a Gilbert Stuart portrait of the first president, Washington, dark-suited, erect, and with hand outstretched over his desk, as if to indicate the business of the new nation before him. The other early presidents draw crowds too—an unidentified artist's interpretation of a somber Madison, an unfamiliar-looking Monroe by John Vanderlyn, George Caleb Bingham's John Quincy Adams, a striking Andrew Jackson in uniform by Ralph Earl. But there are, as well, substantial clusters of observers taking in portraits of the lesser-known sequence of nineteenth-century presidents—one-termers we studied in school, albeit often forgetting details of their administrations, not to mention years of their terms.

I cite, for example, the Mathew Brady daguerreotype of Martin Van Buren, who came from the village of Kinderhook, near my hometown of Albany, New York; and studies, as well, of both William Henry Harrison and the later Benjamin Harrison, Tyler and Polk, Taylor and Fillmore, Pierce and Buchanan; later post–Civil War chief executives like Hayes and the assassinated Garfield (only half a year in office), Arthur and Cleveland, the also-assassinated McKinley and 300-pound William Howard Taft (whose portrait by Robert Lee MacCameron, painted in 1909, is one of the most riveting in the hall). Understandably, we give time to Lincoln (George Peter Alexander Healy based his 1887 study on sketches made while Lincoln lived), and to Lincoln's successors, Andrew Johnson (saved by a single vote from impeachment), and Civil War commanding general Ulysses S. Grant (painted in uniform during the conflict by a Norwegian named Balling).

Later presidents' administrations are mostly more familiar to us—Teddy Roosevelt and World War I–era Wilson; Harding, who died in office before his first term expired, "Silent Cal" Coolidge and the pre-Depression Hoover, FDR in familiar cloak and with familiar holder-held cigarette, by Douglas Chandor; an atypically serene Truman by Greta Kempton; a uniformed Ike; a superb oil by William Franklin Draper of Kennedy in the rocker he used because of his bad back; Johnson in bronze; a flattering Nixon, *almost* smiling, by Norman Rockwell; and later leaders through to today's White House occupant. Not to be missed, either, are collections of *Time* magazine cover portraits, the gallery's third-floor Great Hall, whose décor is a nineteenth-century masterwork; and paintings throughout, from, say, self-portraits by John Singleton Copley and Mary Cassatt through to representations of a young Frederick Douglass (the black leader whose Washington home you may visit, below) and of America's Saint Elizabeth Seton.

What makes the *National Museum of American Art* significant is that it alone among museums in the American capital concentrates on art by Americans, running a gamut, colonial to contemporary, with works from each era. There are, to be sure, fine American paintings at the National Gallery of Art (above) and the Corcoran Gallery of Art (below). But here, your route through three floors is logical and absorbing—a Charles Wilson Peale miniature of two eighteenth-century youngsters; an early-nineteenth-century oil portrait of not one but five Indian chiefs in full regalia; an 1820 view of Niagara Falls by Alvin Fisher; a room of George Catlin's nineteenth-century Indian studies; landscapes by the likes of Thomas Cole, Asher Durand, Thomas Moran, and Albert Bierstadt; a fine group by Albert Pinkham Ryder; memorable Winslow Homers and Childe Hassams, John Singer Sargents and James McNeil Whistlers. Under no circumstances leave without ascending to the third floor, in whose generously proportioned arched-ceiling Lincoln Room (so called because it was the scene of Lincoln's second Inaugural Ball)—and neighboring galleries—the museum's twentieth-century art is concentrated, including, to give you an idea, Edward Hopper's *Cape Cod Morning 1950* and Thomas Hart Benton's *Achilles and Hercules* (1947).

National Museum of American History (on the Mall with entrances on Constitution Avenue and Madison Drive, between 12th and 13th streets NW)—despite its name, only somewhat less formidable than the title when I first knew it (National Museum of History and Technology)—this museum is the Smithsonian at its wittiest. Most creatively conceived museum of the group, its three exhibit-packed floors interpret the American genius—the theme might be called social history, but it's actually more than that—affording the viewer more chuckles than any other museum in town. Themed exhibits, each occupying considerable space, entertain as well as educate. "Information Age: People, Information and Technology"—which cost $10 million to mount—surveys the evolution of mass communications, from such early objects in the museum's collection as the Morse telegraph components of Bell's first telephone and a piece of the first transatlantic cable. It includes mockups of, for example, a 1939 living room in which a floor-model console radio of that era plays snippets of such then-classic shows as "Fibber McGee and Molly," "The Shadow," "Abbott and Costello," and "Superman"—with commercial announcements of the period as well. There's a mini-movie theater, as part of this same exhibit, in which visitors watch scenes of Hitler's rallies, a form of mass communications that led to expansion of the Nazi party and World War II. Other museum sections develop other themes— "Men and Women, A History of Costume, Gender and Power" demonstrates the relationship between clothing and grooming (early toothpaste and "hair-restorer" through nineteenth-century corsets and hoop skirts to 1920s Cutex nail polish and 1930s swimsuits and streetwear. "After the Revolution: Everyday Life in America, 1780–1800" deals in part with slave life in the South and reveals how African culture survived in the New World. "A Nation of Nations," stressing America's multiethnic composition, presents facets of Indian life, the voyage of the *Mayflower,* and objects from early Jamestown, Virginia; it reproduces in toto an early grist mill, a long-ago New England farmhouse, even a World War II Army barracks-cum-latrine. Inaugural gowns of first ladies is an exhibit that few visitors pass by. Nor do they forgo the fifteen-star American flag—to aid in preservation, enclosed in a case that is opened every half-hour. It's the actual flag Francis Scott Key observed, flying over Fort McKinley, Maryland, in 1814—which served as inspiration for the lyrics of "The Star Spangled Banner," America's national anthem. The museum's basement book and gift shop (chapter 6) is among the Smithsonian's biggest and best. There's a pair of restaurants (chapter 5). One of them specializes in ice-cream sodas and borders the interior of a 1900 candy shop and a white wicker-furnished visitor lounge; it's the most fun of any of the Smithsonian's eateries. Indeed, my only complaint, with respect to the American History Museum, is that it is responsible for the now-tired exhibit—objects of American life in 1876—that has occupied the Smithsonian's nineteenth-century *Arts & Industries Building* on the Mall, since as long ago as 1976, the year of America's Bicentennial—and is overdue for replacement.

National Air and Space Museum (on the Mall, with entrances at Independence Avenue and 6th Street NW and at Jefferson Drive): I don't know the names of the architects or building contractors for the Air and Space, but if I did, I would want to honor them on this page. That the building they erected in 1976—the year of the American Bicentennial—still appears to be in apple-pie order is no small feat; something like 104 million visitors have come to call. Constant crowds notwithstanding, still another marvel of this building is that it never seems hopelessly overcrowded as can, for example, those sections of the National Gallery of Art, the Art Institute of Chicago, or New York's Metropolitan Museum of Art, when they house short-term blockbuster exhibitions. Which is hardly to say the Air and Space is placid. Youthful exuberance—there is a kid-filled space— precludes tranquility. Still, with a gratis map from the information counter in hand, you have no difficulty in negotiating just under two dozen galleries occupying two floors.

This Smithsonian Institution–operated museum undertakes—and with extraordinary success—to tell us what air and aerospace technology are all about. The most spectacular exhibits are in double-level Gallery 100. They include the plane used by the Wright Brothers as the first powered, controlled, and sustained flight by man in a heavier-than-air craft at the turn of this century, in 1903; Lindbergh's *Spirit of St. Louis*, the little craft on which was made the first solo, nonstop flight across the Atlantic, New York to Paris, on May 20–21, 1927 (flying time 33½ hours); a model of *Explorer I*, the first U.S. satellite to orbit the earth, dating to 1958; a Soviet-constructed replica of *Sputnik 1*, the first artificial satellite to orbit the earth, in 1957; *Friendship 7*, on which astronaut (later U.S. Senator) John Glenn became the first American astronaut to orbit the earth; *Gemini 4*, the two-seat spacecraft from which an astronaut took the first space walk in 1965; the *Apollo 11* command module, which carried astronauts Neil Armstrong, Edwin Aldrin, and Michael Collins to the moon and back on the first-ever manned lunar landing in 1969; a 243-pound moon rock sample (which you may touch) that's said to be four billion years old and was brought to earth by *Apollo 17* astronauts in 1972.

Not even old-fashioned airplanes are passed over. Another gallery devoted to historic models displays, for example, a Douglas DC-3, on counterparts of which I have made considerable flights in the course of my work. Aviation in the two World Wars is the subject of a stellar section. I was drawn to World War II memorabilia—uniforms and medals, photos and medals, induction orders and passes for leaves; even a copy of the early 1940s War and Navy departments' *Short Guide to Britain*—for Yanks then

stationed in the U.K. There is, as well, a section given over to
forecasts from my childhood of the space age, for kids: disin-
tegrator guns, rocket pistols, and pop-up-paged books including
Buck Rogers in the 25th Century.

And there is, as well, to satisfy francophiles like me, a beautifully prepared exhibit of French ballooning in the eighteenth
century (an Anglo-French duo piloted a balloon across the
English Channel in 1785, two years after France's Montgolfier
balloon took to the skies). Airships like Germany's Graf Zep-
pelin, which crossed the Atlantic in 1937 (including tableware
used by its passengers) are the subject of still another display.

It's small details that make the Air and Space fun; the Space
Food section, for example, shows the kind of puréed pap John
Glenn ate in the early 1960s, and the specially canned containers
of Coke consumed by a space shuttle crew in the mid-1980s.
(Earthbound food of this very moment is an Air and Space
specialty, too; you don't want to miss its relatively recently
constructed restaurants, one atop the other—chapter 5.) But
there's more: movies about aviation and America's space program, shown in the museum's Samuel P. Langley Theater, and a
spectacular show in its Albert Einstein Planetarium; performances of both are repeated the day long, may be reserved in
advance, and require admission tickets (charges are nominal)—
unlike the museum proper, which is free.

Mount Vernon (Mount Vernon Memorial Highway, Mount Vernon, Virginia, 8 miles south of Alexandria, Virginia, below; and
16 miles from Washington): It is hardly surprising that the
country seat of the first president of the United States is so close
to the federal capital; George Washington himself selected the
city's precise location—not far from his own home. Mount
Vernon's situation is a boon to the visitor in Washington. And so
is the fact that it has been preserved over a two-century period
with mementos of the significant era when its owner was the
first leader of the new republic.

At once gentleman farmer and country squire, as well as
politician and soldier, Washington took his bride, Martha Dan-
dridge Custis, to Mount Vernon in 1754, enlarging and expanding it until it became one of Virginia's leading estates, embracing

five independently managed farms totaling 8000 acres, with wheat and other grains the chief crops; and slaves—all of whom were subsequently freed in Washington's will—the laborers. Washington was called away from Mount Vernon on two noteworthy occasions. First was in 1775 when he was elected commander-in-chief of the new American army (coming home on leave twice during the eight years of the Revolutionary War). Then, in 1787, he was off to Philadelphia to preside over the Constitutional Convention, and in 1789 he went to New York—the first federal capital—to begin two terms as our first president.

By the time he turned over the government to John Adams in 1797, the capital had moved to Philadelphia, from where he journeyed south to Mount Vernon, keeping busy as master of Mount Vernon until he died in 1799, to be buried in the family vault on the estate. (Martha Washington, after her death in 1802, was buried alongside her husband.)

The house remained in the family, albeit with increasing financial difficulty, until, in the mid nineteenth century, John A. Washington, Jr., attempted to sell it to either the federal government or the State of Virginia, to no avail. But Mount Vernon's clouded future became known to a South Carolina woman named Ann Pamela Cunningham. A gifted organizer, she banded together—long before women were operating multistate enterprises—a group of women from around the country in the nonprofit Mount Vernon Ladies Association of the Union, which was chartered by the Virginia legislature in 1858. With funds raised throughout the United States, the association purchased Mount Vernon, restored and refurnished it (an ongoing task these many years), and opened it to the public.

The same association, with its original quaint—if hardly inaccurate—title continues to run Mount Vernon through an all-female board of 35, from as many states, who gather for semiannual meetings, still receiving absolutely no government funds, the while luring a million visitors a year to the nation's No. 1 historic house.

The Washingtons lived the good life. Main-floor rooms—including a pair of parlors (one with the silver urn and porcelain service from which Martha would have presided at tea) and as many dining rooms (one for big dinners, with a Palladian window and plaster decorations, the other smaller, for family dinners)—are stunners. So is the capacious central hall with doors at both front and rear of the house—the latter giving onto lawns overlooking the Potomac River. There's a downstairs bedroom (common in big Virginia houses of the period), and a library on the same floor with the president's secretary-desk, his swivel chair, a French-made dressing table, and a globe created in England to the president's specifications, first used by him at the original (and, sadly, long since razed) capitol in New York.

The Washingtons' bedroom—with the fourposter, canopy-covered bed in which the president died—is the most important of five second-floor rooms, one of which was used by Nelly Custis, Martha Washington's youngest granddaughter and a Mount Vernon resident since childhood. You want to visit also the pantry with the family's original blue-and-white tableware; the kitchen in a detached building (breakfast was at 7, dinner at 3, tea at 6, and, upon occasion, supper at 9); a museum (also in its own building) chockablock with Washingtoniana, including a Houdon bust of Washington, Martha's ivory fan, portraits in miniature of family members, silver wine cooler and coffeepot, the president's drafting instruments, and satin slippers worn by the first lady.

Beyond are a diverse range of outbuildings—reconstructed slave quarters (the original quarters burned in 1835), overseers' quarters, flower and kitchen gardens, and last but hardly least, the tomb, a little brick house with remains of the presidential couple and other family members. There are a pair of shops on the grounds as well as a pair of eateries (chapter 5).

If you drive your own or a rented car (rather than going by tour bus or Potomac River boat), spend the whole day, taking in also three other important area houses: *Woodlawn Plantation*—so close to Mount Vernon that you can walk it (although motor transport is recommended), believed to have been designed (1803) by William Thornton, first architect of the U.S. Capitol (above), on land that was a gift from the president to his foster daughter and nephew, Nelly Custis and Lawrence Lewis, with handsome parlor, delightful dining room, and furnished-in-period bedrooms; neighboring *Pope-Leighey House,* designed by the celebrated architect Frank Lloyd Wright in 1940 and a prototype of today's middle-category American family house; and *Gunston Hall* (southwest of Mount Vernon, on the Potomac at Mason Neck, near Lorton, Virginia), the home of George Mason (who helped draft the Constitution and Virginia's Declaration of Rights, a model for the U.S. Constitution's Bill of Rights), a 1755 brick house, backed by formal gardens, with nicely furnished period interiors and a detached one-room schoolhouse where Mason's nine kids studied, the lot of them sharing a common teacher.

ALL AROUND THE TOWN: A WASHINGTON SAMPLER, ARCHITECTURAL AND OTHERWISE

Adams-Morgan is neither a house nor a museum, but rather the name of a neighborhood in the northwest part of town centering on Columbia Road, between 18th Street NW and Kalorama Park, west of upper Connecticut Avenue. It has blossomed in recent years as the nucleus of ethnic restaurants—Ethiopian are the most exotic, perhaps, and there are more such than in any other city. But there are Mexican, French, and Italian restaurants as well, with cafés and art galleries, antique shops and specialty delis; and the populace is a congenial mix of professionals and artists, Americans and newcomers. I make a point of including a number of Adams-Morgan restaurants in chapter 5.

Alexandria (Virginia) Old Town (easily accessible by D.C.'s Metro to King Street station, thence via city bus to South Fairfax Street, on which—at No. 221, eighteenth-century Ramsay House—the Alexandria Visitor Center is situated, and where you may purchase a discounted ticket for three of the Old Town's historic houses and a museum): Easily vying with Georgetown in the beauty of early nineteenth- and eighteenth-century houses in its central portions, Alexandria (again like Georgetown) predates the District of Columbia (except that, unlike Georgetown, it is not a part of D.C., but rather just over the Potomac in Virginia). Indeed, it was in Alexandria—founded by Scottish settlers in 1749—that George Washington participated in crucial political meetings during the formative period of the Revolution and attended church and the theater. Old Town, centered on King Street with the Potomac River its eastern frontier, has been so well organized for tourism that, if you arrive from Washington after a fairly early breakfast, you can take much of it in without rushing, pausing for lunch in one of its restaurants (chapter 5), in the course of a single day. And be glad that you did.

The three historic houses and the museum that are visited on the reduced-rate ticket (sold not only at the Visitor Information Center, above, but at any of the houses) include the *Boyhood Home of Robert E. Lee* (707 Oronoco Street), a Federal period townhouse known to George Washington, with mostly eighteenth-century furnishings of considerable style in the Lafayette Parlor, Morning Room and Dining Room on the first floor, with a Guest Room and Nursery upstairs highlights; *Carlyle House* (121 North Fairfax Street)—most elegant of the lot, where General Edward Braddock and five colonial governors made plans for what became the French and Indian War, with fine interiors including classically detailed Front Parlor, the general's desk and papers in the Study, and, via an overlarge Front Hall, up a stairway punctuated by a Palladian window at midpoint, Master and Children's Bedrooms, with an interesting shop en route out; *Lee-Findell House* (614 Oronoco Street)—built in 1785 by a Lee descendant of white clapboard, and the home (1937–1969) of labor leader John L. Lewis, with mostly mid-nineteenth-century furnishings, Formal and Family Parlors and a Dining Room downstairs, two bedrooms and a Nursery up a flight; and *Gadsby's Tavern Museum* (134 North Royal Street, above still-in-use Gadsby's Tavern (a restaurant about which I write in chapter 5), embracing a pair of attractive Georgian houses, with exhibits on two floors (the best is about Colonial-era foods), including a small Dining Room, big Assembly Hall, trio of restored tavern bedrooms (which slept as many as fourteen guests to a room, and as many as four, sleeping crosswise, per bed!), and lovely Ballroom, still the site of annual parties celebrating George Washington's birthday. To be visited also, in the course of an Alexandria day, are *Christ Church* (Cameron and North Washington streets)—Georgian in style and period (it went up between 1767 and 1733), handsome and squarish, brick-walled and trimmed in white, with a fine tower and an impressive interior, among whose pews is that of George Washington, who was a vestryman (General Robert E. Lee was confirmed within and was a longtime parishioner, even after he moved to Arlington House, below); *Lloyd House* (220 North Washington Street)—built in 1797 and restored two centuries later as a historical library (Alexandria and Virginia are the specialties), with changing exhibits from the library's collection and aged paintings as well; and the *Lyceum* (201 South Washington Street), colonnaded-cum-portico Greek Revival, dating to 1939 and now Alexandria's historical museum. (The graceless six-story tower that hovers over town, and about which you may be curious, is a modern-day Masonic temple, with some Washington memorabilia, none of it requisite to an appreciation either of Washington or of Alexandria.)

Arlington National Cemetery and Arlington House (just west of Arlington Memorial Bridge spanning the Potomac, in Arlington, Virginia, with Arlington Cemetery Metro station adjacent, and with service also to both cemetery and house by buses of the Tourmobile system) are conveniently taken in tandem, with the latter—Arlington House—on the territory of the former. Ideally, go on a weekday rather than on a weekend, when crowds are heavy; in summer, when temperature and humidity can be high, long Tourmobile queues—in the open sun—can be, to understate, disagreeable.

Arlington National Cemetery, although not the nation's largest, is certainly its best known. Within 612 acres are buried some 200,000 military and naval veterans and their dependents and a considerable number of historical, political, and military figures, the range World War I's General John J. Pershing and World War II's General George C. Marshall, beyond to boxing champ Joe Louis and William Howard Taft (the only American who served both as president and as chief justice of the United States), explorer Richard Byrd and astronaut Dick Scobee, baseball's Abner Doubleday and President John F. Kennedy. Indeed, the grave of President Kennedy—assassinated on November 22, 1963—is believed to be the most visited grave in the United States. Two of his infant children are buried with him, beneath a plaque bearing only his name and the years of his birth and death, with an eternal flame, lit by his widow when he was buried. The grave of the president's brother, Robert, whom he had appointed attorney general, who was later a United States senator representing New York—himself assassinated in 1968— is alongside.

Nearby is the severely simple *Tomb of the Unknown Soldier,* under which are buried four unidentified members of the military— from World Wars I and II and the Korean and Vietnam wars. The tomb is guarded around the clock the year long by soldiers from the Army's Third Infantry, mostly specially trained volunteers for this duty, who remain at these demanding posts for periods ranging between a year and 18 months, with Changing of the Guard hourly on the hour, October through March—every half-hour the rest of the year. While on duty at the tomb, guards take 21 steps before turning and facing the tomb for 21 seconds, the figure corresponding to the number of guns—21—in a traditional salute. A visit is a moving and memorable experience.

Arlington House, atop the cemetery hill and affording fine views of the Potomac and Washington, is on land originally owned by the family of General Robert E. Lee, commander of Confederate forces in the Civil War. An outstanding example—one of the best in the United States—of the Greek Revival architecture popular in this country in the nineteenth century, it was built by George Washington Parker Custis, a grandson of Martha Washington by her first marriage, to Daniel Custis. Young George was raised by George and Martha Washington at Mount Vernon (above). Built between 1802 and 1817, the house was first inhabited by Robert E. Lee when he married a Custis heir.

Restoration began in the 1920s under the aegis of the War Department, continued in the 1930s when the house became part of the National Park Service, under whose authority, in 1955, it was officially declared a memorial to General Lee. (Lee, after surrendering to General [later U.S. president] Ulysses S. Grant at Appomattox Court House, Virginia, on April 9, 1865, became president of Washington College [now Washington and Lee University], where he died in 1870).

When you consider the crowds that hike though the not-overlarge house, especially in summer, its mint condition is extraordinary. Costumed hostesses are dotted about at strategic points, but the tour is self-guided. You want to take in the view of Washington from the Center Hall as you enter, noting, as you amble about at your own speed, the green silk–covered early-nineteenth-century furniture in the Family Parlor, the family's own china on the handsomely set Dining Room table, the quite grand White Parlor, the eighteenth-century chest-on-chest in the Lees' bedroom, as well as simpler and smaller Boys' and Girls' Bedrooms, also on the second floor; and the Kitchen and Servants' Quarters (Lee freed the house's slaves in 1862) on the grounds.

Bureau of Engraving and Printing (14th and C streets SW): Next time you're given a pack of new bills at the bank, I wager you'll think of your Engraving and Printing tour. If, that is, you've the patience to wait in line as long as an hour and a half during the spring-through-summer season for an expedition that lasts 20 minutes. Still, it's fascinating. The journey is self-guided with commentary provided through a loudspeaker system. You are on the premises of the division of the Department of the Treasury that is termed the government's "security printer," responsible for the design of U.S. currency, postage stamps, and Treasury and other U.S. securities. What you see is the manufacture of paper money—notes as they're officially termed, bills as we call them. "The Buck Starts Here," says the first sign. You're told that bills are not paper but rather 75 percent cotton and 25 percent linen, and as you move along, you see them engraved, printed in large sheets, chopped down to size, sorted into stacks of a hundred bills, and banded and packaged into "bricks" containing 400 bills, which are sent to twelve branches of the Federal Reserve Bank around the nation for distribution to local banks. You're informed, as you move along, about what's printed on bills—with Washington ($1), Jefferson ($2), Lincoln ($5), Hamilton ($10), Jackson ($20), Grant ($50), and Franklin ($100) on the front of the various denominations; and but four Washington landmarks—Lincoln Memorial, Treasury Building, White House, and U.S. Capitol—among subjects on backs of bills. Bills may not portray living persons; dollar bills have an average life of 18 months (although $100 bills tend to last 23 years); and the signature of the Treasurer of the United States (by tradition a woman) appears on 16.5 billion dollar bills over a five-year period. Interesting shop.

Canadian Embassy (501 Pennsylvania Avenue NW, opposite the National Gallery of Art): It's agreeable to stroll past facades of Embassy Row, mostly on Massachusetts Avenue NW between Scott Circle and Wisconsin Avenue NW. There are some 140 embassies in that area, most if not all occupying posh mansions. But they are to be entered only if you've official business or have been especially invited—to a lunch, reception, or dinner.

The new-in-1989 Canadian Embassy, on the other hand, is not on Embassy Row, and it *does* welcome visitors intent on inspecting one of the most talked-about of Washington's contemporary buildings, with the schedule—subject to change, of course—Monday, Wednesday, Friday, and Saturday at 10 A.M., for 40-minute stays including guided walk-through and slide show.

Additionally, you may have a look at the current exhibition of Canadian works, in an open-to-the-public art gallery that keeps regular hours. The embassy of the United States' important next-door neighbor to the north is bold and big and unconventional enough to attract detractors as well as enthusiasts. Designed by a Vancouver-origin architect named Arthur Erickson, it's a massive marble mix of styles that's mostly modern, albeit with classic architectural accents, impressing visitors with such features as a rotunda ringed with a dozen columns (one each for Canada's ten provinces and two territories), a plaza centered by a reflecting pool, several levels of office floors whose windows are hung with plants, snazzy rooms for embassy parties, impressive auditorium, and library.

Chesapeake and Ohio Canal (Foundry Building ticket office, alongside the canal between Jefferson and 30th streets NW): How about a boat ride on this historic body of water, linking Georgetown with Cumberland, Maryland? The C and O Canal dates to the presidency of John Quincy Adams 160 years ago and is now a national historic park—the only such solely embracing a body of water. The mule-drawn boats traditionally operate spring through fall. The canal is 184 miles long—but don't worry, you won't go anywhere near that far.

Chinatown: If you're from San Francisco or New York, the capital's Chinatown is not going to make much of an impression. Still, Washington takes it seriously enough, and there's no question but that neither of its much larger counterparts can boast a vivid, unmistakably Chinese-design archway like that of Washington's—traversing H Street NW at 7th Street, in the core of a compact restaurant-dotted quarter (see chapter 5) due east of the Convention Center.

Dupont Circle is the quarter—taking the name of the circle centering it—that links Embassy Row and upper Connecticut Avenue to the north with downtown to the south. It's a trendy mix of museums, smart (and often delicious) restaurants (chapter 5), hotels (chapter 4), and shops (chapter 6) with a convenient Metro station whose escalators are among the system's steepest. An interesting, convivial, stimulating part of town.

Embassy Row—the northwest quarter wherein are located the majority of the capital's 140-plus seats of foreign envoys (albeit with important exceptions), in that part of upper Massachusetts Avenue NW between Sheridan and Observatory Circles and spilling into adjacent streets. Embassies occupy either long-on-scene mansions or townhouses (this is the case with most) or buildings their governments have designed, like the sleek, low-slung marble-facaded *French Embassy* at 4101 Reservoir Road NW; the *British Embassy,* among the larger in this part of town, at 3100 Massachusetts Avenue, with a statue of Sir Winston Churchill out front; and the *Brazilian Embassy* (3006 Massachusetts Avenue NW). Other purpose-built embassies include those of the *Soviet Union* (1225 16th Street NW); *Mexico* (1911 Pennsylvania Avenue NW)—where a sleek contemporary building has been cleverly built over a pair of early nineteenth-century townhouses still with original facades; and *Canada* (501 Pennsylvania Avenue NW)—to which I devote a separate entry (above, in this chapter) not only because it is architecturally distinguished but because it has open-to-the-public visiting hours for tours; other embassies are closed to the general public. Bronze or brass plaques—often in English as well as the national language—and, frequently, national flags identify embassies. And it is worth noting that in many cases embassies scatter divisions in several buildings, sometimes considerably detached from one another. If you've business at an embassy, double-check the proper address in advance.

Federal Bureau of Investigation (Pennsylvania Avenue at 10th Street NW, but with the tour entrance on E Street)—not unlike the Bureau of Engraving and Printing, above—packs in kid-filled crowds, with a wait for the hour-long guided tour as long as an hour and a half in summer. The FBI—a unit of the Justice Department in a big but ungainly building wherein 900 of the 8000 workers are agents—effectively puts its best foot forward on the expedition through its headquarters. Exhibits run a wide gamut—the gun, hat, cigar, and eyeglasses of infamous criminal John Dillinger who was killed in 1934 in Chicago, and photos of other much-chronicled FBI enemies of that era, including Al Capone, Alvin Karpis, Bonnie Parker, Baby Face Nelson, and Machine Gun Kelley. There are gangland weapons, Ten Most Wanted posters (with a majority of criminals in the posters, the tour guide advises, invariably apprehended), fingerprint cards (of which there are no two alike, with millions in FBI files since they were first used in 1924), displays of drugs (cannabis, crack, heroin, opium, and cocaine), guns and pistols from a collection totaling 5000, a gambling exhibit including loaded dice ("the odds are always against you," the guide makes clear), and, among much else along the route, cases containing 1930s FBI-themed games and toys, including titles of the then-widely-read Big Little Books series about agents' exploits, "Jr. G-Man" badges, "G-Man Automatic" toy guns, G-Man toy cars and G-Man handcuffs.

You learn that agents' average ages are 23–35, that they hold university degrees, that they take a 15-week training course at Quantico, Virginia, generally retiring from the field at age 55, and that there are 950 women out of a total of some 9700 agents. But I save most exciting for last (the kids go for this): The tour concludes in an auditorium where, from the stage—actually an indoor shooting range—an articulate, impeccably groomed agent welcomes the crowd and then fires a submachine gun at his target. Needless to say, it's a bull's-eye.

Folger Shakespeare Library (201 East Capitol Street SE) is a feast for Shakespeare buffs, with the largest collection extant of Shakespeareana, including precious early editions of the Bard's plays and other rare books and manuscripts dating back centuries. The library stages short-term exhibitions, not necessarily Shakespearean but invariably absorbing, as for example the relatively recent "The Cathedral: Faith in Stone," which, by means of various artistic representations, delineated the design and history of seats of bishops in nine European countries. If you won't be attending a performance in the Folger's authentic Elizabethan-design theater (chapter 3), try for a peek while you're inspecting the library; the theater doors are often open— and it's a charmer. Note that the Folger presents concerts of early music, as well as poetry readings and a lecture series. A commendable institution, easily inspected when you're in the neighborhood at say, the Capitol or Supreme Court (above) or Library of Congress (below).

Georgetown (like Alexandria, Virginia, above) was a thriving community before the District of Columbia (of which it is now a part) was created. It happily retains its name and a special ambience—a felicitous blend of a youthful clientele in its M Street and Wisconsin Avenue shops, restaurants, cafés, and late-hours bistros, together with affluent residents (the clientele and residents can be, and often are, one and the same) of impeccably maintained eighteenth- and nineteenth-century houses lining residential streets, again not unlike those of Old Town Alexandria. I call to your attention such specific Georgetown standouts as Georgetown University, Dumbarton Oaks, Tudor Place, and the Old Stone House, as well as a number of hotels and restaurants, on other pages. At this point, I want to emphasize the wealth of old houses—many originally restored with the encouragement of Eleanor Roosevelt during the years when her husband, FDR, was luring professionals to Washington who needed homes. A post–World War II Act of Congress protects Georgetown's aged buildings. Its fine houses are, with less than a handful of exceptions (like Tudor Place) private, but it's rewarding to pass them by in the same way you do the mansions of Embassy Row. Streets to stroll include P Street NW, with early-nineteenth-century houses, and the Victorian houses of Q Street NW. But don't limit yourself to the foregoing. Virtually all Georgetown streets M north to Q, especially between 30th and 31st streets NW, constitute old-house territory.

Jefferson Memorial (East Basin Drive SW, flanking the Tidal Basin on an intentionally planned axis—with the Washington Monument and White House due north) appropriately honors the vigorously multitalented man who was not only the third president, but also an architect and author, vice president under John Adams, President Washington's secretary of state and, earlier, one of our first diplomats to serve abroad, as a negotiator (with Benjamin Franklin and John Adams) of treaties with major European powers. Architect John Russell Pope (who designed the National Gallery's West Building and other major works)—after the memorial was decreed by a 1934 Act of Congress—created a building reflecting Jefferson's partiality toward the dome-topped Pantheon in Rome and the houses of Andrea Palladio (see *Italy at Its Best*), which influenced Jefferson in the case of his University of Virginia rotunda and Monticello, his Virginia mansion. The memorial is a variation on this theme: impressively domed (height is 67 feet) fronted by a colonnaded portico, and still additional columns—topped by severe Ionic capitals—encircling the building. Within, the centerpiece is a statue of a standing Jefferson, the work of sculptor Rudolph Evans, a New Yorker who was victorious in a nationwide competition for the commission. A smaller sculpture is a representation of Jefferson with fellow Declaration of Independence authors Adams, Franklin, Robert Livingston, and Roger Sherman.

Before leaving, your eye lights on four meaningful Jefferson quotations inscribed on as many walls. Most famous—we learn it in school and we don't forget it—is this eloquent excerpt from the partly Jefferson-authored Declaration of Independence: "We hold these truths to be self-evident: that all men are created equal, that they are endowed by their Creator with certain inalienable rights; among these are life, liberty, and the pursuit of happiness, that to secure these rights governments are instituted among men. We . . . solemnly publish and declare that these

colonies are and of right ought to be free and independent states.
. . . And for the support of this declaration, with a firm reliance
on the protection of divine providence, we mutually pledge our
lives, our fortunes, and our sacred honor." The Jefferson Memorial, like the Lincoln, is traditionally open late—until midnight.

Library of Congress (with the main entrance of its principal, or
Jefferson, building on 1st Street, between East Capitol Street and
Independence Avenue SE; the newer Adams and Madison buildings are just opposite to the east and to the south, respectively)
has become, in less than two centuries, a wonder of the world of
the printed word. Quite literally overshadowed by the domed
Capitol, its near neighbor, and situated in a wonder-filled city, it
remains for all too many Washington visitors woefully underap-
preciated. You owe it to yourself to become acquainted with
what President John Adams created as a little reference library in
the Capitol for members of Congress. It has become the largest
library in the world, with 86 million items (including 4 million
maps and atlases, 10 million prints and photos, a 7-million piece
music collection, 80,000 movies, and—on permanent display—a
Gutenberg Bible along with many other rare volumes and precious prints, and 26 million books, of which three-quarters are
published in 470 languages other than English). The library's
5000 employees (of which 900 fulfill the library's original
mission—researching legislative matters for members of Congress) provide services for the blind and otherwise disabled, staff
the U.S. Copyright Office (all of my books are, of course,
copyrighted by the Library of Congress, and on one visit I
checked them all out, to have a look), manage computerized
library data that is available to libraries around the world, and
offer auxiliary services that include concerts and literary programs, imaginatively created exhibitions of its fabulous treasures, movies, and guided tours. Besides the dramatically domed
Main Reading Room of its Jefferson Building, there are a score-
plus additional reading rooms, the range African and Middle
Eastern, European and Hispanic, through Motion Pictures and
Television, Rare Books and Science, as well as a Performing Arts
Library in the Kennedy Center (chapter 3).

The oldest of the library's building trio was named in recent
years for Thomas Jefferson who contributed the books of the

library at his Virginia home, Monticello, amassed over half a century, to the still-fledgling Library of Congress—destroyed when the British burned the Capitol in the War of 1812. The *Jefferson Building*, costliest library structure in the world when it opened in 1897, is a veritable Italian Renaissance palazzo. You are wowed from the moment of entry by a Great Hall that is one of the truly stunning Washington interior spaces, a magnificent mix of marbles and mosaics and murals, stained glass and statuary, of tremendous height and scale. The Jefferson's extravagantly decorated Main Reading Room (reopened in 1990 after closing for major renovations) is at the same exalted aesthetic level as counterparts in London's British Library (see *London at Its Best*) and Paris's Bibliothèque Nationale (see *Paris at Its Best*), with a 160-foot-high coffered ceiling embellished with griffins and garlands. It has its own collection of 45,000 reference books, desks for 250 readers, and an adjacent Computer Catalogue Center for public access to the library's automated catalog files through computer terminals.

Both the other buildings are of this century; the *John Adams Building* (1939) has murals of Chaucer's *The Canterbury Tales* decorating its big and handsome fifth-floor reading room, while the newer *James Madison Building* more than doubled the library's space when it opened in 1980. Restaurants (in the Madison Building, chapter 5) welcome visitors, and that same building's shop is a good one. Open-hours impress, too; traditionally, they're the most generous in Washington. The library's head is the presidentially designated librarian of congress; political appointments though they are, the librarians, or at least their professional staffs, have quite obviously been top rank. We can all be proud of the Library of Congress.

National Aquarium (Department of Commerce Building, 14th Street and Constitution Avenue NW) is a Washington oddity in that—location within a government building notwithstanding—it charges admission. Withal, it claims to be run by a nonprofit group, and is so well located—near the Mall—that an inspection is not out of order. Go, if you can, at shark-feeding time—customarily Monday, Wednesday, and Saturday at 2 P.M., or if you prefer, piranha-feeding time at 2 P.M. Tuesday, Thursday, and

Sunday. All told, there are more than 1200 aquatic creatures—sea turtles, alligators, and, if you will, tropical clown fish among them—peering out at you, when the spirit moves them, from some 70 tanks, most novel of which is a "touch" tank whose residents—sea urchins, hermit and horseshoe crabs—you may pick up.

Commerce's cafeteria welcomes visitors through lunch on weekdays.

National Archives (Constitution Avenue at 7th Street NW) is so well located—at the eastern edge of the Federal Triangle almost opposite the National Gallery of Art—and with such significant contents that virtually every visitor in town goes inside. As well they might. The building itself is one of the city's dazzlers, designed by the same John Russell Pope who is responsible for the National Gallery of Art's West Building, the Jefferson Memorial, and New York City's Customs House. It is one of the great Neoclassic works, with 8 of the 72 Corinthian columns surrounding it supporting a superbly sculpted portico, framing bronze entrance doors a foot thick and weighing 190 tons between them.

Chances are you will queue up, but lines move fairly rapidly and your goal at the far end of the rotunda is worthwhile: bronze and glass cases in which are exhibited the Declaration of Independence (drafted by Jefferson, Franklin, John Adams, Robert Livingston, and Roger Sherman, June 11-28, 1776; adopted July 3, 1776, and signed August 2, 1776, by John Hancock, the Continental Congress's president, and other members, that day and later); the Constitution (drafted by the Constitutional Convention in Philadelphia May–September 1787, signed September 17, 1782, by twelve of the first thirteen states, taking effect in March 1789, a month before Washington was inaugurated president); and the Bill of Rights (the first ten amendments to the Constitution). All the documents are sealed in cases in which air has been replaced by protective helium. At closing time each day the documents are lowered into a subterranean vault, the better to preserve and protect them.

But you want to look around, before departing, at murals of Jefferson presenting the Declaration to Hancock, and of James

Madison presenting the Constitution to Washington, not to mention a riveting clutch of historic D.C. photos. The Archives has considerable other holdings, the range the Emancipation Proclamation and slave ship manifests through Japanese surrender documents and captured German records from World War II, Indian Treaties and the Louisiana Purchase document (the purchase doubled the nation's territory). And it's the Archives that operate eight of the presidential libraries, coast to coast. Shop.

National Zoological Park (a.k.a. The Zoo, with its main entrance a few blocks north of the Woodley Park–Zoo Metro station on upper Connecticut Avenue NW), despite operation as a unit of the Smithsonian Institution, is, at least to this aficionado of zoos, something of a disappointment. The fault is only partially the Smithsonian's. Location is unfortunate, especially on a sizzling hot summer day when so many out-of-town visitors go. Exhibits straddle what is, in effect, a minimountain, and if you want to see them all you must descend it if you've entered on Connecticut Avenue (necessary also if you're hungry enough to want lunch in its cafeteria) and then ascend to exit to the Metro. By no means all exhibits are modern style—by that I mean with animals roaming in really wide open spaces. But you go, in my view, principally to say hello to Ling-Ling and Hsing-Hsing, the black-and-white giant pandas presented to the United States by the People's Republic of China in 1972. At least if they're awake, visible, and eating bamboo—their principal activity (feeding times are 11 A.M. and 3 P.M.) other than snoozing. The zoo's collection of invertebrates—animals without backbones such as butterflies, spiders, and leeches—is considered outstanding, and of course you will come across such familiars as elephants and zebras, rhinos and hippos, lions and tigers, monkeys and apes, not to mention seals that are fed daily at 11:30 A.M. National Friends of the Zoo, an organization of contributors that operates the hot-dog stand at the summit of the mountain near the main entrance, needs more staff to handle summer crowds, and places other than open benches for eaters to sit down with what they've ordered, seating that offers no protection from the elements. Pandas and an amusing shop (chapter 6) notwithstanding, the zoo is hardly in a class with those of the Bronx in New York, of San Diego, or of London.

Old Executive Office Building (Pennsylvania Avenue at 17th Street NW): Would that its name conveyed its historic significance as its facade conveys its grandeur. Still, the Old Executive Office Building served as the seat of three of the then four most important cabinet departments simultaneously—State, War, and Navy—from the 1880s until (at least for State) 1947. And it is hardly run-of-the-mill today, given its occupants: Executive Office of the President (which operates it), certain additional segments of White House staff, and the National Security Council. It is as well the location of one of the three offices of the vice president (others are in the Capitol and the White House). Derided when it went up between 1871 and 1888—the expectation was that a building to the west of the White House would be a Greek Revival clone of the Treasury (above) on the White House's east flank. Alas, it is anything but. In contrast to the colonnades and porticos of the Treasury, the OEOB is easily the most exuberant of the capital's principal government buildings: French Second Empire—rich in detail and complexity—with a facade deftly teaming porticos and dormer windows, Mansard roofs and pilasters, Doric and Ionic columns (900 all told), and a network of chimneys; along with interiors that are arguably the most luscious and lavish in the capital.

What lay behind architect Alfred Mullett's design was the optimism of the post–Civil War period—a period of expansion and increasing prosperity. Over the years, though, OEOB deteriorated. In the 1980s the Executive Office of the President began an ongoing restoration program, with emphasis on the most spectacular of the building's historic interiors. And it offered first-time-ever public tours. Not unlike the State Department Diplomatic Reception Rooms and the Treasury Department (below), guided tours of the OEOB are relatively unheralded, must be reserved in advance, and are requisite for buffs of architecture, interiors, and American history.

When you consider that this building was the site, simultaneously over a sustained period, of three cabinet departments, it is not surprising that the alumni roster is stellar—Theodore and Franklin Roosevelt (both as assistant secretaries of the Navy), William Howard Taft, and Dwight D. Eisenhower are among the presidents who worked on the premises, as have two dozen secretaries of state (including Cordell Hull, who met in the building with Japanese diplomats immediately after the Japanese bombed Pearl Harbor in 1941); 25 Navy secretaries, and 21 secretaries of war (who headed what is now called the Department of the Army).

The building's interior architecture is dazzling. Features that can be mundane in a modern building—like corridors and stairways—are minor masterworks here.

Intricately coffered domes cover stairwells at each of the OEOB's corners. Rotundas are stunners: East Rotunda, embellished with gilded busts and carved wood, West Rotunda with stained glass. And those of the important rooms that have been restored (more are to come, as part of the long-range program) represent the building at its best. The onetime secretary of the Navy's office is lit by chandeliers hung from a painted ceiling, with Victorian chairs surrounding a conference table at one end and, on the secretary's desk, a gilded vertical-design telephone of the kind used through the 1920s.

The former War Department Library—now serving as the White House Law Library—embraces three levels of cast-iron stacks and still boasts its original skylight. The present White House Research Library, originally containing volumes used for research by the State Department, is constructed entirely of cast iron, with its three intricately designed balconies painted white; before the National Archives (above) opened, this library displayed the Declaration of Independence and the Constitution. You know you're near tour's end when you arrive in the romantically titled Indian Treaty Room, named for a succession of international and other agreements signed on its tables. Its décor—bronze lamps in each corner representing Arts and Science, Industry, Liberty, and War and Peace, patterned tile floor, marble-paneled walls, wrought-iron balcony setting off a second level on all four sides—reflects its original use as a naval reception room. Although you will have entered the building at a side door on 17th Street NW, you exit very grandly indeed from the imposing north lobby, down the steps along a stone-paved walkway to Pennsylvania Avenue, just opposite the Smithsonian's Renwick Gallery (below), a compatible neighbor that was completed a decade and a half earlier but is of the same Second

Empire style, albeit much smaller and a good deal less flamboyant. (Make a note of the phone number for tour reservations: [202] 395-5895.)

Old Post Office (Pennsylvania Avenue at 12th Street NW): The good news about this quite marvelous turn-of-century architectural masterwork—with its distinctive neo-Romanesque facade in an area of Classical-style structures—is that it still is with us. When the Post Office Department took over more contemporary quarters nearby, some years back, government planners favored razing, with a replacement more in keeping with the architecture of neighboring Federal Triangle buildings. Common sense prevailed, and the building was restored, reopening in 1983 with "Old" preceding "Post Office" in its title, and rangers of the National Park Service, the current operator, leading groups up a glass elevator in the nine-story atrium for views from the 315-foot tower. The bad news is budget-category commercial occupants. Unlike restored Union Station (below), where shops and restaurants are largely a class act, mercantile activity at the Old PO is pretty much run-of-the-mill stores and fast-food joints. (I recommend none of them in chapters 5 and 6.) Still, you want to pay your respects, perhaps en route to or from museums on the nearby Mall.

Organization of American States (17th Street at Constitution Avenue NW) was known as the Pan American Union when I first visited. The current title makes clear that it's the headquarters of the intergovernmental association of hemisphere countries, whose Latin-American accents—a tropical patio, tropically planted, and an Aztec garden especially—constitute the building at its most interesting. You want especially to have a look at the handsome Council Chamber where OAS member countries deliberate. (And note that paintings by artists of the hemisphere are displayed at the neighboring *Museum of Art of Latin America* at 201 18th Street NW.)

Pentagon (Pentagon station of the D.C. Metro, or U.S. 395 south to Boundary Channel Drive exit, Arlington, Virginia): A hike through corridors (some, to be sure, with exhibits extolling the military whose headquarters this structure houses) is hardly to everyone's liking. Still, you may want to be the first on your block. Completed in 1943, the seat of the Department of Defense is one of the world's largest office buildings, twice the size of Chicago's Merchandise Mart, with three times the floor space of New York's Empire State Building, so capacious that the U.S. Capitol could fit into any of its five wedge-shaped sections. Its work force of 23,000 (including the secretaries of Defense, Army, and Navy, and the admirals and generals of the Joint Chiefs of Staff) climbs 131 stairways, rides 19 escalators, tells time by 4200 clocks, drinks from 691 water fountains, and makes 200,000 phone calls a day. I am indebted to Pentagon researchers for these figures, and for the intelligence that despite its 17½ miles of corridors, it takes only 7 minutes to walk between any two of the most-distant-from-each-other points in the building. Tours (starting with an explanatory film) are Monday through Friday only, departing half-hourly, customarily 9:30 A.M.–3:30 P.M. and lasting an hour and a quarter. Employee cafeterias are not open to visitors, but the very next station on the Metro is Pentagon City, with restaurants (chapter 5), shopping mall (chapter 6), and even a Ritz Carlton hotel (chapter 4).

Union Station (50 Massachusetts Avenue NE) is called to your attention herewith should you be a first-timer in town who has arrived by plane, car, or bus and thus not had a look at what is once again one of America's great railway terminals—as well as the site of a number of creditable restaurants (chapter 5) and a hundred shops, a number of them of good quality (chapter 6). A glorious Beaux Arts palace—in the manner of so many of its counterparts coast to coast during the era when trains were the favored means of long-distance transport, the station fell into near oblivion when the airplane took over following World War II. As a well-intended means of rescue and to avert razing, the National Park Service spent $100 million in the 1970s, turning the station into an information center for visitors to Washington—which hardly any visitors bothered using. America's Bicentennial came and went—and so did the Visitor Center.

Still, as the 1980s evolved, passengers, myself among them, were shunted to nether regions of the complex to board and alight from Amtrak trains; refurbishment was underway. There's little that a budget of $160 million can't do to restore a building of this caliber. In 1988, the thoroughly rebuilt, revamped Union Station—retaining the ebullience of architect Daniel Burnham's original 1908 design—reopened to widespread acclaim. When you go in—passing under a sculpture-embellished entrance defined by Ionic columns to either side—the aesthetics of the interior prove exciting. Vaulting of the 90-foot barrel-vaulted ceiling in the soaring Main Hall has been meticulously restored, with a wealth of architectural detail, balustrades through spiral staircases, gold leaf embellishing ceilings, and fountains playing at strategic sites.

The business of buying tickets for, boarding, and exiting trains is as contemporary as can be. You go from Main Hall to Main Concourse to a glass-enclosed structure known as the Train Concourse, en route to trains. There's a Metro station, a 1400-car garage, and in addition to the network of attractive restaurants and classy shops, a high-ceilinged lower level devoted to mostly fast-food eateries sharing a vast common seating area.

U.S. Department of State Diplomatic Reception Rooms (2201 C Street NW): When it left what is now called the Old Executive Office Building (above) after World War II, the State Department moved into modern government-issue quarters in the Foggy Bottom area, not far north of the Lincoln Memorial. The building was then, and remains now, nondescript, unattractive, and not worth calling to your attention, except for one standout feature: a suite of rooms—used by the secretary of state for official entertaining—that has in the last three decades been transformed architecturally and with respect to furnishings (period is the eighteenth and early nineteenth centuries) into a complex housing one of the greatest collections extant of American antiques and antique accessories, with a current value—I learned from the guide on my most recent tour—of $50 million. With its worth increasing as a result of an ongoing campaign for funds and appropriate furnishings by State's Fine Arts Committee—composed of rich contributors, with wives of half a dozen past secretaries of state and the current secretary as honorary members. A paid curator manages operations. Since I first visited the rooms as a guest at a reception during the Carter Administration, they have evolved considerably. A Georgian lounge, dubbed Ceremonial Office of the Secretary of State, and an elliptical, classically colonnaded Treaty Room paid for by tobacco companies on the seventh floor of the building— down a flight from the reception rooms—are not shown on guided tours. What you see is the gala sixth-floor suite embracing three principal salons and a number of satellite spaces. It is possible to fault the Diplomatic Rooms' décor as being, in certain rooms, a case of too much of a good thing, jampacked with magnificent objects albeit upon occasion in excessive quantity.

Which is hardly to say you want to miss these salons, if you have even a whit of interest in American decorative arts—or for that matter, fine arts. For paintings are museum-caliber, with many by noted artists whose work you'll recognize. Even the architectural design of each room is significant; architects and designers worked with artisans to transform standard office building amenities—acoustical ceilings and plain plaster walls— into spaces embellished with columns and pilasters, cornices and friezes, panels and pediments, arched doorways and draped windows.

After being pointed in the right direction by a stony-faced receptionist in State's severe 23rd Street lobby (don't arrive appreciably early as there's no place to sit except on the steps outside), you are impressed as you alight from the elevator. The corridor is crystal-chandeliered, with marbleized pilasters and entablatures against its walls. Your next stop, the Entrance Hall, could be the drawing room of an eighteenth-century house. You pass, then, along a hallway called the Gallery, with Palladian windows at either end and walls lined with American Chippendale and Queen Anne furniture. Then comes the John Quincy Adams State Drawing Room, where the secretary of state welcomes lunch and dinner guests. A Philadelphia highboy is its dominant piece, complemented by yellow-and-red-damask-covered eighteenth-century furniture, fine paintings, and precious Oriental rugs, with illumination from a trio of crystal chandeliers. Most restrained in décor of the principal areas, the

Thomas Jefferson State Reception Room, comes next—coolly neoclassical, with walls of celadon and eighteenth-century sculpture in white-framed niches, the lot reflecting the well-documented taste of the third president, who was, as well, the first secretary of state. Biggest for last: Benjamin Franklin State Dining Room, able to seat 500 for lunch or dinner, with the seal of the United States carved into the plaster of a ceiling hung with eight Adam-style chandeliers, and walls edged by *faux-marbre* columns, topped by gilded Corinthian capitals. (Just beyond, albeit not shown to groups, are a pair of contiguous smaller rooms named for James Madison—a Federal Period reception room and a dining room with a table flanked by sixteen Sheraton chairs. Both are the exclusive province of the secretary, the former for pre-meal drinks, the latter for VIP lunches and dinners.) My notes brim with exclamation points of approbation for the rooms' paintings. (You wish the group moved more slowly so that you could look at more of them.) I recall with pleasure portraits of James Monroe by both Thomas Sully and Samuel F. B. Morse; Martha Washington by Rembrandt Peale and her husband George by Charles Willson Peale; a painting each of Mr. and Mrs. Winthrop Sargent by Gilbert Stuart; still another Stuart of John Jay; the French portraitist Greuze's study of Benjamin Franklin executed while Franklin represented us in Paris; Jefferson by Charles Willson Peale, and also by Sully; a Miss Alice Hooper by John Singleton Copley; another Copley of a Mrs. John Montresor; and a Benjamin West study of the signing of the Treaty of Paris, with John Jay and Franklin among the signers. There are other nonportrait works of consequence, including *A Glimpse of the Capitol, 1844* by William McLeod; Asher Durand's *Departure of Columbus for the New World;* a Wyoming river scene by Thomas Moran; a mountainous New Hampshire landscape by Jasper Cropsey; Lake Tahoe, unrecognizable today, by Albert Bierstadt. Try glancing, as you are rushed past, at extraordinary Chinese Export porcelain dating to the eighteenth century and exquisite American silver.

I want to emphasize that this is a tour for which you must reserve well in advance by phoning the State Department's tour office (202-647-3421), ideally before arrival in Washington, if your stay will be relatively brief. Along with the State Rooms of the White House and relatively recently redecorated interiors, featuring American furnishings, of early-nineteenth-century *Blair House* (1651 Pennsylvania Avenue NW), the presidential guest house not open to the public, more's the pity—these State Department rooms are the finest period interiors in town.

U.S. Department of the Treasury (Pennsylvania Avenue NW between 15th Street, site of the public entrance, and East Executive Avenue)—most paranoid and, again in my experience, downright nastiest, with respect to security, of any government department—opened its doors to the public as recently as 1989 on an extremely limited basis: every *other* Saturday morning, on hour-long guided tours at 10 and 10:20 A.M. Making advance arrangements for tour reservations is bothersome but, if you're a buff of architecture and/or history, worthwhile. The Treasury, along with the onetime U.S. Patent Office, now housing a pair of Smithsonian museums (above), is one of the finest examples extant of the Greek Revival style in the United States. It is, as well, the third-oldest federal building in town (following the White House and the Capitol) and the oldest building, bar none, specifically designed to serve as an office workspace for government personnel. (Construction began in 1836.) You've looked at likenesses of the Treasury countless times, possibly without realizing it (see the reverse side of any $10 bill). Until you study it, you don't appreciate the grandeur of the thirty 36-foot-high Ionic columns constituting the Treasury's east facade, nor for that matter, the porticoes at its north and south entrances. What impelled the brass to allow public tours was a recent multimillion-dollar refurbishing (so meticulous that the Treasury hired a professional art historian as its curator) with funds both public and private, the latter raised by a group called the Committee for the Preservation of the Treasury Building. The tour takes you through the building's south, west, and north wings, along authentically refitted corridors (some hung with portraits of past secretaries), to the capacious reception and conference rooms recently created for the secretary's official parties and meetings. This pair of rooms is in the style of mid-nineteenth-century American Renaissance Revival, with vaulted ceilings, stencil-patterned walls, electrified gas chandeliers and wall sconces, period furniture (some with dollar signs on chair backs, some with gilded U.S. shields from the 1860s), carved wood and gilt cornices over window draperies, specially woven Wilton and Brussels carpets, and paintings including a Thomas Sully portrait of Secretary Salmon Chase, as well as a fine bust of the first secretary, Alexander Hamilton.

Important, too, is the area now occupied as an office by the Treasurer of the United States (the post is invariably held by a politically appointed woman; treasurers' signatures are reproduced on paper money, as you'll note on bills in your wallet or handbag). It was originally a vault, during the mid-nineteenth-century period when currency was still being made and stored in the building. The vault was rediscovered by accident in 1985 in the course of a renovation. It was built a hundred years earlier but hidden from view for nearly 80 years, sandwiched between two later vault extensions. You'll see the restored federal symbols decorating it, and a cross section of its burglarproof lining.

A space now serving as the office of one of the undersecretaries (our taxes support upper-echelon federal bureaucrats in splendid style) is still another tour stop—as well it might be. After President Lincoln's assassination in 1865, it was used by his successor, Andrew Johnson, as the presidential office—a temporarily detached bit of the White House where President Johnson headquartered for six weeks, allowing Mrs. Lincoln time to pack before leaving the Executive Mansion.

The room shown at the conclusion of the tour—a case of best for last—was open to the public as a Treasury-operated bank until as recently as the year of the American Bicentennial, 1976. Called the Cash Room, its walls and floors are of nine types of marble in tones of gray, white, black, pink, and red; its chandeliers are glass-globed; its Ionic pilasters are highlighted in gold; the balcony, of exquisitely wrought bronze in agricultural and marine motifs, is as handsome as it is history-laden. Although the room is not overlarge (dimensions are 32' X 72'), it was selected as the venue for President Grant's inaugural reception in 1869. Two thousand invitations were sold, each valid for a gent and two ladies, or in other words, 6000 persons. The crush was intense—people danced in corridors throughout the building—and advance planning was virtually nil on such matters as seating, adequate food at buffet tables (women are reported to have fainted en route to obtaining sustenance), and, oddest of all, the checking of coats—with some guests staying on, the press reported, until as late as 4 A.M. searching for outer wraps. Next time you throw a party or go to one, think of Ulysses S. Grant and the Treasury's Cash Room.

U.S. Marine Corps Memorial and The Netherlands Carillon (just west of Arlington Memorial Bridge, off Route U.S. 50, Arlington, Virginia) are taken in tandem at this point—and might well be, by you—because they're immediate neighbors, between Arlington National Cemetery and the Potomac. The *U.S. Marine Corps Memorial,* frequently called by the name of the Pacific Island—Iwo Jima—which is 660 miles south of Tokyo and was the site of a key battle toward the end of World War II. The memorable monument is a three-dimensional emulation, if you will, of a prize-winning photo by a news photographer named Joe Rosenthal, taken on February 23, 1945, when a Marine company, having climbed Iwo Jima's peak, Mount Suribachi, raised the flag on its summit. Rosenthal's Pulitzer Prize–winning photo captured American hearts, was sculpted by Felix W. de Weldon, then cast in bronze before removal to its present site and dedication by President Eisenhower in November 1954. June through August, Marines parade at sunset adjacent to the memorial, usually between 7 and 8:30 P.M.

The Netherlands Carillon is a gift from the Dutch people to the American people in appreciation of World War II aid. A symbol of the gift—a small silver bell—was presented to President Truman by then-Queen (now Princess) Juliana in 1952. Several years later the 49-bell carillon—whose construction was paid for with funds raised by the Dutch people—was shipped transatlantic, and in 1960 the carillon in its specially constructed tower, designed by a Dutch architect, was dedicated. It's 125 feet high, surrounded—not surprisingly—by tulips whose bulbs are Dutch imports, and it is heard in concert traditionally Saturday afternoons and some holidays between 2 and 4 P.M., during which time visitors may ascend (via a stairway) to the top of the tower to watch carillonneurs play.

Washington Monument (south of Constitution Avenue NW, at the western edge of the Mall, between 15th and 17th streets NW, and encircled by American flags): The best known of early American figures served as commander in chief of the revolutionary army, president of the Constitutional Convention, and for two terms (1789–1797) as first president of the United States—and his principal memorial is surely the capital city that takes his name. Mount Vernon, the Washington mansion in nearby Virginia (above) is still another major memento. As is, of course, the Washington Monument, inspired in the simplicity of its design (and from a period—the mid nineteenth century—when simplicity was not a design hallmark) and in the strength it conveys of the man it memorializes. Not to mention its height: 555 feet, especially important because it has long been the practice in Washington to build no structure any taller.

The monument was anything but an overnight construction project. By no means as elaborate as the original design submitted in the 1840s, the monument—a hollow shaft with a plain, undecorated facade—was begun in 1848; the trowel used for the ceremonial beginning of the construction was that employed by the first president himself at the cornerstone ceremonies for the U.S. Capitol in 1783. In 1850, construction stopped—a delay attributed to political squabbles. Later, the Civil War was an impediment to continued construction. Only in 1885, during the Cleveland presidency, did the monument open to the public.

Time was when you could ascend the 897 steps to the summit. (Views are fabulous.) But because the walk up is arduous, it's no longer allowed. Now, take the elevator—the second, installed in 1955, makes the trip in 70 seconds. But, if you like, you may walk *down* this 90,854-ton structure, taking in nearly 200 memorial plaques on stairwell walls, one each from the 50 states and others from assorted organizations and foreign countries. *Caveat:* The summer months see long queues for the ascent, even though the elevator departs every five minutes. Try to arrive early—the monument traditionally opens at 8 A.M. April through Labor Day, during which period it closes at midnight. Hours the rest of the year are customarily 9 A.M.–5 P.M.

MUSEUMS AFTER THE BIG FIVE

There is a wealth of Washington museums—no other city its size has anything like as many, and quality is right up there with quantity. Five of these museums are significant enough, in my view, to rank among the top ten destinations in town—and I include them, for that reason, in "The Essential Washington" (above). They are the National Gallery of Art, National Portrait Gallery/National Museum of American Art, National Museum of American History, and National Air and Space Museum. Still, they're only a starter for museums. Here are a score-plus more.

Anacostia Museum (1901 Fort Place SE)—a relatively recent off-Mall addition to the Smithsonian Institution's network—occupies space in a clean-lined 1987 structure, and is, in effect, a contemporary artistic portrait of black America, interpreted by short-term exhibits, whose subject matter can range from the Anacostia community in which the museum is located, through to black cultural and historic highlights and the achievements of black Americans, aviators through coloratura sopranos. Whenever you go, displays are absorbing.

Art and Industries Building of the Smithsonian Institution (Jefferson Drive at 9th Street SW) is a next-door neighbor of the Smithsonian Castle (below), and the second-oldest Smithsonian building after the Castle. It opened with a bang—in the form of President Garfield's inaugural ball—in 1881. There's no disputing its spirited good looks, embracing a network of towers framing a main section with a farther-back dome atop an octagonal rotunda. The problem, or at least so it seems to me, is that the Smithsonian has never known quite what to do with Art and Industries. Prior to the U.S. Bicentennial in 1976, it had been the repository of any number of objects. Then, for the nation's 200th birthday, it was spruced up and put to use as the setting for a display of objects in use a hundred years earlier, in 1876: the range printing presses and machine tools through to an actual railway locomotive, the lot reposing in four principal galleries. Still, on my recent visits, I have found fewer visitors in Art and Industries than in any other downtown Smithsonian museum.

Why not move the best of this collection over to the National Museum of American History (of which Art and Industries is a satellite) and come up with something new and different for this lovely building?

Capital Children's Museum (800 3rd Street NE): I am not sympathetic to a museum policy—even when the theme is children—whereby kids (from two onward) pay the same relatively stiff entry fee as their parents. This museum—without any distinctive relationship to Washington, and which could be in virtually any city, where children would no doubt enjoy it—made its mark with hands-on exhibits: computers, scientific objects, and an unusual sculpture garden among them. But if you're with youngsters and with limited time in town I would concentrate on, say, the Washington Monument, the Air and Space Museum, or the pandas at the zoo.

Corcoran Gallery of Art (17th Street and New York Avenue NW) occupied what is now the Smithsonian Institution's Renwick Gallery (below) before it moved to its present quarters—a formidable Beaux Arts building a hop and a skip west of the White House—in 1897. Until the National Gallery of Art opened prior to World War II, the Corcoran was D.C.'s principal art museum. The relatively recent criticism to which it was subjected (as a result of its having refused to open a 1989 exhibition—partially homoerotic—by the late photographer Robert Mapplethorpe, out of fear that Congress would cut grants) was deserved. Withal, the Corcoran—refurbished, with its Main Hall's wine-shaded walls set off by white marble nineteenth-century busts—is an important museum with an important collection of American as well as European art. The museum's founder, banker William Wilson Corcoran, started buying American work in the latter decades of the last century, and the museum has expanded its American holdings since Corcoran's time. You see today early greats like Gilbert Stuart's likeness of Mrs. Thomas Lea, Benjamin West's *Cupid Stung by a Bee,* Rembrandt Peale's *Washington before Yorktown*, the inventor-artist Samuel F. B. Morse's *The Old House of Representatives,* Thomas Cole's unusual pair, *The Departure* and *The Return,* Fredrick Church's *Niagara Falls* with additional

American paintings by the likes of Mary Cassatt and Thomas
Eakins, Helen Frankenthaler and Childe Hassam, Winslow
Homer and George Inness, Maurice Prendergast and Mark
Rothke.
  The European galleries are standouts, too. You remember
Degas's *École de Danse*, Pissarro's *Seine à Paris*, Daumier's *Print
Stand*, Chardin's *Woman with Saucepan*, Turner's *Ships in Strong Sea*,
not to mention De Hooch and Steen, Gainsborough and Law-
rence, Monet and Renoir, Corot and Vlaminck, Reynolds and
Titian. In no event bypass the Grand Salon, transported in toto
from a Paris mansion, to portray eighteenth-century French
interior design, its furniture quite literally museum-caliber
Louis XV, its wall panels and pilasters gilded, its floor the original
parquet. The Corcoran operates a prestigious four-year fine arts
college granting the B.A. degree; there are tours, lectures, and
chamber-music concerts. And a shop.

Daughters of the American Revolution Museum (1776 D Street
NW): If you are of a certain age, you remember how, when you
were a kid, Eleanor Roosevelt, the First Lady, resigned as a
member of the DAR when it objected to black contralto Marian
Anderson performing in its Constitution Hall. Mrs. Roosevelt,
along with Interior Secretary Harold Ickes, was instrumental in
moving the Anderson concert to the Lincoln Memorial; the
president's wife's widely publicized pullout had historic significance, serving as a kind of warm-up for the later civil-rights
movement. Indeed, for many Americans, the DAR remains
synonymous with organizational racial prejudice. Which is my
way of explaining that it took a while—the final research trip for
this book (following many D.C. visits over a sustained period)—
until I paid a call at the DAR's museum.
  Staff reception at the entrance bordered on the hostile, but the
volunteer docent to whom I was assigned (you move about in a
smallish group—not on your own) was kind and knowledgeable.
There's no question but that the exhibits—centering on period
rooms whose contents are themed to 33 American states and are
contributions from DAR members in as many states—are top-
rank. There's not enough tour time for all 33 rooms, but the
docent packs in as many as possible, including, for example, an

Oklahoma farm kitchen chockablock with domestic implements of the last century; a New Hampshire attic serving to display games, dolls, and toys of the late eighteenth and early nineteenth centuries; Chinese export pieces in the smart New York State salon; a late eighteenth-century interior from what must have been a handsome Massachusetts house; and, in contrast, an adobe California parlor—to give you an idea. Note that this museum is customarily closed Saturdays and Sunday mornings; on weekdays last tours usually commence at 3 P.M.

Dumbarton Oaks (703 32nd Street NW) is a principal pride of Georgetown, and with reason. An early-nineteenth-century Georgian-style mansion, it was deeded to Harvard by its past owners in 1940. First, see its museums. One is devoted to Byzantine art—an illuminated manuscript, "Moses Receiving the Law," labeled CONSTANTINOPLE, CIRCA 1084, is a stunner among many—including ivory, silver, and jewels. The other, in a Philip Johnson–designed pavilion (1963) is a trove of pre-Columbian treasures, a mosaic-embellished early Peruvian mirror, and superb textiles from that same period, with other pieces from Mexico, Guatemala, Panama, Costa Rica, and Colombia. Museums behind you, move along to the house's tapestry-walled, beam-ceilinged Music Room, site of the 1944 Dumbarton Oaks Conference that led to the creation of the United Nations, and beautifully furnished with a mix of Renaissance and eighteenth-century pieces, the focal point an immense stone fireplace. Just around the corner on R Street is the entrance to the complex's gardens—a dozen acres punctuated by reflecting pools, gazebos, and terraces. Shop.

Fondo del Sol Visual Arts Center (2112 R Street NW) can come up with super short-term exhibitions from just about anywhere in the hemisphere, especially south of the United States. That can mean island nations of the Caribbean (so often culturally slighted in American museums), Mexico, Central America, and South America.

Ford's Theatre Museum and the House Where Lincoln Died (the theater and its museum are at 511 10th Street NW, and Petersen

House is just opposite, at 516 10th Street NW) is a tripartite destination of significance. The theater—where President Lincoln was assassinated in the course of a performance on the evening of April 14, 1865—has been nicely restored, and although it is used commercially for plays (chapter 3), it welcomes visitors at no charge during the same daytime hours (except on matinee afternoons—Wednesday and Saturday—when it's occupied) as the fascinating museum in its basement (operated by the National Park Service). The museum was updated and enlarged in 1990; its exhibits relate to the fatal shooting of the president by actor John Wilkes Booth. Keeping the same hours as the museum, and also operated by the National Park Service in conjunction with it, is the House Where Lincoln Died (a.k.a. Petersen House) just opposite.

Go first to the theater. Closed by the federal government after Lincoln's death, it went through a long period of ups and downs (more of the latter than the former) until Congress appropriated funds for a meticulous facelift completed in 1968. Note the presidential box to the right as you face the stage; it contains a red damask sofa quite as it did the night of the shooting and is edged by American flags appropriate to the period, with a framed print of President Washington attached to the railing in view of the audience, again as was the case on the evening of the assassination.

Descend, then, to the basement and the museum's exhibits focusing on the assassination, the assassin, and his cohorts: including the frock coat Lincoln wore to the theater, the diary in which Booth justified his actions, even the weapon with which the president was shot. Finally, cross 10th Street to the Petersen House to which the wounded Lincoln was rushed, and where in the back bedroom he lay on a bed too short for him (he was laid diagonally across it), with his wife and son Robert present— much of the time in the front parlor—while Secretary of War Edwin Stanton, in the back parlor, began an investigation of events surrounding the tragedy.

Stanton issued orders for the arrest of Booth, who was killed while being apprehended by Union Army troops, on April 26— less than a fortnight later.

Freer Gallery of Art (on the Mall, Jefferson Drive at 12th Street SW) is the Smithsonian Institution's oldest art museum, dating to 1923 when only it and the Smithsonian Castle were at the Mall's western edge. The graceful Classic-style building houses the collection of a Detroit railway car manufacturer turned collector named Charles Freer, who donated his valuable art— an oddball mix of Asian treasures along with one of the two largest groupings extant of the paintings, drawings, watercolors, pastels, and etchings of the late-nineteenth-century American artist James McNeil Whistler.

Freer's gift hinged on the Smithsonian's agreeing not to break up the Asian and American meld, although it has been allowed to add to the Oriental portion. Upon completion of its Arthur M. Sackler Gallery—one of the nation's choicest holdings of Asian art—next door in 1987 (see below), the Smithsonian, closing down the Freer for several years, embarked upon a renovation of the Freer and the construction of new exhibit space, through which the Freer and Sackler were connected, thus actually uniting the two Smithsonian Oriental collections, the while leaving the Whistlers in the Freer, according to the agreement with the late Mr. Freer. Whistler's Oriental-influenced Peacock Room, with representations of the bird species taking its name inset in paneled walls, is the Freer at its most spectacular. But the Asian art—a fourth-century gilded silver dish from Persia, a fourteenth-century scroll of a boldly inked drawing of a monk in profile, lacquered and gilded Bodhisattva sculpture dating to the sixth century, Chinese bronzes, centuries-old daggers studded with rubies and emeralds—is splendid, too. Not without reason, the Freer is a Smithsonian favorite with many Mall regulars.

Hirshorn Museum and Sculpture Garden (on the Mall at Independence Avenue and 8th Street SW): First-timers can be diffident toward the Smithsonian's Hirshorn. Its circle of a reinforced concrete building—three stories high and atop a quartet of massive supports 14 feet above ground, creating an open-sculpture area—can take getting used to. But you like it more after you enter, your opinion of the environment aided without question by its contents: a representative selection of the 4000-plus paintings and drawings and more than 2000 sculptures given to the Smithsonian by the late Joseph Hirshorn, a Latvian-born immigrant of fabulous wealth. Besides his collection, Hirshorn contributed a million dollars toward the construction of the Skidmore, Owings & Merrill-designed building, which opened as the Smithsonian's museum of modern and contemporary art in 1974—seven years before his death.

The Hirshorn's principal attribute is its benefactor's taste. You find yourself exclaiming and approving, one work after the other, as you make your rounds, first in the Sculpture Garden across Jefferson Drive from the museum, then among the sculptures at ground level within the museum, and finally, inside, because of the paintings. My notes abound with enthusiasm from my most recent visit: the plethora of Henry Moore sculptures (more than in any other U.S. museum) with *Seated Figure against Curved Wall* and *King and Queen* my favorites; Dame Barbara Hepworth's *Large and Small Forms;* typically black, typically stacked Louise Nevelson boxlike forms; David Smith's unusually small *Bolton Landing;* and other sculptors' work, including Arp and Noguchi, Anthony Caro and Claes Oldenburg, Auguste Rodin and Richard Serra. Paintings are more American than foreign—the last century's William Merritt Chase, Thomas Eakins, John Singer Sargent. More recent U.S. works are by Rockwell Kent (a memorable seascape), Maurice Prendergast *(Beach Resort),* Childe Hassam *(The Union Jack, New York, April Morning)* along with other household-name painters such as George Bellows and Edward Hopper, Thomas Hart Benton and John Sloan, Milton Avery and Marsden Hartley, Georgia O'Keeffe and Stuart Davis. There are Europeans, too: Britain's Bacon, Belgium's Magritte, Spain's Miró, France's Matisse, Italy's Marini; and a substantial group of artists who came to the United States as immigrants, not unlike the museum's benefactor: German-born Albert Bierstadt, Dutch-origin Willem de Kooning, Yasio Kuniyoshi from Japan. And not a lemon in the lot! Take your time at the Hirshorn, bearing in mind, especially if it's summer, the possibility of a pause in the outdoor café (chapter 5). Short-term exhibitions can be top-rank, but the shop is smaller than you expected.

National Building Museum (F Street NW, between 4th and 5th streets): Not unlike the Renwick Gallery (below), you visit the

National Building Museum more for the building than for its exhibits, although these can be of interest when their emphasis is more on aspects of architecture than on construction. The kicker of this museum, though, is its Great Hall. Visitors utter a spirited "Wow!" at first glance, and then absorb the magnitude of what lies before them: a space 316 feet long, 116 feet wide, and 159 feet at its highest point. But it's not size alone (even though this is believed to be the largest room in town). It's the Corinthian columns—eight all told—that support it; each is 8 feet across, 25 feet around, 75 feet high, and built of 70,000 bricks, painted to resemble marble. (They're considered to be the largest such extant.) Seventy-two Doric columns line the first-floor Arcade, and the same number of Ionic columns embellish the Arcade on the second floor. Urns decorate the third-floor Parapet, while the fourth floor is set off by a wrought-iron Balcony. And there's a central fountain. All hail to the Civil War general—Montgomery C. Meigs—who designed this masterwork (it opened in 1883) as the Pension Building, for the distribution of pensions to Union Army veterans. Not surprisingly, it's been the site of not a few presidential inaugural balls.

National Museum of African Art (on the Mall, edging Independence Avenue SW, between 9th and 10th streets) occupies one of the pair of exquisite buildings constituting the newest of the Smithsonian Institution's museums (the other is the Arthur M. Sackler Gallery, below), which opened in 1987. Though not identical twins (African Art has curved domes, while the Sackler's domes are peaked, and there are other differences in detailing), the two museums, separated by a charming garden, are similar (each has an above-ground entrance pavilion and two levels below ground, a subterranean connection between the pair) and bring pride to the Smithsonian. Warren M. Robbins began this collection considerably before it became part of the Smithsonian.

There are bigger African art museums—Musée des Arts Africains et Océaniens, in Paris, for example—but none, I am sure, with finer specimens of the three-dimensional works that dominate sub-Saharan African art, taking the form of sculpture in carved wood and ivory, cast or forged metal, and modeled clay, often with utility as household wares, as architectural elements, and as religious objects. I became enamored of African art in the course of researching *Africa A to Z*, my first book, and no one has been more pleased to see such fine examples in so lovely a setting. There are, to be sure, temporary shows—such as "Art of the Yoruba People of Nigeria," and "Icons in the Art of Africa," along with lectures by experts and workshops. But the permanent collections are this museum's dazzlers: a golden pendant from the Ivory Coast; a harp fashioned from wood, leather, and metal, from Zaire; a metal-decorated carved-wood stool from Angola; a stone figure from Sierra Leone: a Nigerian headdress made from seeds, resin, fiber, and wood; a pottery vessel in beige and brown from Malawi; examples of the world-famous textiles—Kente cloths, they're called—from the Ashanti people of northern Ghana; and an extraordinary selection of ritual masks, from many countries. Excellent shop (chapter 6).

National Museum of Natural History (on the Mall, at 10th Street and Constitution NW), although a link of the Smithsonian chain, is nothing like as big or multidepartmental as the American Museum of Natural History in New York (see *New York at Its Best*) or the also-massive Museum of Natural History in London (see *London at Its Best*). Which is hardly to say you want to miss a visit, especially if you're with children and from a city without a similarly themed museum. And there's no question but that this one opens with a bang. Its central dome frames a capacious rotunda centered by an immense African bush elephant, trunk extended.

There are two principal floors of exhibits on the main level, leading from the elephant-centered rotunda. You find American Indian, African, and Pacific cultures; and even more to the point for a museum of this type, dinosaurs and fossils. But my favorite exhibits are upstairs: the Hope Diamond (at 45 carats the largest blue diamond extant), still in the setting made for its last private owner; not to mention rubies, sapphires, and a pair of earrings France's King Louis XVI gave to Queen Marie-Antoinette—all in the Gems Gallery.

At the other end of the same floor is the Insect Zoo, ants to tarantulas—and fascinating. Worth noting, too: the Discovery

Room, where you may feel, smell, and taste assorted natural objects (hours are limited and free passes are required weekends); the Naturalist Center, with rocks, animals, plants, and anthropological materials that can be handled or observed through microscopes by visitors over twelve. One of the best museum shops in town (chapter 6) and a cafeteria (chapter 5).

National Museum of Women in the Arts (1250 New York Avenue NW) seemed to me somewhat sexist when it opened in 1987. Still, mine is a male point of view, and there may well be a need for such a museum. At any rate, I made a visit in the course of researching this book, to find that the entire permanent collection was missing—on display for a year, an attendant at the desk explained, in foreign parts. A couple of the short-term exhibits scheduled to be displayed, according to the museum's quarterly bulletin, were nonexistent, as well. And the restaurant was closed. Only the shop and a single relatively small short-term show were to be seen. I had not come a great distance on my visit, but it is possible that you may, so I suggest you telephone in advance to learn what you'll be able to see (202-783-5000). I'm advised that painters in the permanent collection include Dame Barbara Hepworth, Mary Cassatt, Georgia O'Keeffe, and Helen Frankenthaler. The elaborately restored building—a former Masonic Temple—is very attractive.

Navy and Marine museums constitute a valid reason for an expedition to the Washington Navy Yard, 9th and M streets SE. The former, bigger of the pair and in Building 76, a rebuilt gun factory, does not stint in its exhibits, with the range an anchored destroyer at the pier, the famed sailing ship *Constitution's* gun deck, an actual submarine's inner cabins, flags and paintings, weapons and uniforms, medals and model vessels. Indeed, at journey's end, I was tempted—well, *almost* tempted—to extract my old sailor's uniform from mothballs. The *Marine Museum* is in Building 58, which had long been used as a barracks and where there's a graphic interpretation of the Corps's most celebrated battles, "Shores of Tripoli" to the current era, and a wealth of Marine Corps paraphernalia, natty uniforms included.

Phillips Collection (1600 21st Street NW), in a sense Washington's counterpart of New York's Frick and London's Wallace collections, constitutes the brilliant cache of a rich art patron—the scion of a steel tycoon—housed in the turn-of-the-century family mansion to which additions have been made (the latest in 1989) to the two painting-filled rooms of the original house, opened to the public in 1921.

Duncan Phillips had started collecting only a few years earlier, but he knew what he wanted—Phillips paintings are mostly but not entirely modern—and he had a good eye. By the time he died, he had accumulated 2,500 works. His wife Marjorie succeeded him as director, and their son Laughlin followed his mother. Although its exhibition space doubled with the opening of the Goh annex (named for its Japanese benefactor), the charm of the Phillips remains its relative intimacy, and the significance of the Phillips lies in the brilliance of its holdings.

There's an entire gallery devoted to Bonnard (*Woman and Dog* and *The Open Window* are my favorites), and still other galleries are allotted to Mark Rothko and Georges Braque. As you move about, you spot paintings you know you'll remember—Renoir's *The Luncheon of the Boating Party* (the museum's trademark), a relative handful of older works including two entitled *Repentant Peter* (one each of the saint by El Greco and Goya), Chardin's *A Bowl of Plums*, Daumier's *The Uprising*, and an unusual Daumier self-portrait, predecessors of the Impressionists like Corot and Courbet, even England's John Constable. Impressionists on hand include Boudin and Monet, Sisley and Degas, Berthe Morisot and Gauguin. The Phillips has a number of Cézannes, splendid Matisses (especially *Interior with Egyptian Curtain*) and painters whose work we see too little of in many U.S. museums, like Gris and Kandinsky, Kokoschka and Douanier Rousseau (whose 1909 *Notre Dame* is like no other you will have observed). There are a number of fine Klees, Modigliani and Soutine, Edward Hicks and Thomas Eakins. But you may take in, as well, works of such other Americans as Whistler and Albert Pinkham Ryder, John Henry Twachtman and Winslow Homer, John Sloan and Edward Hopper, Maurice Prendergast and Stuart Davis, Georgia O'Keeffe and Jacob Lawrence. Not that more recent names are lacking. Consider Jackson Pollock and Milton Avery, Willem de

Kooning and Clyfford Still, Morris Louis and Robert Mother-well. Be aware, too, of the restaurant (chapter 5), shop (chapter 6), and concerts (chapter 3). The Phillips is special.

Renwick Gallery (a non-Mall museum of the Smithsonian Institution, at Pennsylvania Avenue and 17th Street NW): The principal point of a visit to the Renwick is the Renwick. By that I mean the building itself, rather than—at least in my experience—the often insipid temporary exhibits of American crafts, staged by the Renwick's "parent" museum, the otherwise estimable National Museum of American Art, which I consider important enough to be included in "The Essential Washington" on the opening pages of this chapter. But the Renwick building is something else again: a stunning specimen of French Second Empire, splendidly embellished of facade, with Mansard roofs, balcony-topped towers, pilasters, niches, and carved stone—including an inscription "Dedicated to Art," dating to the period when the gallery was built as the first home of the Corcoran Gallery of Art. Work started on the building in 1858 but was impeded by the Civil War. President and Mrs. Grant hosted a fund-raiser for the Washington Monument in the still-uncompleted, then-Corcoran in 1871, with the grand opening three years later. Between 1899 (by which time the Corcoran had moved to its much larger present quarters) and 1964, the Renwick was a courthouse. The Smithsonian then took it over and wisely named it for the architect James Renwick, who designed, among much else, the Smithsonian's Castle; still another Castle at Syracuse University, which was the School of Journalism (where I studied) until the university tragically razed it; and New York's St. Patrick's Cathedral.

My hope is that the Smithsonian will come up with a scheme for more effective use of the Renwick. Meanwhile, go—regardless of the current short-term crafts show. What you want to see are the ever-so-grand Grand Salon, on whose walls the Corcoran once jammed 115 paintings. Now there are considerably fewer. But the furnishings are delightfully Victorian, the high-ceilinged room skylit. Much more intimate is the Octagon Room, originally designed to set off a nude sculpture that the Corcoran took with it when it moved, but still quite a special interior space.

Arthur M. Sackler Gallery (on the Mall at 1050 Independence Avenue, SW) is a Smithsonian jewel, and a near-twin to the National Museum of African Art (above) just across the pretty garden that separates them, and linked with the African by a subterranean passage, off the lower of two underground levels of exhibit space. The Sackler comprises a thousand objects of Asian (mostly Chinese) art given to the Smithsonian by a rich physician-collector who died just before the gallery (part of whose construction costs he paid) opened in 1987.

Like the also-beautiful African Art Museum, the Sackler is entered through a ground-level pavilion of granite and glass, and you descend to discover its treasures. Chinese work—in jade, bronze, and lacquer, not to mention a wealth of scrolls and paintings—is reason enough for a visit or two or three: pendants and disks and figures and rings and vases of carved jade; a rarely seen collection of garment hooks—used to suspend swords or secure belts—of turquoise, gold, and silver, inlaid with diamonds and other precious stones; exceptional carved lacquer—trays, boxes, platters; scrolls of the Ming, Yuan, and Qing dynasties and of later centuries; and bronzes (so often boring to look upon, even if you appreciate how valuable and venerable they may be) that are the most interesting and handsome I've come across, their range wine containers made fifteen centuries B.C., through drinking vessels only a few centuries younger, to bells and bowls as relatively recent as the tenth century B.C. But there's more: an ancient Anatolian copper bull, Indian sculpture a millennium old, other Near East and Asian objects. It's all so beautiful you find yourself heading for the shop (chapter 6) before you depart. Note, too, that the Sackler's temporary exhibits can be exceptional.

Smithsonian Institution Castle (on the Mall at 1000 Jefferson Drive SW), though not a museum in and of itself, constitutes the core—the headquarters—of the Smithsonian Institution's multiplying family of museums. (The *National Museum of American Indian Art* is next on line.) The Castle—first building of a clutch of museums that now extend as far as Fifth Avenue in New York City (Cooper Hewitt Museum, devoted to decorative arts), and even include the National Zoo, an official relationship with the autonomously operated Kennedy Center for the Performing Arts and also autonomously operated National Gallery of Art—is so called because it looks like a medieval château from without. Named for James Smithson, a rich English scientist who willed, upon his death in 1829, half a million dollars (a lot of money in those days), to the U.S. government for "an Establishment for the increase and diffusion of knowledge among men," the Smithsonian today is substantially federally funded (some $266 million per year), albeit with private-sector income as well. Its board is nothing if not impressive—with the chief justice of the United States, the vice president, a trio of members from each House of Congress, and nine private citizens, with its chief executive modestly titled "Secretary." Both of the Smithsonian museums that occupy the old Patent Office Building beyond the Mall (National Museum of American Art and National Portrait Gallery), as well as the Mall's National Museum of American History and National Air and Space Museum, are included in the opening section of this chapter, "The Essential Washington," while the other Smithsonian museums are in this section. There is no question but that the James Renwick–designed Castle (1855) is not only the Smithsonian's headquarters, but its principal symbol. It was relatively recently renovated, with its main floor now resembling a fairly decent motel lobby, constituting (despite an information desk) what appears to this observer largely wasted space that could—given the Smithsonian's vast holdings (only a portion of the total of a hundred million objects are displayed)—be put to considerably better use.

Textile Museum (2320 S Street NW): You have to be more of a nut about textiles than I am to fall in love with this museum, although there's no denying that it occupies a pair of handsome contiguous houses. Exhibits are of both domestic and foreign textiles and carpets. You might want to pop in, in conjunction with a visit to the nearby Woodrow Wilson House (below).

U.S. Department of the Interior Museum (18th and C Streets NW): It is, of course, the Department of the Interior that operates the great American network of national parks through the National Park Service, which—through its National Capitol Region subdivision—is also the landlord of many points of interest in the District of Columbia, Washington Monument through, say, Theodore Roosevelt Island. So it's not surprising that Interior has a museum of its own. It's strong on Indian artisanship, headdresses through totem poles (Interior oversees Indian Reservations countrywide); but also interprets facets of early American life through dramatic dioramas, shows off the national parks in well-designed displays, even operates an Indian Crafts shop (chapter 5). Art buffs will want to wander the building's corridors, noting pre-World War II murals, much of it commissioned by Roosevelt administration arts projects—and frequently top-rank.

Washington Project for the Arts (400 7th Street NW), though more gallery than museum (its specialty is temporary exhibitions) achieved national prominence in 1989 when it exhibited a retrospective exhibit of photographs by the late Robert Mapplethorpe, after the Corcoran Gallery of Art (above) canceled the show it had been scheduled to exhibit, citing concern that Mapplethorpe's photos—many of them explicitly homoerotic—would alarm Congressional appropriators of funds for the arts. The Washington Project's headquarters include a multifunction theater.

HISTORIC HOUSES

Anderson House (2118 Massachusetts Avenue NW) is a Washington sleeper. It's the onetime home of the late Lars Anderson, completed in 1905, after its owner had served as ambassador to Belgium and to Japan, returning home with superb European art and equally outstanding Oriental objects. Mr. and Mrs. Anderson had good taste and a sense of style. And the Society of the Cincinnati—whose members are descendants of American and French officers who served with the Revolutionary Army (to whom the Andersons willed the house)—has wisely retained the original décor, adding only a series of exhibits relating to its organization (originally criticized for an exclusively hereditary membership) and to the Revolution. You are impressed with the

Classic-style mansion even before you pass through one of the twin gates punctuating the wall separating it from Massachusetts Avenue. The front door is framed by a semicircle of a portico supported by Corinthian columns. And interiors are hardly anticlimactic. Flags of the original thirteen states are among those in the front hall. The so-called Choir Stall Room is named for the fragments of Italian Renaissance church choir stalls with which its walls are paneled.

The Great Stair Hall's walls are painted in trompe-l'oeil to convey the impression of sculpture in *grisaille*, or gray tones, which are a fine foil for floors of red Italian marble and an antique marble fireplace. The Billiard Room is more than a table and cues. How about paintings by early American artists like Gilbert Stuart and John Trumbull? (Their work is complemented elsewhere in the house by British artists, including Hoppner, Raeburn, and Reynolds.) Note the First Landing's Baccarat crystal eagle; the marble floors and frescoed walls of the Key Room; Louis XV and Régence furnishings of the French Parlor contrasting with English paintings (one a portrait of the Duke of Wellington by Sir Thomas Lawrence) and American Hepplewhite (as well as eighteenth-century French) furniture in the English Parlor; a tapestry-hung Long Gallery that takes you back to the great country houses you've toured in Europe; and still additional tapestries in the crystal-chandeliered Dining Room, whose paneled walls are carved in the style of the seventeenth-century's Grinling Gibbons, one of the great English wood sculptors.

Quite as striking are the Musicians' Gallery, 60 feet long, 30 feet wide, and 30 feet high, with eighteenth-century Japanese screens its primary décor; and the smashing two-story Ballroom (you may enter from its balcony, by means of a wrought-iron stairway). End in the garden, noting the immense eighteenth-century Japanese Buddha. If anybody invites you to a luncheon or dinner here (the Society rents the mansion for social events), be sure to accept! And note, too, that it sponsors lectures and concerts.

Arlington House (See under "All around the Town," above.)

Mary McLeod Bethune House (1318 Vermont Avenue NW): Mrs. Bethune, who died in 1955, was a widely known activist for black women's rights who advised presidents. This nineteenth-century townhouse—more than a century old—served as headquarters for the National Council of Negro Women from the mid-1940s to the mid-1960s and is now a ranking museum of the black women's movement.

Boyhood Home of Robert E. Lee (See under "All around the Town: Alexandria Old Town," above.)

Carlyle House (See under "All around the Town: Alexandria Old Town," above.)

Decatur House (748 Jackson Place NW, and pronounced Dee-KAY-tur) is not without historic interest. It's named for the War of 1812 naval officer who built it, retaining an architect—Benjamin Henry Latrobe, who was involved in design of the U.S. Capitol. After Decatur died from duel wounds, the impressive Federal house passed among a series of owners until a rich California family bought it in the 1870s, updating it in the Victorian fashion of that time, and subsequently later periods. Nicely restored from without, the pity of its interiors is that they represent a not necessarily felicitous mix of the elegant Federal with the exuberant Victorian and even later eras. Best spaces are the still-Federal Entrance Hall, a first-floor Bedroom dominated by a honey of a canopy bed that had been owned by Commodore Decatur's parents, the architecturally outstanding staircase and second-floor Hall, and the two generously proportioned North and South drawing rooms. I'm surprised the owning National Trust for Historic Preservation, a private membership organization, hasn't furnished the house throughout with pieces from its original Federal period—one of the really outstanding eras of American interior design. Disappointing.

Frederick Douglass House (1411 W Street SE) was the last home—before he died in 1895—of the extraordinary man who fathered the black civil-rights movement. Though born a slave (in 1838), he joined the Abolitionist movement after fleeing north as a young man, exhibiting talents as a writer and speaker to the point where President Lincoln called upon him for counsel. This attractive, capacious white-frame house, Cedar Hill by name, became Frederick Douglass's seat after the Civil War, during the period when he received a presidential appointment as U.S. marshal of the District of Columbia. Later, he pioneered black participation in the Foreign Service as minister to Haiti. He was an eloquent pleader against discrimination against blacks until he died. His widow organized a volunteer group to maintain Cedar Hill after her husband's death, and in 1962 the National Park Service took it over. A visit is conveniently combined with the Smithsonian Institution's nearby Anacostia Museum (above).

Dumbarton Oaks (See under "Museums after the Big Five," above.)

Christian Heurich Mansion (1307 New Hampshire Avenue NW): Well, there's always a first time. In the not inconsiderable period of my experience with volunteer docents—in any number of American and foreign locations—I have never come across one I didn't like. Withal, I found the two encountered at this house— headquarters of the Historical Society of Washington, D.C., and with a commendable multifaceted community program— unfriendly and crotchety. The house, which the society bills as the only open-to-visitors specimen in town from the later 1890s, is, with its single circular tower and red-stone facade, formidable from without and lugubrious within. The tour you pay for takes you to heavy-handed spaces on three of the five floors. If you become bored at, say, midpoint, and want out, there's no escape; the guide tells you, in no uncertain terms, that the house's insurance policy allows for no individual, mid-tour exits. Rest assured, though, that in the course of your odyssey, you will learn more about the German-origin brewing family that put up the place than you dared anticipate. I can't recommend this one.

Hillwood (4155 Linnean Avenue NW) is the 1925 Georgian-style brick mansion to which the late Marjorie Merriweather Post, of the Post cereals empire, moved in 1955 and remodeled to shelter her collections of both French and Russian decorative arts of the eighteenth and nineteenth centuries. The United States is not without other fine French holdings, but the Russian collection left by Mrs. Post (1887–1973) is the largest of its type outside the Soviet Union. Set in 25 acres of visitable gardens, considerably away from the center in northwest Washington, Hillwood is visitable only by means of reserved-in-advance tours. But if utterly fabulous art treasures interest you, the trek to this house will not disappoint. My notes brim with exclamation points, starting with the Front Hallway, with an oil of the Marquis de Lafayette by the French portraitist Largillière; a portrait by another French eighteenth-century artist, Van Loo; and a Louis XVI commode by one of the great French cabinetmakers, Riesener; Catherine the Great as the subject of a tapestry, and as the subject of several paintings by as many Russian subjects.

The Porcelain Room's name suggests contents—Russian china made for Catherine the Great and for other Russian rulers as well. The French Drawing Room—most beautiful interior in the house and one of the most beautiful in Washington—is as notable for paintings (Empress Eugénie by Winterhalter, for example) as for furniture (Marie-Antoinette's rolltop desk by Roentgen, with a dozen chairs that same French queen presented to a brother of Frederick the Great of Prussia. China belonging to the last Russian rulers and imperial photos highlight the Pavilion. The Icon Room is rich in Russian Orthodox art and objects of silver, gold, ormolu, and malachite, a precious trio of imperial Easter eggs enameled by Fabergé, and other Fabergé objects embellished with diamonds, rubies, and emeralds, as well as the diamond-studded crown worn at their weddings by the last three tsarinas.

Grinling Gibbons wood carving stands out in the English-accented Library; Russian glass and French Sèvres (including a tureen of Madame de Pompadour's) set against French Régence oak paneling distinguish the opulently furnished and accessorized Dining Room. Superb Louis XVI furnishings set off Mrs. Post's Bedroom. And the capacious gardens are a mix of styles—French formal and Japanese among them.

Lee-Fendell House (See under "All around the Town: Alexandria Old Town," above.)

The Octagon (1799 New York Avenue NW) is not, you should be advised at the outset, eight-sided; alas, it has but six sides. The first architect of the U.S. Capitol, English-born William Thornton, created it for a wealthy Virginia planter, Colonel John Taylor, with Washington—rather than Philadelphia, which had been considered—its site, thanks to a suggestion from Colonel Taylor's friend, President George Washington, who was optimistic about the Federal City's future. Completed in 1800, the Octagon was offered by the Taylors to President James Madison and his wife Dolley after the British burned the White House in the War of 1812.

Only in 1897 did the American Institute of Architects take it over and rehabilitate a onetime presidential residence that had been allowed to deteriorate by a succession of ten families that had occupied it over the years.

The architects, as certainly would be expected of members of their profession, did a good job. The signature architectural feature of the house—a delicate oval staircase linking the house's three stories—was set to rights. The Drawing Room, with pale-toned walls and draperies, has a fine crystal chandelier and an elegant mantel, and is furnished in Federal period, lighter in style and less elaborate than the eighteenth-century's earlier, more exuberant Georgian motifs. The house reflects the Federal era's partiality to curved spaces, not only with its oval stairway but with the diagonally placed rooms that a six-sided house made possible. Concentrate, as you go through, on the circular Entry Hall with a Robert Adam–style coal stove, urn-topped, and marble-floored; original Taylor chairs and sofa in the Stair Hall, Dining Room with Hepplewhite chairs and table and Chinese export porcelain in its breakfront; with an authentic Kitchen in the basement. Most important for last: the Treaty Room, a circular study on the second floor, with a carpet conforming to the room's shape, centered by a circular desk at which President Madison is believed to have signed the Ghent Treaty, with wedge-shaped drawers marked for alphabetical-order filing, moss-green walls set off by gold-toned draperies, and, between the three windows, a pair of candle sconces of the period, a gift of the Royal Institute of British Architects to their American colleagues. Former bedrooms are now used as galleries for short-term, often excellent, exhibitions.

Old Stone House (3051 M Street NW) is the only pre-Revolutionary building in Washington. Somehow or other, Georgetown's busy main thoroughfare, M Street, did not gobble it up, although the Feds—through the National Park Service—did not take over its operation and maintenance until as recently as 1950. It's not only bigger than it looks, but more attractive than it gives the impression of being, as you enter. Ascend to the second floor, taking in an ivory-paneled Sitting Room—fairly grand—with bedrooms divided between the second and third floors. One is red-textiled with ladderback chairs and a carding wheel; another is in blue with a lovely Adam-influenced mantel. The bedroom on the top floor is supplemented by a cradle. Both Kitchen and Dining Area on the first floor warrant inspection as you exit. The house went up in stages, between 1764 and 1770, with two families inhabiting—and building—it during the period when Georgetown was a prosperous tobacco center.

Petersen House, a.k.a. The House Where Lincoln Died (See "Museums after the Big Five: Ford's Theatre," above.)

Sewall-Belmont House (144 Constitution Avenue NE) is historic as regards age (it is late-eighteenth-century Federal)—the Sewall in the title was its initial occupant—and noteworthy with respect to politics (the Belmont of the title founded the National Woman's Party). Sewall-Belmont remains party headquarters (location is Capitol Hill) and is as well what might be called Washington headquarters for the women-in-politics movement, paying tribute not only to the woman who wrote the Equal Rights Amendment, Alice Paul, but to others who spearheaded earlier landmark legislation, including women's right to vote as embodied in the 19th Amendment to the Constitution, passed in 1920, and consisting of two brief but significant sentences: "The right of citizens of the United States to vote shall not be denied or abridged by the United States or by any state on account of sex." And "Congress shall have power to enforce this article by appropriate legislation." Exhibits are of pioneering women's-rights movement personalities and of events. With a bonus of attractive period rooms.

Tudor Place (1644 31st Street NW): I first learned of Tudor Place—one of Washington's best-kept secrets—when an issue of the National Press Club's *Bulletin* arrived, announcing a tour for members. You are not surprised at its beauty when you learn that it was designed by English-born William Thornton, first architect of the U.S. Capitol ("The Essential Washington," above) and the planner, as well, of the Octagon (above). Thornton's Neoclassical 1805 house had original owners of note. It was built for Thomas Peter and his wife, Martha Parke Custis, who was a granddaughter of another Martha—the first lady of President Washington—who willed her the $8000 the Peters used to buy the land—now a city block—on which Tudor Place stands. Owned nearly two centuries later by descendants of the original Peters, and still with pieces from eighteenth-century Mount Vernon, this is a house at once history-laden and handsome.

Composed of a principal central portion (whose circular two-story Doric-columned portico is an all-Washington architectural standout) and with lower wings to either side, the house does not disappoint within. A severe but smart Entrance Hall, whose floor-to-ceiling doors give onto the garden, leads to the Drawing Room—with an original mantel, original shutters, walls in a shade of the original yellow—and to the Parlor, with lovely pieces—Philadelphia Chippendale chairs, an 1800 piano shipped from England, a piano stool from Mount Vernon, the source also of a tea table. The Dining Room, still with its first chandelier, has half a dozen Philadelphia-made chairs, and, of all things, a dinner bell, also from Mount Vernon. Bedrooms upstairs have Mount Vernon pieces too: most significantly a chest-on-chest and a stool (one of a pair) whose mate is owned by the Smithsonian Institution. You must reserve a tour in advance to see this Georgetown mansion—and I urge that you do so.

Woodrow Wilson House (2340 S Street NW): If you exclude the Octagon (above) where President Madison lived temporarily, after the British burned the White House in the War of 1812; Blair House, the current closed-to-the-public presidential guest house where Harry and Bess Truman were quartered while the White House was being repaired; and an office in the Treasury that was used by President Andrew Johnson while he awaited

Mrs. Lincoln's departure from the White House—well then, Woodrow Wilson House is the only other former presidential residence in the capital. President Wilson and his wife Edith moved to this Georgian Revival house (built in 1915) in 1921, upon leaving the White House, remaining until Wilson died there in 1924. The house is fascinating, not only because of its associations with the president with whom we associate World War I and the Treaty of Versailles, but because it portrays, better than any other museum exhibit I know in any city, the American 20s—old-style phones and console radios; Ivory Flakes and Rinso, Kellogg's Pep and Knox gelatin, an early GE refrigerator, an even earlier icebox, and metal screw-top Mason jars in the Kitchen; bathrooms and clothing (president's and first lady's duds, at that) of the era; sheet music for "Oh, You Beautiful Doll" at the piano. There are a dozen principal rooms, with Wilson's portable typewriter, record player (are you old enough to re-member Victrolas?), home-movie screen, and contemporary books in the paneled Library, Solarium for casual meals at which Mr. Wilson did not wear the tuxedo indicated for dinner in the Dining Room; Reception and Drawing rooms and the couple's bedrooms-cum-open closets, including the bed in whichWilson died, as well as furnishings he had used in the White House.

CELEBRATED PLACES OF WORSHIP

Christ Church (31st and O streets NW) is an Episcopal beauty in Georgetown—Gothic style out of the 1880s, intricately wood-paneled, with fine stained glass and generous proportions. Lovely.

Franciscan Monastery (1400 Quincy Street NE)—a near neighbor of the Immaculate Conception Shrine and Catholic University (both below) brings to mind Renaissance-era churches you have visited in Rome and Florence, although it dates only to 1899. Within, friars welcome you to visit a reproduction of an Assisi chapel associated with St. Francis's founding of his order, and reproductions, as well, of Roman catacombs and of distant shrines and grottoes. The monastery's rose gardens are at their best in May and June. There are frequently scheduled guided tours.

Islamic Center (2551 Massachusetts Avenue NW)—Washington's mosque—has been an Embassy Row landmark since its 1949 opening, with a garden fronting its white facade, a super-slim minaret towering over the entrance, and an art-filled interior, embracing Persian carpets, a pulpit made from some 10,000 pieces of wood, elegantly embellished columns supporting decorative arches, and a massive chandelier. The mosque is open daily for visitors (remove shoes before you go in and better long trousers or skirts than shorts) with a midday service Fridays. Washington's mosque—a joint effort of Moslem countries represented in the capital—was the first purpose-built mosque in the United States.

Metropolitan African Methodist Episcopal Church (1518 M Street NW): In a city some 70 percent black, the leading black church is significant. That distinction is Metropolitan A.M.E.'s—on scene since its founders broke away from mostly white congregations to establish this one, core of downtown. The facade is broad and of brick and has pointed arches in the Gothic Revival style; it was completed in 1885. This big church has a seating capacity of 2,500, a variety of social concerns, not least of which has been the civil-rights movement, and prestige that has attracted speakers of consequence, the range Frederick Douglass and Eleanor Roosevelt, Martin Luther King, Jr., and Winnie Mandela. Open weekdays to visitors.

New York Avenue Presbyterian Church (1313 New York Avenue NW)—though replaced by a newer edifice since Lincoln's time— is the church where the Civil War president worshiped. The original Lincoln pew remains, and among the Lincolniana displayed is a draft—reputedly the first—of the Emancipation Proclamation, the Lincoln edict of January 1, 1863, that freed the slaves. Traditionally open to visitors Tuesday through Friday.

St. John's Church (16th and H Streets NW): The same Benjamin Latrobe who was involved in design of the Capitol and the White House was St. John's first architect. It opened in 1818, although its Doric-columned portico and bell tower are somewhat later. The bronze bell in the tower is the work of a son of Paul Revere, and the stained glass is mostly late-nineteenth-century, French-designed and installed in collaboration with James Renwick (the architect of the Smithsonian Institution's Castle and of St. Patrick's Cathedral in New York), who designed an 1883 enlargement. This Episcopal church has welcomed every president since Madison, a communicant at its opening, with pew 54 traditionally reserved for presidential occupancy. Half a dozen-plus alterations over long years notwithstanding, St. John's remains classic in ambience, still with original features, including its saucer-shaped dome. Situated just opposite Lafayette Park, a near neighbor of the White House, St. John's remains open the day long. You want to drop in, perhaps for one of its organ recitals. The adjacent Parish House at 1525 H Street NW, aged too, dates to 1836 and was for some years the British Legation.

St. Matthew's Cathedral [Roman Catholic] (1725 Rhode Island Avenue NW)—red-stone seat of the Catholic Archbishop of Washington—too often goes unappreciated by visitors, frequently attracted by the mock-Gothic splendor of Washington National—the Episcopal cathedral—and by the tremendous size of the Shrine of the Immaculate Conception (below). Withal, it was St. Matthew's—No. 1 in the pecking order of Catholic churches in the area, with the archbishop's throne edging its high marble altar—where a high mass was said for President Kennedy after his 1963 assassination (a plaque indicates where he lay before burial in Arlington National Cemetery). Completed in 1899, the cathedral melds—with considerable success—the Byzantine and Romanesque styles. You are impressed from afar by its immense 200-foot dome. Within, mosaic murals distinguish a rich décor—behind and above the High Altar, beneath the dome, in the Baptistry, even on walls backing some of the side chapels. A principal exception to the motif of mosaics is the Wedding Chapel, its gold-leafed wood sculpture backed by black marble. Pop in.

Shrine of the Immaculate Conception (Michigan Avenue and 4th Street NE) went up in 1920 as a neighbor of both the Franciscan Monastery (above) and Catholic University (below). It is the largest Catholic church in the United States and one of the largest in the world. Its Byzantine-Romanesque profile—a slim and very tall bell tower complementing a blue and gold dome with an immense rose window over the principal portal—is dramatic enough. But the interior is special, too: a main or upper church seating 2000; a second church in the crypt below; a network of chapels, with an extraordinary wealth of mosaics lining the dome and vaults. Look up as you move about, either on your own or with one of the regularly departing guided tours. The cafeteria is open breakfast through lunch, and there's a shop.

Washington National Cathedral [Episcopal] (Massachusetts and Wisconsin Avenues NW)—officially the Cathedral Church of St. Peter and St. Paul—is the seat of the Episcopal Bishop of Washington. Despite its way-away-from-the-center location on Embassy Row, the cathedral—spectacularly mock-Gothic—is eminently visitworthy. Construction started when this century was but seven years of age—Teddy Roosevelt spoke at the dedication—to be completed only in 1990 (President Bush spoke at the ceremony), by which time every intervening president has been a visitor. The cross-shaped structure is in English Decorated style, at its peak in the fourteenth century. It is one of the largest churches in the world, with a strikingly vaulted Nave that's a tenth of a mile in length, not one but a trio of rose windows, and a facade embracing pinnacles and finials, buttresses and gargoyles, arches and towers created by talented stone masons and sculptors over long years. Wander about slowly, noting the medieval-style sarcophagus that is President Wilson's tomb; the so-called Space stained-glass window with a sliver of moon rock—presented by the Apollo II crew—embedded within; the exquisitely detailed Children's Chapel and the crypt's Bethlehem Chapel—two of nine chapels all told; along with especially pretty gardens. There are guided tours, concerts, and recitals, and not one but a trio of shops.

Other D.C. Places of Worship include *All Souls' Unitarian Church* (16th and Harvard streets NW), a *Christ Church* other than that above (at Cameron and North Washington streets in Alexandria Old Town), *First Baptist Church* (16th and O streets NW), *Metropolitan Memorial Methodist Church* (3401 Nebraska Avenue NW), *Georgetown Lutheran Church* (1566 Wisconsin Avenue NW), and *Washington Hebrew Congregation* (Reform—at 3935 Macomb Street NW).

PRETTIEST PARKS

The Ellipse (15th to 17th streets, Constitution Avenue to Pennsylvania Avenue South NW, a.k.a. E Street) is the well-manicured green that lies strategically between the White House to the north and the Washington Monument to the south. If your visit to Washington is in summer, you may well wait on a grandstand in the Ellipse until it's your turn to tour the White House (above). If you arrive in December you'll see the National Christmas Tree, traditionally lit by the president. There are a pair each of ex-White House gatehouses and fountains on the grounds.

Kenilworth Aquatic Gardens (Douglas Street at Anacostia Avenue NE) is the nation's only national park whose principal subject matter is water lilies. It covers a dozen acres, mostly of ponds, on the east bank of the Anacostia River, a tributary of the Potomac just seven miles upstream from where the two rivers meet. The park derives from a pond that was lily-planted after the Civil War by a local family, and expanded. Besides the lovely lilies, you'll see water birds, frogs, and ducks, among other wildlife. Not to mention iris and cattails and water hyacinths. Customarily open early—at 7 A.M.

Lafayette Park (15th to 17th streets, Pennsylvania Avenue to H Street NW) is a kind of north-of-the-White House counterpart to the Ellipse (above) to its south. It's flanked by the New Executive Office Building and Renwick Gallery (above) to the east, and Decatur House to the north, with an equestrian statue of President Jackson in its center. It's tempting to want to relax on one of this pretty square's benches. But these days they're pretty much occupied by the homeless, stretched out and sleeping, day or evening.

Rock Creek Park—a National Park Service–operated area of some 1750 acres in the northwest part of the city, extending from Beach Drive NW, just below the D.C.–Maryland border, south to Klingle Road NW, with the stream called Rock Creek cutting through it—is one of America's oldest and largest urban parks, a verdant valley where you may drive winding roads, walk serene pathways, relax over a picnic, play golf and tennis (18 holes, 16 courts), ride horseback, admire contemporary paintings (at the *Art Barn*), rent canoes and boats (from *Thompson's Boat House)* to gain the Potomac via Rock Creek), and watch flour milled at restored *Pierce Mill.* Park headquarters are at its *Nature Center* (changing exhibits, films, a planetarium), 5200 Glover Road NW. *Montrose Park* (with tennis courts) and contiguous *Dumbarton Oaks Gardens* (see "Museums after the Big Five: Dumbarton Oaks," above) edge the park to its southeast.

Theodore Roosevelt Island (in the Potomac River, accessible via a footbridge leading from George Washington Parkway, paralleling the island, in Arlington, Virginia, and reached from Washington via Theodore Roosevelt Bridge) is an 88-acre nature reserve operated by the National Park Service. Its anchor is a 17-foot bronze statue of the conservation-conscious president it memorializes, by Paul Manship, which tops a 30-foot-high shaft of granite, with an adjacent quartet of granite tablets in which quotations of Teddy's are inscribed. Roosevelt Island's game is exercise—walks along four miles of nature trails, for views of cattails and pickerelweed, woodpeckers and wood thrushes, turtles and frogs—maybe a muskrat if you're lucky. Customarily open as early as 8 A.M.

U.S. Botanic Garden (Maryland Avenue and 1st Street SW) is a core-of-the-city surprise package of no little charm. At the base of Capitol Hill (and under supervision of the Architect of the

Capitol), it combines nicely with a visit to either the National Air and Space Museum or the National Gallery of Art (both above, "Essential Washington"), if not the Capitol itself. Conveniently compact as botanic gardens go (it's an easily walkable fraction of the size, for example, of New York Botanical Garden in the Bronx) and entirely under glass, it's based on a pair of reflecting pools divided by a pavilion of lush subtropical plants, with masses of orchids—in abundant variety—in its central region, and on the side nearest Independence Avenue, plantings of cactus, of palms, and of ferns. Some species are labeled, some are not. And there are, at least in my experience—when they are no special exhibitions underway—no guards or attendants, no shop (can you believe it?), and no admissions counter, there being no entrance fee. You simply wander about on your own, relaxing on a bench when you will, to enjoy this concentration of natural beauty. The garden stages shows—begonia, iris, Christmas poinsettia, daffodil—throughout the year, usually for month-long periods. Delightful.

U.S. National Arboretum (3501 New York Avenue NE) is, like the U.S. Botanic Garden above, a Washington surprise. Within its 444 acres not far northeast of Union Station is a joyously color-drenched Department of Agriculture–operated complex of flowers, flowering plants, and trees, the range azaleas and magnolias, cherries and peonies, rhododendron and daffodils, hibiscus and roses, the unusual National Herb Garden, and—most unusual of its pluses—22 splendid Corinthian columns that once supported the East Portico of the U.S. Capitol, removed in the late 1950s as part of a renovation, considered too fragile to be used again, and stored away until a private citizens' campaign raised $2 million and lobbied Congress for a quarter-century, finally succeeding in gaining approval to install the columns at the arboretum over a platform of paving stones cut from Old Capitol steps. The columns flank a reflecting pool and, surrounded by dogwood and daffodils, are a special treat in spring. There are picnic grounds, and local garden-club members volunteer as guides. A lovely place.

LEADING UNIVERSITIES

American University (4400 Massachusetts Avenue NW) is the poshest-located of the universities, with its main campus (centered by the Eric Friedheim Quadrangle) and satellite Tenley campus in the Embassy Row area of Northwest Washington, a fair distance, alas, from the Metro. Founded in 1891 by the Methodist Church as a graduate school, it has evolved into a nondenominational university of 11,000 students, with a college of arts and sciences as the umbrella for schools of communication and education; there are, as well, schools of public affairs and international service, plus colleges of law and business administration. Both music and art departments are strong, with multifacility buildings of their own; in the latter, *Watkins Gallery,* with frequently changing art exhibitions and a permanent collection, welcomes visitors, as does *Bender Library*—for short-term exhibits. And there are campus tours, primarily for would-be undergrads, several times each weekday—and on Saturday, autumn through spring.

Catholic University of America (620 Michigan Avenue NE) dates back more than a century and occupies a substantial campus in northeast Washington. (Shrine of the Immaculate Conception, above, is adjacent, as is a Metro station.) There are 7000 students, coming from most of the states and many foreign countries. Occupying a 145-acre campus, the university comprises 9 schools, with its courses in music and drama (and America's oldest continuous classical repertory touring company) perhaps the best known. There are frequent performances of plays and musicals in the university's *Hartke Theatre* and other venues, and some 300 concerts annually (many of them free) by CUA music groups, which include a symphony, a chorus, and the *Summer Opera Theatre.* Campus tours for prospective students take place three days a week, fall through spring, somewhat less frequently the rest of the year.

Georgetown University (O and 37th streets NW) takes the name of the area of D.C. on whose eastern flank its 60-building, 104-acre campus is situated. Georgetown opened its doors in 1789, which makes it not only the oldest university in town, but the oldest Catholic university in the United States and, as well, the oldest U.S. university operated by the Jesuits—Catholicism's most intellectual priestly order (with more than 60 Jesuits on Georgetown's staff). President Washington spoke to students from the south doorway of *Old North*, the senior-in-age campus building (in use since 1795). But the university is especially proud of the *Healy Building*, formidably Gothic Revival (it dates to 1877) albeit with its open-to-visitors Carroll Parlor classic in the style of England's eighteenth-century Robert Adam, and with assorted treasures, including paintings by Gilbert Stuart (a portrait of Georgetown's founding priest, John Carroll), Anthony Van Dyck, and Luca Giordano, as well as Louis XV, Queen Anne, and later nineteenth-century furniture, and among much else, an unusual music stand made of Meissen porcelain confected a couple of centuries back. There are close to 12,000 students, in 5 undergraduate schools (foreign service and foreign languages are perhaps the best-known of these), with ranking medical and law schools as well; the last-mentioned, in downtown Washington, is the largest such in the United States. Regularly conducted campus tours.

George Washington University (801 22nd Street NW)—with its campus to the east and south of a Metro station (Foggy Bottom) often used by visitors, is perhaps the most familiar to out-of-towners. Undergrad schools include business, education, and arts and sciences, with medicine and law schools, as well. This is among the biggest of area universities, with some 14,000 students. Campus tours are frequent, as are art exhibits in *Gelman Library* and *Dimock Gallery.*

Howard University (2400 6th Street NW) embraces a dozen-plus colleges (including medicine, law, engineering, dentistry, and architecture), a number of research centers, a 500-bed hospital, a 150-room hotel (*Howard University Inn* at 2225 Georgia Avenue NW) on a northeast Washington campus (albeit with an "NW" address), and several satellite campuses. With some 12,000 students from all 50 states and 100 countries and a faculty of 1900 (no university has more black Ph.D.'s) it is, hands down, the No. 1

dominantly black university in the U.S. (There are, of course, non-black students, too.) President Jackson signed the bill incorporating the university. It's named for the head of the post-Civil War Freedman's Bureau whose house, on Georgia Avenue—one of the university's original buildings—is a national historic landmark. Georgian-style *Founders Library* towers over the main campus, where visitors are welcome, as they are also at *Rankin Chapel* and the *Gallery of Fine Arts,* with choice African sculpture in its Alain Locke Collection.

3

Washington to Watch

SETTING THE SCENE

While you may not have been looking—or listening—the nation's capital has become an all-U.S. ranker of a performing arts city. It was not always so. When the multi-auditorium Kennedy Center opened in 1977, skeptics doubted that multitheater complex would fill its seats. But the center came along at the right time—in the 1970s, a period when Washington was becoming increasingly important on the international scene, drawing not only more diplomats but substantially increased numbers of educated middle-class Americans to the capital as well as to Maryland and Virginia suburbs. Not to mention pleasure, business, and convention visitors in the millions.

It all adds up. Approaching the twenty-first century, Washington—for long a world leader with respect to the fine arts—now holds its head high in performing arts as well, with top-of-the-line theater, including its own repertory companies, symphony, opera, and ballet, not to mention visits by important touring groups and soloists, and a nearby summer performing-arts center that's the only such constituted as a national park.

John F. Kennedy Center for the Performing Arts (edging the Potomac at the foot of New Hampshire Avenue and the western tip of F Street NW): It is an irony of the Kennedy Center that the assassinated president—John Kennedy—whom it memorializes

Tickets info
202 - 467 - 4600

named the chairman of a campaign that raised more than $13 million for its construction. That was in 1961, not long after Kennedy's predecessor, Dwight Eisenhower, signed a bill authorizing the center, providing land for it and designating its first trustees. Following Kennedy's death, Congress appropriated $15.5 million toward building the center, stipulating that private money be contributed as well, and moreover, that it be named for the slain president as a national memorial. A then-fashionable architect, the late Edward Durrell Stone (whose credits include New York's glitzy General Motors Building and the American Embassy in New Delhi), was selected to design the complex; it is functional if hardly beautiful. (Stone adored masses of marble, expanses of glass, glossy facades.) Withal, the Kennedy—opened in 1979—works very well indeed.

The center is unique in that it's an official presidential memorial, toward which federal funds are committed, as well as a nonprofit performing arts center with private money contributed to it. And even though it's a self-sustaining bureau of the Smithsonian Institution, it operates under the direction of its own 45-member board of trustees, including 30 presidential appointees and wives of ex-presidents (Mesdames Carter, Ford, Johnson, Nixon, Onassis, and Reagan), with maintenance by still another agency, the Department of the Interior's National Park Service. There are, to be sure, a lot of fingers in the Kennedy pie.

It is neither central nor heart-of-downtown, and it's half a dozen blocks from the nearest Metro station. Still, Washington has long since come to accept this acoustically sound, 630-feet long, 300-feet wide building, its terraces edging the Potomac.

There are three lobby ticket office areas—*Hall of Flags,* named for colors of the 50 states displayed in the order in which they entered the Union, and of the territories, as well; *Hall of Nations* flying flags, hung in alphabetical order, of all countries recognized diplomatically by the United States government; and, focal point of the trio—leading from both Hall of States and Hall of Nations—*Grand Foyer,* serving as principal lobby for the three major auditoriums, extending the length of the building, with its best feature a well-executed bronze bust of John Kennedy by Robert Berks, and—hardly an aesthetic match for the Kennedy

bust, a series of chandeliers contributed by the Swedish government and a mass of Belgian-contributed mirrors. The *Roof Terrace*
is the center at its loveliest, with an al fresco walkway cum
panoramas and restaurants (chapter 5). And there's space for
1450 cars on three subterranean levels.

Which leaves the auditoriums: *Concert Hall* (the largest), with
2700 seats and white-and-gold décor; *Opera House,* in red and
gold, with 2200 seats; *Eisenhower Theater,* wood-paneled and with
1100 seats; *Terrace Theater* (a chamber-concert addition to the
original complex, given by Japan in 1976, America's Bicentennial
year), in tones of rose and silver with 500 seats; *Theater Lab,*
seating 380; *American Film Institute Theater,* seating 220; and, as
mentioned in an earlier chapter in connection with the Library of
Congress, the co-operator, the *Performing Arts Library.* There are
guided tours daily.

Guests at the center have ranged from great symphonies—
Vienna Philharmonic, Leningrad Symphony, Philadelphia Orchestra—through visiting ballet troupes—Bolshoi, Royal Dan-
ish, New York City—and theater companies like London's Royal
Shakespeare. But the center has regular tenants as well, to wit:

Washington Opera, with annual seasons autumn through spring,
supertitles imposed over the stage (with dialog of foreign-
language productions sensibly translated into English), expert
direction (Martin Feinstein is artistic boss), and a wide-ranging
repertoire of classical and contemporary works, including
Verdi's *Aïda* and Mozart's *Così fan Tutte,* Donizetti's *Lucia di
Lammermoor* and Rossini's *The Barber of Seville,* through to such
modern works as Argento's *The Aspern Papers* and Gershwin's
Porgy and Bess, Menotti's *The Consul* and Paulus's *The Postman
Always Rings Twice.* Performances take place both in the Opera
House and in the Eisenhower Theater. All told, Washington
Opera has produced some 170 operas since its maiden season in
1956.

National Symphony Orchestra, dating to 1931, became internationally known in its middle years, when Howard Mitchell succeeded the first director, Hans Kindler, and the orchestra began
to tour. Anatol Dorati was the third leader, and under the

fourth—and current—director, Mstislav Rostropovich, the orchestra has recorded extensively, toured the globe (USSR and Japan, western Europe and our own continent), appearing often on TV, playing annually in summer at Wolf Trap in nearby Virginia ("Summer Specialties," below), at presidential inaugurations, annual Independence Day and other celebrations on the West Lawn of the U.S. Capitol. Not to mention the Kennedy Center, with which the symphony is affiliated and where it performs regularly in the Concert Hall, with Maestro Rostropovich often handing over the baton to such guest conductors as Lorin Maazel, Sir Neville Marriner, and Rafael Frubeck de Borgos.

American Ballet Theater: Though other dance companies perform each season at the center, American Ballet Theater is on scene annually, with the Kennedy Center and New York's Metropolitan Opera House (see *New York at Its Best*) its principal homes. ABT goes back to 1940, with Lucia Chase and Oliver Smith its co-directors over a sustained period and two leading Soviet dancers in artistic slots in recent seasons: Natalia Makarova became artistic director in 1990, succeeding Mikhail Baryshnikov, who had served as artistic director since since 1980. Performing both contemporary as well as traditional ballets, ABT is as celebrated for productions of, say, Jerome Robbins's *Fancy Press* and Antony Tudor's *Pillar of Fire* as well as old favorites like *Giselle* and *The Sleeping Beauty.*

Mostly Mozart Festival is an annual summer offshoot of the original festival, an annual warm-weather-months event for the past quarter-century at Avery Fisher Hall in New York City's Lincoln Center. The festival's chamber orchestra, beloved of New Yorkers, departs en masse each year for an early summer season at the Kennedy. Not surprisingly, given its title, programs are dominantly of works by Mozart, with composers like Beethoven and Haydn, even occasionally Mendelssohn, often part of programs, and with soloists—Spanish pianist Alicia de Larrocha is the perennial favorite—complementing the orchestra.

CONCERT SERIES

Supplementing the National Symphony at the Kennedy Center (above) are annual seasons of orchestras in a number of felicitous settings, as for example:

Corcoran Gallery of Art (17th Street and New York Avenue NW) is known for its annual autumn-through-spring Musical Evening Series, with chamber music concerts by varied groups, the Cleveland Quartet and Tokyo Spring Quartet invariably among them, often performing on matched sets of precious Stradivarius and Amati stringed instruments owned by the gallery.

Hirshorn Museum and Sculpture Garden (Independence Avenue at 8th Street NW) has presented chamber groups seasonally for a dozen years. The orchestra in recent seasons has been the 20th Century Consort.

Library of Congress (Jefferson Building, 1st Street and Independence Avenue SE) has a winner with its annual Summer Chamber Festivals, welcoming the public both to certain rehearsals (usually weekday mornings at 11) and scheduled evening performances, usually weeknights, by the festival's own chamber orchestra. Admission is free.

National Gallery of Art (West Building, Constitution Avenue at 6th Street NW) presents its own ensemble, the National Gallery Orchestra, in concert, invariably with soloists accompanying, on Sunday evenings (traditionally starting at 7 P.M.), October through June, in the attractive West Garden Court. A treat. Admission is free.

Phillips Collection (1600 21st Street NW) offers guest groups and soloists at Sunday concerts, customarily beginning at 5 P.M., September through May. Setting is the paneled Music Room with string quartets and violinists, pianists and cellists, flutists and harpsichordists. Admission is free.

Pop Concerts at the Kennedy (New Hampshire Avenue and F Street NW, above): Various theaters of the Kennedy, often the biggest-of-the-lot Concert Hall, are venues for pop art concerts by such performers, over past seasons, as Lena Horne, Liza Minelli, Frank Sinatra, Loretta Lynn, the Pointer Sisters, and Johnny Mathis.

THEATERS AND OTHER ENTERTAINMENT

Arena Stage (occupying a three-theater complex—800-seat Arena, 500-seat Kreeger Theater, and 180-seat Old Vat Room—at 6th Street and Maine Avenue SW) is an internationally distinguished repertory group founded some four decades back—and until 1990 directed by the multitalented producer-director Zelda Fichandler (now artistic director of the Acting Company in New York, and succeeded at the Arena by Douglas C. Wager as artistic director, with Stephen J. Richard the managing director). The Fichandler era saw the company produce 400 plays in 40 years, 7 or 8 per season, October through June, with the scope extensive. By that I mean Oliver Goldsmith's *She Stoops to Conquer*, Chekhov's *The Seagull* and Shaw's *Pygmalion*, beyond to contemporary works by playwrights from abroad—the Soviet Union's Viktor Slavkins, for example—and, from our own country, Cheryl West. The Arena is nonprofit and, when all three of its theaters are operating, employs a staff of 200, including directors, actors, and designers, who among them present 19 performances each week. Traditionally, Tuesday and Wednesday performances start at 7:30 P.M. (instead of 8), and the Arena is noted for its after-performance discussion series following certain Tuesday and Thursday evening presentations. Matinees are on the usual days—Wednesday, Saturday, and Sunday.

Folger Theater (in the Folger Library, 201 East Capitol Street SE) is charming Elizabethan in design (see chapter 2, "All around the Town," above), with a resident company started in 1970 (producer Richmond Crinkley brought it national attention) under Michael Kahn's artistic direction that presents a season—September through June—mostly of Shakespeare. Recent productions have included *The Merry Wives of Windsor, Twelfth Night, As You Like It, The Winter's Tale,* and *Romeo and Juliet*—as well as other works: John Gay's *The Beggar's Opera* and Schiller's *Mary Stuart,* for example. Primarily, though, this is where you want to see Shakespeare, the specialty of the house. There are just over 250 seats, so you had better reserve as well in advance as possible.

Legitimate Theaters (without resident companies) presenting new productions, dramatic and musical, prior to and post-Broadway, include *Ford's Theatre* (511 10th Street NW), where President Lincoln was assassinated, with a National Park Service–operated museum related to the events in its basement and, just opposite, the open-to-visitors Peterson House (a.k.a. The House Where Lincoln Died)—all the subject of an entry on an earlier page; and the *National Theater* (1321 Pennsylvania Avenue NW) with nineteenth-century origins and some 1100 seats, which is, because of its capacity, selected often for splashy musicals, but it presents dramas, too.

Other Concert Halls and Theaters include *Constitution Hall* (18th and D Streets NW, in the D.A.R. complex) with frequently important concerts; *Carter Barron Amphitheater* (Rock Creek Park, with box office at 4850 Colorado Avenue NW) summer presentations; and *Sylvan Theater* (Washington Monument grounds), varied warm-weather entertainments.

Movies: Watch the papers, of course, for what's playing where, but bear in mind that there are frequent film performances at the *American Film Institute Theater* (John F. Kennedy Center for the Performing Arts) and *Pickford Theater* (Jefferson Building, Library of Congress); the popular Pickford, where admission is free, is small (64 seats), so that you must reserve in advance by phone.

SUMMER SPECIALTIES

Festival of American Folklife is sponsored annually by the Smithsonian Institution. This popular festival takes place on the Mall, traditionally for eight late June–early July days, late morning through early evening, with specific American regional themes varying season to season, but invariably including songs and instrumental music, crafts, foods, and dancing in the evening. Big crowds (about a million per festival), much fun, many families.

Independence Day (July 4) is special in the capital, traditionally beginning with a gala parade along Constitution Avenue, entertainment the day long at the Sylvan Theater on the grounds of the Washington Monument, an evening concert by the National Symphony at the U.S. Capitol, and fireworks—usually at 9:30 P.M.—over the Washington Monument.

Military Bands—those of the *Air Force, Army, Navy,* and *Marines*—present outdoor concerts the summer long, Memorial Day through Labor Day; they invariably begin at 8 P.M. and they're free. Here's the breakdown.

Mondays:	U.S. Navy Band, U.S. Capitol, west steps
Tuesdays:	U.S. Army Band, Sylvan Theater on the grounds of the Washington Monument
	U.S. Air Force Band, at the Capitol
Wednesdays:	U.S. Marine Band, at the Capitol
Thursdays:	U.S. Marine Band, at the Capitol
Fridays:	U.S. Army Band at the Capitol
	U.S. Air Force Band at Sylvan Theater
Sundays:	U.S. Marine Band, Sylvan Theater

Twilight Tattoos (traditionally mid-July through August) meld music and pageantry, with military troops and military bands, on the grounds of the Ellipse, between the White House and the Washington Monument, traditionally beginning at 7 P.M., and free.

Navy Concerts on the Avenue traditionally take place Thursdays and Saturdays (when the sailors take turns with other military musicians) at the Navy Memorial on Pennsylvania Avenue between 7th and 9th streets NW.

Marine Corps Evening Parades are warm-weather treats, on Tuesdays at the Iwo Jima Memorial in Arlington, Virginia, with the Marines' Drum and Bugle Corps and Silent Drill Team featured; and Fridays at the Marine Barracks, 8th and I streets SE. Starting times of each series of parades vary and you're advised to reserve by phone for the Barracks parade. (Note, too, that the Marine Band and Chamber Orchestra or Chamber Ensemble present concerts Sunday afternoons March through May at the Marine Barracks.) All are free.

Netherlands Carillon Recitals, at The Netherlands Carillon on the grounds of the Iwo Jima Memorial in Arlington, Virginia (above), take place Saturday evenings June through August, customarily between 6:30 and 8:30 P.M. Free.

Wolf Trap Farm for the Performing Arts (Trap Road, Vienna, Virginia) constitutes America's only national park functioning exclusively as a venue for the performing arts. It goes back to the mid-1960s, when the federal government accepted a private gift of a hundred Virginia acres in pretty countryside west of Washington. Wolf Trap's summer theater, the 6800-seat *Filene Center*, opened in 1971 (and was rebuilt after a 1982 fire). Land and funds were donated later, for the 1981 opening of *The Barns*, an indoor theater used in winter. Summer sees regular performances of the *Wolf Trap Opera Company* and the *National Symphony Orchestra*, with other groups on scene, as well—the *New York City Opera* and the *New York Philharmonic* usually among them. There are performances of singers and solo instrumentalists, trios and quartets—pop, jazz, and classical—and guest ballet troupes, too; these latter have included both Moscow's Bolshoi and the Joffrey. And you don't need a car; take the Metro to West Falls Church station, transferring there to Wolf Trap's own shuttle bus to Filene Center, and returning via the same route in reverse. If you like, watch performances from the lawn, with a picnic supper that you've brought along (along with a blanket to sit on) or ordered in advance from Wolf Trap's own caterers. Wolf Trap is special.

Sports in Washington: RFK *Stadium,* named for Robert F. Kennedy, a younger brother of President Kennedy, and like the president assassinated (he had served as his brother's attorney general and as a New York senator), is at the termination of East Capitol Street, adjacent to a Metro station; it's the home of the *Washington Redskins,* the capital's football eleven. Other D.C. teams include the *Washington Capitals* (hockey) and the *Washington Bullets* (pro basketball): they play at *Capital Center,* in nearby Landover, Maryland.

Ticket-Purchasing Services: Though with nothing like the volume of pioneer discount-ticket centers in New York and London, Washington's *Ticketplace* (F Street between 12th and 13th streets NW, at the Metro Center subway station; phone 202-842-5387) keeps busy vending cash-only tickets discounted by half, for day-of-performance tickets to certain local presentations, including ballet, concerts, and athletic events at RFK Stadium—all with a service charge tacked on. Ticketplace is, as well, a source of tickets at regular prices for future showings of most events. I suggest phoning in advance for details, ifs, and buts. The same *Ticketron* you know from other U.S. cities is in Washington (phone 202-626-1000). Bear in mind that when you order from it with a credit card, the tickets are yours—and will be charged to you—whether you make use of them or simply leave them uncalled-for at the box office.

4

Washington to Stay

SELECTING YOUR HOTEL

Not at all surprising—the city is, after all, a world capital and a global destination for diplomats, executives, and pleasure visitors, foreign as well as domestic, not to mention convention-goers in quantity—Washington's hotel facilities are way out of proportion to its size.

They're situated all over the District, rather than in a single central-city location, and they spill into bordering Maryland and Virginia. Washington's primary hotel strength is Luxury category. Still, the middle, or First Class, ranks are well represented, and I include in this chapter a group of Moderate-category hotels as well.

There's a wealth of choices. Decide first on your (or your employer's) budget. Determine next what part of town might be most convenient for you—the area of Downtown near the Mall, or north of the Mall; the so-called West End, lying between Dupont Circle and the zoo; way east to the area between the Capitol and Union Station; or beyond the D.C. borders where, unless you're with car, it pays to stay at a hotel close to a Metro station, so that you may gain the center of the city effortlessly.

Actually, proximity to a Metro station is important in the selection of in-the-city hotels, too. With the group that follows, I make it a point to concentrate on hotels located near the Metro. When that is not the case, I so signify, suggesting that you'll be happier as a guest if you have a car at your disposal.

Just about all the major hotel chains and hotel groups are represented in Washington, along with the occasional individually owned hostelry. You'll recognize hotels associated with *Leading Hotels of the World;* they're accepted into LHW by invitation only. Washington-based *Marriott* has a considerable number of area hostelries. Three *Hyatt* groupings—Hyatt Regency, Park Hyatt, Grand Hyatt—are on scene. So are links of globe-girdling *Inter-Continental* and *Hilton International's* Vista division, the elegant *Four Seasons* and *Ritz Carlton* chains, *Holiday Inns* and its upscale Crowne Plaza division, *Ramada Inns* and its premium-category Ramada Renaissance group, *Stouffer's, Trusthouse Forte, Loews, Embassy Suites, Guest Quarters, Sheraton, Best Western, Comfort Inns, Days Inns,* and *Quality Hotels.*

If you're from a non-English-speaking country, you may be surprised to learn that hotel staffs—executives, middle-level personnel, and the people serving you in the restaurants and keeping your room spic and span—are from points throughout the planet: Germany and the Philippines, France and China, Holland and Switzerland, Nigeria and India, Ethiopia and Colombia. Invariably there will be someone on staff to speak your language. Although New York is universally considered to be America's prime melting-pot city, contemporary Washington easily matches it.

ABOUT SPECIAL RATES
AND BARGAIN PACKAGES

Masses of summer vacationers notwithstanding, rates tend to dip in the hottest months, July and August—when only the most intrepid business and professional travelers and lobbyists travel to Washington. Additionally, most hotels have excellent-value weekend packages even during the busy cooler months, the better to fill empty rooms Friday and Saturday nights, when they're vacated by business guests. Even if you're staying longer, it can pay to work a weekend package into your visit; often they include extras like the morning paper, a basket of fruit, a bottle of wine, sometimes breakfast and/or dinner.

There are other special rates, as well, corporate (your company will know about these) and convention especially. One of the newest rate gimmicks—emulating advance-purchase reduced-rate air tickets—is called Supersavers; with it, if you book say a month in advance, you may save as much as 25 or 30 percent. Certain chains—Inter-Continental has innovated in this area—now offer excellent-value packages for frequent visitors.

If you're interested in minimum tabs, bear in mind that when you or your travel agent make a reservation, you want to ask for the *lowest possible* rate or package (don't be bashful about using the term "lowest possible"), remembering also that high-up rooms are costlier than those on lower floors, at the rear of the hotel, overlooking its parking lot, or inside on a court. Note, too, that the Washington Convention and Visitors Association ("Phone Numbers," chapter 1) can provide you with up-to-the-minute hotel rates and package plans.

Evaluations following, as in all the books of my *World at Its Best* series, are alphabetical, within each of three groups: *Luxury, First Class,* and *Moderate.*

SELECTED LUXURY HOTELS

Capital Hilton Hotel (16th and K Streets NW; phone 202-393-1000): Go back some years and you may remember this hotel as the Statler Hilton, its former first name that of a onetime premier chain that joined forces, for a period, with the Hilton group. Recent seasons have seen this hotel thoroughly and tastefully refurbished, lobby through on-high suites, in a contemporary-traditional mix of styles. It's handsome and it hums. Those of the 549 rooms and suites I have inspected are in tones of beige and brown, with Louis XVI accents and brass fittings, marble counters, TV, and phone-equipped baths. Top four floors comprise the Towers—extra-amenity, with complimentary breakfast, afternoon tea, and cocktail canapés (if not the cocktails—for which you pay). Locals and guests mingle at the main bar, and there are three restaurants. Trader Vic's, with Chinese-inspired Polynesian fare and jungle-bungalow décor, is a perennial favorite. Twigs Grill (chapter 5) is posh, and just plain Twigs is mid-category. Alert service.

Four Seasons Hotel (2800 Pennsylvania Avenue; phone 202-342-0444): If, like me, you're an Italy buff, what strikes you upon

arrival at the Four Seasons is the detached bell tower—or *campanile*, a feature of Italian churches—that distinguishes this hotel's red-brick profile. Go inside, then, and there are additional treats in this Skidmore, Owings & Merrill–designed complex. What the architects respected was space. They had a lot to work with and they took full advantage. The lobby is long and broad, leading to the casual restaurant, light and airy Garden Terrace. It's evaluated in chapter 5, as is the main restaurant, Aux Beaux Champs. The Fitness Club, opened in 1990, is the most impressive I have come upon in a hotel, with a 60-foot-long lap swimming pool just short of Olympic length (swim eight laps and you've swum a mile) and aerobics classes, massage, and an impressive battery of workout equipment. Look of accommodations—197 all told, including 30 super suites—is soft and svelte, with English-style furnishings of the late eighteenth and early nineteenth centuries (including canopied beds in some suites) melded with contemporary art on walls and fabulous state-of-the-art baths. Guest services stand out here—complimentary shoe shines, complimentary limo service to the center of town on weekdays, quick-as-a-wink pressing, an early-morning coffee urn in the lobby. The Four Seasons' location is significant: at the eastern entrance to Georgetown, where Pennsylvania Avenue leads into M Street. It's a fair walk, but the Metro is closer to the Four Seasons than to any other major Georgetown hotel. Withal, the principal factor in this hotel's success is attention to detail. The staff not only smiles, but it is skilled. A link of the Four Seasons chain that is affiliated with Leading Hotels of the World.

Grand Hotel (2350 M Street NW, phone 202-429-0100) is indeed grand. Thirty-two of its 265 units are suites, one of which, the Royal, with its trio of bedrooms, quartet of baths, dining room, and kitchen, has served as Washington quarters of the king of Saudi Arabia. (The hotel is popular with Arab potentates.) All suites have wood-burning fireplaces, but even in ordinary rooms—good-sized and traditionally furnished—bathrooms are marble-surfaced and with separate stall showers supplementing tubs. Restaurant, bar-lounge, and formal courtyard with a heated pool lead from the circular lobby. Its impeccable luxury notwith-

Sept. 15, 16 th.

$201.00
210.00

standing, the Grand appears, at least to this inspector, to not quite make it in the sense, say, of its West End neighbors, hotels that appear more lively and relaxed.

1-800-233-1234

Grand Hyatt Hotel (1000 H Street NW, phone 202-582-1234): Diversity is the Grand Hyatt's ace-in-the-hole. If you don't like the view of the city from your outside room or suite, move across the corridor for a vista of the 12-story atrium lying beneath a 13,000-square-foot glass skylight, with its focal point a 7000-square-foot lagoon interspersed with waterfalls and fountains. You've dined at Hamilton's, poshest of the restaurants? Then try lunch or breakfast at the Grand Café (chapter 5), edging the lagoon. Have a pastrami on rye at the Zephyr Deli (chapter 5), play video games at the sports bar called Grand Slam, or enjoy a quiet drink at Palladio's, a three-level lounge. The health club extends to two stories, with a lap pool, exercise rooms, sauna, aerobics, and juice bar. Those of the 907 rooms and suites I have occupied or inspected are Hyatt-handsome (suites are especially zingy) and a couple of floors are given over to the Regency Club, the extra-amenity section, with complimentary hot breakfasts, day-long snacks, cocktails, and canapés. You're heart of Downtown, just across from the Washington Convention Center, with underground access to Metro Center station—focal point of the D.C. subway system, through which all lines pass; and convenient as well to Woodward & Lothrop, headquarters emporium of the No. 1 Washington-based department-store chain (chapter 6). Nobody does a hotel like this—big and bold and eye-filling and fun—better than Hyatt. And, despite its size and enormous guest-count, staff is cordial and professional.

1-800
424-5054

Hay-Adams Hotel (800 16th Street NW; phone 202-638-6600) takes the names of a pair of literary/political figures whose homes, turn of the century, were contiguous houses fringing Lafayette Park. They were John Hay, who accompanied Abraham Lincoln to Washington from Springfield, Illinois, co-authored a ten-volume history of Lincoln, and later became secretary of state. Henry Adams, a novelist, historian, and onetime U.S. minister to Britain, befriended Hay, and their townhouses were centers of Washington politics and society. When—decades before the preservation movement—the houses were razed to be replaced by a hotel, the hotel's builder named the hostelry in their memory. Recent seasons have seen the Hay-Adams stylishly and meticulously refurbished, paneled and tapestried lobby through to presidential suite with a catty-cornered fireplace in its living room and views from its windows of the White House, the Washington Monument, and the Jefferson Memorial. All rooms on the Lafayette Park side (the most expensive) have memorable vistas, but accommodations throughout that I have inspected—suites, junior suites, doubles, and twins—are distinctively decorated in traditional style; although the marbled baths I've seen could do with additional updating. But I have no other qualms about the Hay-Adams or its trio of restaurants (chapter 5). Nor with the service, concierges through waiters.

Henley Park Hotel (926 Massachusetts Avenue NW; phone 202-638-5200) is a gemlike smaller house just north of the Convention Center, within walking distance of F Street stores, the Mall, and (four blocks distant) Metro Center subway station. A mock-Tudor structure dating back to World War I, it saw a major 1980s refurbishing, with the lobby's principal architectural features not only left intact, but enhanced with the addition of decorative detail, not least of which are four sculpted gargoyles rescued from the original facade of the Commodore Hotel in New York (now that city's glass-surfaced Grand Hyatt). You pass through the lobby to distinctive public spaces—Wilkes Room, where afternoon tea is served, Marley's Lounge, a club-like bar with mauve-tinted leaded windows and tapestry-upholstered chairs; Coeur de Lion, the restaurant (evaluated in chapter 5) that is based on a glass-roofed atrium. Those of the 96 rooms and suites I've inspected evoke the eighteenth century, with Chippendale and chintz the principal design components—and fine baths. Service, based on my experience, is top-rank. A special spot.

Hyatt Regency Washington Hotel (400 New Jersey Avenue NW; phone 202-737-1234)—eldest of the trio of Hyatt hotels in Washington—is a near neighbor to the Capitol (two blocks) and to Union Station and the Metro (three blocks). You enter a five-story atrium, with one of the trio of restaurants, popular-priced Park Promenade, at its edge; the two others, Jonah's Oyster Kitchen and Hugo's way topside on the roof, are evaluated in chapter 5. Besides two busy bars, there's a health club anchored on a 43-foot, glass-roofed pool-cum-bar. There are 834 smartly styled rooms and suites, including a Regency Club floor—with premium-tabbed accommodations and the use of a lounge in which on-the-house hot breakfast and cocktails are served.

Jefferson Hotel (16th and M Streets NW; phone 202-347-2200): You immediately perceive what the Jefferson is all about when I tell you that fully a third of the 100 units are suites. Erected in the 1920s as an apartment house, it turned hotel in the 1940s accommodating World War II military personnel. By the time I first knew it, in the late 1980s, it had become one of Washington's best kept small-hotel secrets. Come the 90s, it was completely refurbished, with décor essentially eighteenth-century Georgian and early-nineteenth-century Regency, aided and abetted by antique accents and fine textiles. There's a bust of Jefferson in the smallish lobby, the bar is red-walled and clublike, and the restaurant (chapter 5) is hung with historic prints. Each suite and room has two-line speaker phones with hold buttons, speed dialing, conference calling, computer connections, and fax. Location is central; the Soviet Embassy is just opposite, the White House is less than a quarter-hour's walk, and the Metro is a couple of blocks south. *800-228-9290*

J. W. Marriott Hotel (1331 Pennsylvania Avenue NW; phone 202-393-2000): When the international Marriott chain—based in Washington—determined that the time had arrived for a really distinguished D.C. flagship, it covered all bases. Location, to start, was inspired: Pennsylvania Avenue, with the White House due west, the Mall and its museums a short stroll south, department stores and specialty shops of Downtown, along with Metro Center subway station, an easy walk north. So rose the severely striking, easily discernible facade of the J. W. Marriott—first of the chain's hotels employing not only the family name of the boss, but his first two initials as well. The "J.W.," became an instant center-city landmark. Everyone wants to see the network

$ 209.00

of massive crystal chandeliers that illuminate its lobby. The 771 rooms—in tones of gray and pale blue, some with spectacular views and all with state-of-the-art baths—include half a hundred suites among which are a series of standout presidential apartments. There's a premium-tab Concierge Level with its own lounge, for the service of complimentary Continental breakfast and canapés with honor-bar evening drinks. The Health Center—swimming pool, fitness center, and game room—stands out. And so do restaurants and bar-lounges—Celadon (the poshest), Garden Terrace (whose early evening cocktail buffet is one of Washington's more noteworthy bargains) and National Café (chapter 5). And it's worth noting that the hundred-plus stores and eateries of the Shops at National Place (chapter 6) are adjacent to the J.W., with an entrance from its lobby.

Loew's L'Enfant Plaza Hotel (480 L'Enfant Plaza SW; phone 202-484-1000) is unusual in that it's south of the Mall, a block from the National Air and Space Museum, occupying the bottom two and top four floors of a mixed-use office-shop-theater complex that's directly above L'Enfant Plaza Metro station. Recently emerged from a remarkable multimillion-dollar renovation, its 372 rooms and suites are nineteenth-century French in design, all with three phones (with hold capacity), high-tech communications/entertainment centers, and second TVs in new marble and white-tile baths. There's a rooftop pool and fitness center, a busy restaurant, and a congenial bar-lounge.

Madison Hotel (15th and M streets NW; phone 202-862-1600): My publishers booked me at this hotel some years back, in the course of a multicity media tour, but I thought I had better return, in the course of researching this title, for an inspection of the premises, so that I could be up to date on a hostelry that did not, first time around, bowl me over with enthusiasm. On this most recent return—even after presentation of impeccable credentials identifying me and describing my mission—front desk personnel (with one exception, after a long, long wait to be shown representative rooms and a suite) were either rude or ignored me. I remained standing in the lobby nearly an hour (signs state that lobby chairs are for registered guests and the lobby cocktail-lounge is of course for drinkers) until, finally asking to be directed to the general manager, a desk attendant phoned the sales manager; ultimately I was shown around. Rooms and suites are less vivid than I remember them, and refurbished. Still, the lobby, with its registered-guests-only and bar-customers-only seating policy is, to me, insupportable in a luxury hotel, and the lobby's roped-off displays of Louis XVI furniture—each labeled, as in a shop or museum—even to a Francophile author of two books on France such as myself, is, to understate, ostentatious. I declined to look at the restaurant. Heaven knows what the service would be like at its tables, given my experience—even with credentials—at the front desk. If I was treated this way, what might befall you, as an unknown first-timer? The Madison makes a specialty of heads of state; I'm sure they're fussed over, as indeed they should be. But I can't recommend this hotel for the rest of us.

Mayflower Hotel (1127 Connecticut Avenue NW; phone 202-347-3000): Take a look before you go in. The Mayflower, well into its sixth decade, extends a full block from its Connecticut Avenue main entrance, along De Sales Street, flanking its northern facade, to 17th Street at the rear. Sheltering more than 650 rooms, some 70 suites, and a lobby that runs its full length, arguably the most historic (and surely one of the most beautiful) ballrooms in Washington, a baker's dozen meeting rooms (each named for one of the original 13 colonies), a pair each of restaurants (evaluated in chapter 5) and of bars (one with a bartender who doubles as a skilled magician while you're ordering a drink). Designed by Warren & Wetmore, one of the two architectural firms responsible for New York's Grand Central Terminal, the Mayflower opened just in time to provide its ballroom for Calvin Coolidge's 1925 inaugural ball. Since that time it has been the site of an inaugural ball for every president during its existence, which means—so you don't have to look them up as I have—Hoover, Franklin D. Roosevelt, Truman, Eisenhower, Kennedy, Johnson, Nixon, Carter, Reagan, and Bush. Recent years—the hotel is now under the aegis of Stouffer Hotels—have seen $65 million spent on an extraordinary restoration. A 60-foot skylight blacked out in World War II was reopened. More than 56 miles of millwork was used for crown moldings. Almost 47,000 square feet of marble was purchased to resurface upgraded bathrooms. Twenty-three carat gold leaf was employed to gild ceilings and column capitals of the lobby. The vaulted, balconied ballroom was carefully refreshed. Every room and suite has been enhanced with new furniture, textiles, and accessories in coordinated color schemes, with a Federal-period motif. Happiness at the Mayflower is a room—you must specify location when booking—with a view of Connecticut Avenue, and a day beginning with a wakeup call followed by complimentary delivery of *The Washington Post* and a pot of coffee. The weather? No surprise: the chambermaid left you the official prediction when she turned down your bed the night before.

Omni Shoreham Hotel (2500 Calvert Street NW; phone 202-234-0700) was—on the occasion of my first stay—the just plain Shoreham. That was before the Omni chain took over and restored it throughout, when the neighborhood had no Metro station. In those days, you went downtown by cab or bus if you had no car. Today, you simply hop on the subway. The Shoreham's updating—retaining the original look of this big (770 room-and-suite) convention hotel has been tasteful. The 1930 lobby remains vast, gracious, and chandelier-hung. Rooms—those I've inspected are mostly decorated in soft florals and stripes—retain the size that such spaces had half a century back. Grounds include an Olympic-size pool and tennis courts. And on the staff—alert and cordial—is a prize-winning lady concierge who just has to be one of the best in the business.

Park Hyatt Hotel (24th and M Streets NW; phone 202-789-1234): When, some years back, makers and shakers at Hyatt headquarters in Chicago wanted to show guests that they could operate an intimate-scale, personal-service hostelry as well as they do their trademark Hyatt Regency (and now, Grand Hyatt) hotels, they created the first hotel of the Park Hyatt group. And made their point. Washington's Park Hyatt, some years newer and designed by the architectural firm of Skidmore, Owings & Merrill, quickly became a landmark of the hotel-dotted West End. With a triple-level wrought-iron fountain to its side distinguishing it, the lobby is guarded by a pair of oversize Chinese T'ang horses, with conversation groups of Louis XV chairs dotted about. Well over half of the 224 units are suites, in tones of beige, seafoam green, and soft peach, each with living room and one, or, in some cases, two bedrooms; and in the case of the spectacular presidential suite, a library and dining space. Maid service twice a day is the rule, but so is late afternoon delivery of a complimentary snack—to tide you over till cocktails and dinner—from the general manager. Phones are two-line with hold buttons and computer modems. There's a barbershop/hairdresser. I evaluate Melrose, the Park Hyatt's restaurant, in chapter 5. A lounge that could be that of a private club is the venue for drinks and afternoon tea. The Health Club's pride and joy is a big pool with a kid's pool supplementing it. But the Park Hyatt's lure is service. Even on a first visit, everyone knows you by name; when you return, you're a member of the family.

Ramada Renaissance Techworld Hotel (999 9th Street NW; phone 202-898-9000)—just east of the Convention Center edging Chinatown, and a couple of blocks distant from Metro Center subway station—is a relatively recent giant embracing just over 720 rooms and 80 suites, pair of restaurants (the less expensive of which, Café Florentine, can be useful to conventioneers, and is evaluated in chapter 5), bar-lounge, fitness center, and 50-foot swimming pool. A separate wing houses 166 Renaissance Club Tower rooms and suites—extra-tab but including the service of breakfast and canapés with honor-bar cocktails. This is a smartly styled house—one of the best-looking of Ramada's upscale Renaissance division that I have observed. Lobby is engagingly high-tech, with white metal columns supporting a striking steel-and-glass roof. Rooms—note that some are larger than others—are embellished in hues of teal and cinnamon, all with generous writing surfaces (praise be!), good baths, textiles in florals and stripes. (If you're curious, the "Techworld" of the hotel's title relates to Techworld Plaza—a mixed-use office-store-showroom complex—in which it is located.)

Ritz-Carlton Hotel (2100 Massachusetts Avenue NW; phone 202-293-2100): Time flies. I first knew the Ritz-Carlton when it

was the Fairfax, on the occasion of an initial visit to the Phillips
Collection, just across the street, easily a dozen years back. My
introduction to the hotel as the Ritz-Carlton came some years
later—again in connection with a museum visit, that time the
National Gallery of Art, to which the British Tourist Authority
had invited journalists to the exhibit "Treasure Houses of Britain." My most recent stay was the eye-opener of the lot. New
York interior designer Sister Parish—known for interpretations
of the eighteenth and early nineteenth centuries in her work—
had been called in to redecorate, stem to stern. And so she did,
with its 23 suites and 207 rooms in hues of yellow and blue,
antiques and reproductions of period pieces upholstered in floral
chintzes, good eighteenth- and nineteenth-century paintings
and prints—the effect not unlike that of nearby Georgetown's
restored Federal townhouses. With its new look came Ritz-
Carlton attention to service and detail. You're welcomed by
name; the staff's motto, "within ten minutes," means that whatever the time of the request, it will be fulfilled in under a quarter
of an hour. When you ask the concierge where breakfast is
served, you're not simply pointed in the direction of the Jockey
Club restaurant (evaluated in chapter 5), but rather you're taken
to it—and with a smile. Ditto if you're seeking out the Fairfax Bar
for afternoon tea before its fire on a brisk winter day. No hotel in
town—at least in my experience—is more concerned with service. Nor more enjoyable. And location is A-plus, impressive
embassies all about, and Dupont Circle Metro station one short
block distant.

Vista International Hotel (1400 M Street NW; phone 202-479-
1700) catches you up immediately upon entering. You find
yourself in a 14-story, glass-enclosed atrium that is among the
most dramatic of Washington's contemporary spaces. Most of
the Vista's 413 rooms and suites overlook the landscaped atrium.
Those I have inspected or inhabited are good-sized and good-
looking—furnishings are modern, textiles warm, colors relaxing. The half-dozen most special suites are the work of French
couturier Hubert de Givenchy (who doubles as an interior
designer). There are premium-tab Executive Floors way topside
(with extra amenities, including complimentary Continental

breakfast and cocktails and canapés). There are two restaurants, the pricier Harvest and the Veranda, which is combined with a wine bar. Perhaps most fun of all is the high-up Tower Lounge, for drinks-cum-vistas. Location is good; you're a ten- or twelve-minute walk from the White House, and McPherson Square Metro station is a few blocks south. The Vista is part of the domestic U.S. group operated by around-the-world Hilton International.

Washington Hilton Hotel (1919 Connecticut Avenue NW; phone 202-483-3000): If there were not already a Washington Hilton it would have to be created. Which is easier said than done. Hotels that are D.C. institutions like this one are not built overnight.

Presidents of the United States deliver more speeches to larger live audiences at the Washington Hilton than at any other venue. They come often enough for the hotel to have constructed a special presidential entrance area on T Street, at the rear (protected with bulletproof doors, added after the 1981 attempt on President Reagan's life); a specially secured lounge where presidents wait before proceeding to the main ballroom, adjacent so-called Cabinet Room used by VIPs at ranking events; and what the hotel terms Presidents' Walk—the hallway leading from the presidential holding room to the backstage entrance of the main, or International, ballroom. The walk is well worth a stroll, if you can swing it in the course of a hotel visit. Lining its walls are pictures of all the presidents and their wives, or the women who served as official White House hostesses, the range George and Martha Washington along with say, James and Sara Polk and Chester and Ellen Arthur, beyond to William and Ida McKinley and Franklin and Eleanor Roosevelt, through to Jimmy and Rosalynn Carter and George and Barbara Bush.

Reason for the frequent presidential visits is the largest ballroom in town; it will seat 3074 for dinner and 4200 for meetings. And there's a vast exhibit hall, second ballroom, and 31 other meeting rooms to supplement it. Not surprisingly, the 1150-room-and-suite Washington Hilton—which opened in 1965 and emerged from a $27 million renovation in 1990—is no stranger to superlatives. Renée Subrin, its astute public relations whiz, has compiled calculations revealing that it accommodates

425,251 guests per year, uses 892,502 bedsheets per year, serves 898,000 meals per year, included in which are a million pats of butter and almost three million strawberries. And, hey! When you take a postcard from the desk in your room, announcing to Cousin Maude that you've toured the White House, bear in mind that it's one of 50,000 the hotel provides guests annually. To term the Washington Hilton the quintessential convention hotel is to understate; 70 percent of its guests are conventioneers. Newly done rooms are easy to take—in pastel mauves, aquas, and greens, accented by blond wood furniture, and updated baths. The premium-tab Towers has been brightened too, offering complimentary Continental breakfast and gratis drinks at cocktail time. I evaluate the dressy Ashby's Restaurant (with a lively bar-lounge taking its name) in chapter 5; Colonials is the coffee shop—and very nice. In a hotel as big as this, there are other venues for food and drink—especially, during warm weather, the Gazebo, an umbrella-covered café flanking the Olympic-size pool in the garden, with a trio of tennis courts adjacent. Public transportation is nearby: Dupont Circle Metro station is four blocks down Connecticut Avenue.

Washington Hotel (Pennsylvania Avenue at 15th Street NW; phone 202-638-5900): Bless the Washington Hotel. Through the long years of Pennsylvania Avenue's modern-day deterioration, it remained open. Now, of course, that stretch of the thoroughfare on which the president travels from the neighboring White House to the Capitol on his inauguration day, is one of the spiffiest in town, and the Washington has two ranking hotel neighbors: the restored Willard Inter-Continental (below), which had been closed for some years, and the recent J. W. Marriott (above). Dating to the last year of World War I—1918 (it was being constructed while President Wilson reviewed troops marching down Pennsylvania Avenue en route to the front, transatlantic)—the Washington is a beloved D.C. institution. Designed by the noted New York architectural team, Carrere and Hastings, its embellishments, inspired by the Italian Renaissance, include a sculpted frieze depicting Washington, Lincoln, Jefferson, Franklin, and other history-book Americans. In the 1920s, printed reports noted guests' delight with running ice water in the bathrooms. Vice presidents like John Garner, Supreme Court justices like Frank Murphy, House speakers like John McCormack lived at the Washington. (A former hotel employee has recalled to management a period when 50 representatives and five senators called the Washington home.) Recent seasons have seen the hotel refurbished stem to stern (cost was $15 million), the while retaining the look of its high-ceilinged movie-set lobby. Two Continents Restaurant and—special treat this—the rooftop Sky Terrace are both evaluated in chapter 5. There are two bars, one at the lobby's edge—busy both with guests and with Washingtonians at the end of each day—and the other, the Grille, whose walls are hung with blown-up photos of earlier Washington eras. Rooms and suites, in this oldest D.C. building in continuous operation as a hotel, sport new baths and new (albeit still traditional) décor; there are 350 all told, of varying sizes, and when you book, ask for accommodations with a view either of the next-door Treasury Building and the White House, just beyond, or of Pennsylvania Avenue and the Washington Monument. I save staff for last, wagering that no hotel in town has more old-timers still cheerfully serving—more than two dozen with 20-plus years, some with more than 50, who returned post-retirement out of affection for this very special place.

Watergate Hotel (2650 Virginia Avenue NW; phone 202-965-2300): So much continues to be heard about the Nixon-era Watergate scandal—based on a break-in of Democratic National headquarters in the ten-acre mixed-use Watergate complex, in the 1970s—that the perfectly beautiful hotel in this contemporary architectural grouping too often goes by the wayside. A pity. The Watergate—adjacent to the Kennedy Center, edging the Potomac, some blocks southwest of Foggy Bottom Metro station—is one of the city's toniest hostelries. Public spaces—with a chatty cocktail lounge edging the lobby—are antique-accented. Most costly of the 238 accommodations afford views of the river and Georgetown. But all of the suites (constituting almost half of total capacity) and rooms I have inspected are capacious and smartly styled in the traditional English manner. There are a pair of restaurants—mid-category Brighton Grill and ever-so-costly, dinner-only Jean-Louis—both evaluated in chapter 5. The Watergate is a part of the Exclusive Hotels division of Britain-based Trusthouse Forte.

Westin Hotel (2401 M Street NW; phone 202-429-2400)—a kingpin of the hotels cluster in the West End quarter between Downtown and Georgetown—is among the handsomer of Washington's modern hotels. Its lobby—edged at the rear by a glass-roofed and windowed loggia giving onto a fountain-centered courtyard—sets the theme of the interiors. Those of the suites (there are but 4, each with its own design motif) and 412 rooms I have inspected have features that I like, including really large desks, luggage benches at the foot of *each* bed, terry robes in *all* baths, and *two* ice machines per floor. There's a premium-tabbed section of extra-amenity rooms, fitness center-cum-pool, drinking parlors, and a pair of restaurants evaluated in chapter 5. Friendly.

Willard Inter-Continental Hotel (1401 Pennsylvania Avenue NW; phone 202-628-9100): When it reopened in 1986 (I was there to cover the festivities, so I know whereof I speak), the rebuilt, restored Willard—which had been closed for 18 years—became a principal look-see destination for ordinarily blasé Washingtonians. And with reason. They realized that this D.C. institution—the first major such in the revitalization of Pennsylvania Avenue, which had been allowed to deteriorate over a long period—reflected a chunk of the capital's history. Travelers were offered shelter where the Willard stands as long ago as 1816. A few decades later, Henry Willard bought the site and built a hotel that took his name. It hosted every president from Franklin Pierce in 1853 to Dwight D. Eisenhower nearly a century later. There was an unavoidable hiatus during the years of closure, but after the reopening, Presidents Reagan and Bush made visits. And certain earlier presidents made unusual use of the hotel. Lincoln, as president-elect, was smuggled in on February 23, 1861, because of assassination threats; holding staff meetings in the lobby, he stayed until his inauguration on March 4. Grant liked the same lobby as a relaxation spot for brandy with a cigar; power brokers approached him on various causes and he came to call them "lobbyists," thus coining a still-used term. Coolidge lived at the Willard as vice president, remaining as president until the then-newly-widowed Mrs. Harding left the nearby White House. And Wilson held meetings at the hotel, of the League to Enforce Peace—predecessor to the Wilson-founded League of Nations. Architect of the current building (1901–1904) was the same Henry Hardenbergh who designed New York's Plaza and Boston's Copley Plaza. Inter-Continental Hotels, its operators, undertook a $120 million refurbishing, especially meticulous in public spaces like the Pennsylvania Avenue lobby (look up at seals of U.S. states on the ceiling, as in the hotel of yore), and in the passage that connects the lobby to F Street, to the north, off which are the hotel's Willard Room restaurant (chapter 5) and a coffee shop. The circular Round Robin Bar has the same contours as in earlier eras (and still serves its famous mint juleps). Inter-Continental—with expertise gained in pioneering restoration of such landmark hotels as Paris's Grand, Edinburgh's George, Cannes's Carlton, and Amsterdam's Amstel—wisely replaced the original 500 rooms with 400 completely new rooms (including 60 suites) and likewise new baths. Accommodations with Pennsylvania Avenue views are the ones to aim for, but all those I have inspected or inhabited are generous size (some, of course, bigger than others), with little expense spared in details like Louis XVI–style furniture, carefully crafted ceiling cornices, silk-shaded brass lamps and sconces, and marble counter-sinks. Location is among the best in town; White House, Mall museums, F and G street department stores, and Metro Center subway station are all easy strolls.

SELECTED FIRST CLASS HOTELS

Dupont Plaza Hotel (1500 New Hampshire Avenue NW; phone 202-483-6000) is enviably well located, facing Dupont Circle, core of an area chockablock with restaurants, shops, embassies, and the Metro station taking the circle's name. The hotel itself is a winner. Lobby is good-sized with a cordial staff at reception. Stephanie's Restaurant (chapter 5) is busy, talky, and a good value at lunch; popular, too, in the evening. The bar is a congenial mix of neighborhood execs, diplomats, and hotel guests. And those of

the 314 rooms and suites I have inspected are attractively traditional, the lot with refrigerator-equipped wet bars and phones in
baths. Nice.

Embassy Row Hotel (2015 Massachusetts Avenue NW; phone
202-265-1600) is aptly named: the street on which it's located is
the No. 1 embassy thoroughfare of the capital. This clean-lined
contemporary house, a hop and a skip from Dupont Circle
Metro station, lures execs and visiting diplomats, whom it shel-
ters in its 196 rooms (including 28 suites), the lot nicely appointed, with good baths. The restaurant, Lucie by name, is stylishly
Franco-American with well-priced prix-fixe lunches; the bar can
be amusing, and there's a swimming pool on the roof.

Embassy Square Suites Hotel (2000 N Street NW; phone 202-
640-9000)—a couple of blocks south of Dupont Circle and its
Metro station—occupies an architecturally unexceptional modern building. Its ace-in-the-hole is kitchen-equipped accommodations, 250 all told. Choose either a one-room studio (the one I
inspected had a queen-size bed plus a pullout sofa bed, kitchen,
and bath) or a one- or two-bedroom suite. All have balconies,
with those inside facing a big swimming pool-centered garden.
Restaurant, bar.

Embassy Suites Washington Hotel (1250 22nd Street NW; phone
202-857-3388) is located in the hotel-dotted West End between
Downtown and Georgetown; Foggy Bottom Metro station is
four long blocks distant. This is an architecturally striking hotel,
with 318 attractive suites giving onto a waterfall and plant-
embellished atrium. The suites' design is standard throughout
(as it is indeed throughout the Embassy Suites chain) except that
corner accommodations are larger, and there are two-bedroom
as well as one-bedroom options. Living–dining rooms are
equipped with giant TVs. Baths (big, as they are throughout the
chain) can be entered from either the living–dining room or the
bedroom (with either a king-size bed or two double beds and a
second, smaller TV). Special treats are twofold: complimentary
hot breakfasts (not Continental) and complimentary cocktail
parties of two hours' duration, each and every evening. Friendly.

Georgetown Inn (1310 Wisconsin Avenue NW; phone 202-333-8900), appropriately Georgian of facade, lies smack in the center of Georgetown. There are just 85 rooms and 10 suites; those I have inspected are generously proportioned, with eighteenth-century-style décor including fourposter beds in some accommodations. Baths are tub- and stall-shower-equipped, with phones. The bar's happy hour is a Georgetown institution (free nibbles with drinks), and the restaurant, Georgetown Bar & Grill, is evaluated in chapter 5. Friendly.

Guest Quarters Suite Hotel (2500 Pennsylvania Avenue NW; phone 202-333-8060)—amid the hotel cluster of the West End between Downtown and Georgetown—is somewhat larger than its counterpart (below), with 123 suites equipped with bedroom, living room, and full kitchen, off-lobby library, but alas, no swimming pool, and with the Metro farther away than from the New Hampshire Avenue GQ.

Guest Quarters Suite Hotel (801 New Hampshire Avenue NW; phone 202-785-2000)—not far from Foggy Bottom Metro station and convenient, as well, to the Kennedy Center, the State Department, and George Washington University—is a 101-unit house embracing living-room- and bedroom-equipped suites— the look is quietly tasteful—with full kitchens. A swimming pool is on the roof.

Holiday Inn Crowne Plaza (775 12th Street NW; phone 202-737-2200) is a link of Holiday Inns' upscale Crowne Plaza group, a 456-room-and-suite tower that's a hop and a skip from the Convention Center and just around the corner from the Grand Hyatt (above). The lobby is large and low-key, with inviting leather-covered wing chairs and corner sofas. Those of the rooms I have either occupied or inspected are designed around pastel schemes, with striped taffeta draperies and spreads, Washington-motif art on walls (specially commissioned by the hotel), and well-equipped baths. There are two floors of premium-tab rooms with a lounge wherein complimentary Continental breakfast, cocktails, and evening drinks and desserts are provided; a honey of a health club with pool, sauna, and fitness equipment under a striking glass skylight; and both Metro Center Bar (nice for a casual lunch) and restaurant (chapter 5), named for the adjacent subway station, with Hecht's department store and the F Street shops also near neighbors.

Morrison Clark Hotel (1015 L Street NW; phone 202-898-1200) comprises a pair of joined 1865 townhouses. You're central, to be sure, but the neighborhood is not the handsomest in town. Public spaces are Victorian-inspired albeit with contemporary touches; ditto the half a hundred-plus, no-two-alike bedrooms and suites, some more attractive than others. Ambience is not necessarily cordial, at least at reception, but the white-hued restaurant, illuminated by a crystal chandelier, draws diners lured by good modern American cooking.

Omni Georgetown Hotel (2121 P Street NW; phone 202-293-3100) is not, to set the record straight at the outset, in Georgetown, but rather in the neighborhood of Dupont Circle, hardly a quarter to be shunned, what with embassies, restaurants, and shops in quantity, not to mention a Metro station; indeed, Omni Dupont Circle might be a better name. Rooms and suites—300 all told—tend to be large and eye-filling, the décor a modern-traditional mix, with plenty of space on desktops and up-to-the-minute baths. A couple of floors are set aside for premium-tab amenities, and there are both restaurant and bar-lounge. Nice.

One Washington Circle Hotel (1 Washington Circle NW; phone 202-872-1680) is all-suite. By that I mean its 150 units range from living room with one bedroom, kitchen, bath, and foyer beyond to bedroom counts of two, three, and four. West End Café, the restaurant, has seafood among its specialties. And location is a plus: facing a circle intersected by K Street, with Foggy Bottom Metro station a block south.

Phoenix Park Hotel (520 North Capitol Street NW; phone 202-638-6900) is, to understate, a find. Location—a block from Union Station and the Metro, and but a few blocks from the

Capitol and congressional offices—is ideal. Occupying a building that went up as the Commodore Hotel in 1927 (and, even two
decades later, charged D.C.'s going rate—$5 for a double with
bath) its interior was gutted by new owners in the 1980s, who
replaced the original 150 small rooms with the current 87 larger
rooms and 9 suites, embodying a color scheme of jade and rose. A
new name—inspired by a famous Dublin park—was selected,
two restaurants (one among the more elegant and delicious on
Capitol Hill, the other a convivial Irish pub-cum-entertainment,
both evaluated in chapter 5) were opened, and the Phoenix Park
became a Hill institution.

Furnishings throughout are in the style of the eighteenth
century, with framed antique Irish prints on walls. All rooms—
not just top-grade accommodations as in some hotels—have
terrycloth robes in baths. Most important is the personal quality
of the service. With less than 90 rooms, the staff—a number of
whom are Irish, not unlike the names of the hotel, its pub
(Dubliner), and its restaurant (Powerscourt, the original of
which is a great County Wicklow mansion)—finds it easy to
know guests. Not surprisingly, the Phoenix Park has considerable
repeaters.

Quality Hotel Capitol Hill (415 New Jersey Avenue NW; phone
202-638-1616) makes a specialty of visitors with business on the
Hill. This is a modern house with 341 well-fitted rooms, restaurant and bar-lounge, and a swimming pool on the roof.

Quality Hotel Central (1900 Connecticut Avenue NW; phone
202-332-9300)—an across-the-avenue neighbor of the Washington Hilton—is clean-lined and contemporary, with agreeable
public spaces that include restaurant, bar-lounge, and outdoor
pool, along with 150 okay rooms.

Ramada Renaissance Hotel Downtown (1143 New Hampshire Avenue NW; phone 202-775-0800) is not actually downtown, but
rather in the West End area between Downtown and Georgetown. (Don't confuse it with the Luxury-category Ramada
Renaissance Techworld above, which *is* downtown.) This is a

pleasant, modern house with rambling lobby, reliable restaurant, oft-busy bar, and 350 rooms and suites—most are accented with floral pastel textiles and have really big baths, if those I've inspected are typical. There is a premium-tab, extra-amenity floor with Continental breakfast and cocktails included in its rates. Friendly.

Sheraton Washington Hotel (2660 Woodley Road NW; phone 202-328-2000) has room-count as a standout. Its 1505 rooms and suites—more than in any other D.C. hotel—occupy a trio of structures on a 16-acre plot, way north, near the zoo. Accommodations in premium-tab Wardman Tower excepted (they are agreeably traditional in style and were in good condition, when I inspected), this is not, for me at least, an easy hotel to love. Main-building rooms I've checked are minimally attractive (those I saw could have done with facelifts), reception staff (again, in my experience) minimally cordial. There are several restaurants (one a cafeteria) and bars and a pair of pools. Not surprisingly, this is a convention hotel; I can't conceive of any reason to check in other than through assignment as a delegate to one or another conference. Escape is easy, however; the hotel is directly over the Woodley Park–Zoo Metro station.

State Plaza Hotel (2117 E Street NW; phone 202-861-8200) is interestingly located between George Washington University to the north and the Lincoln Memorial to the south, with the Vietnam Veterans Memorial and State Department near neighbors, and Foggy Bottom Metro station five blocks distant. This is a looker of a house, with Georgian-style furnishings, stylishly upholstered in artfully draped and accessorized public spaces and in 215 rooms and suites, all with kitchens. And there's a restaurant-café.

Washington Court Hotel (525 New Jersey Avenue NW; phone 202-628-2100): Go back to the early 1980s and you may remember the then-new Sheraton Grand. It assumed its present name and management a few years later. Tall by Washington standards (there are 16 stories), its 254 rooms' décor is a pleasing mix of traditional—including Queen Anne and Louis XVI—with contemporary. A top-floor presidential suite affording a panorama of the Capitol, Supreme Court, and Washington Monument is the hotel's special pride. The atrium-lobby is striking. There are a pair of restaurants (one dressy, one casual), a bar-lounge with evening entertainment, and a fitness center. Besides proximity to the Capitol, the Washington Court is but two blocks from Union Station and the Metro.

Washington Marriott Hotel (1221 22nd Street NW; phone 202-872-1500) stands out for its staff smiles; I don't know of a hotel in Washington where guests are regarded more cordially by doorman and concierge, registration and coffee-shop staff, cashiers and chambermaids. This buzzing West End house—room count became 472 upon completion of a recent 71-room addition—offers amenities like complimentary breakfast in its premium-tabbed Concierge Floor. But rooms throughout are generous-sized and with good baths. Special treats are the indoor pool and adjacent fitness center/sauna. A congenial lobby bar, the Court Lounge, complements Atrium Grille, with a steak restaurant—independently operated Blackie's House of Beef—on the premises. The Washington Marriott is about midpoint between Dupont Circle and Foggy Bottom Metro stations.

Washington Plaza Hotel (Massachusetts and Vermont avenues NW; phone 202-842-1300) is nicely situated at Thomas Circle, in a hotel-dotted quarter that's a 15-minute walk from the White House, and with the McPherson Square Metro station five blocks south. This is a relatively modern 340-room house, with a spacious lobby, restaurant, bar, and outdoor pool whose problem, when I inspected, was wear and tear. The hotel needed nothing so much as a multimillion-dollar stem-to-stern refurbishing. Until that comes about, this is not a hotel I can recommend.

Wyndham Bristol Hotel (2430 Pennsylvania Avenue NW; phone 202-955-6400)—stylishly comfortable, with its décor traditional—lies just south of the West End hotels cluster, between Downtown and Georgetown. Its rooms are kitchen-equipped.

There are both restaurant and bar-lounge. And Foggy Bottom Metro station is a couple of blocks distant.

SELECTED MODERATE HOTELS

Anthony Hotel (1823 L Street NW; phone 202-223-4320), strategically situated half a dozen blocks north of the White House and but a block from Farragut North Metro station, has just under a hundred rooms and suites, some traditional in look, others contemporary, most with kitchens or wet bars. There is no restaurant, but many are nearby.

Bellevue Hotel (15 E Street NW; phone 202-638-0900), a near neighbor of Union Station and the Metro, and not far from the Capitol, is an elderly albeit updated house with a balconied lobby adjacent to its Tiber Creek Restaurant-Pub, and 140 okay rooms.

Best Western City Center Hotel (1201 13th Street NW; phone 202-682-5300): You're near Thomas Circle at this Best Western, in an attractive Downtown quarter that's not close to the Metro but is within walking distance of the White House and the Mall, to the south. There are just a hundred well-equipped rooms, restaurants, and gym.

Carlyle Suites Hotel (1731 New Hampshire Avenue NW; phone 202-234-3200): Art Deco buildings are a relative rarity in Washington, nothing like as commonplace as in, say, Miami Beach or New York. The Carlyle Suites welcomes with a stunner of a little early-40s-style lobby, and there are Art Deco accents in those of the 170 rooms and suites I've inspected, many good-sized (the hotel opened as an apartment building). There's an attractive coffee shop, nearby health club whose facilities are free to hotel guests, and location is good: on a delightful embassy-dotted street off Dupont Circle and its Metro station.

Comfort Inn (500 H Street NW; phone 202-289-5959): Because it was recommended and because I know that other links in the chain (New York, for example) are satisfactory, I undertook an inspection of this hotel. I didn't like the near-hostility of the reception staff, nor the little lobby, nor the accommodations I was shown. There are 197 rooms and a coffee shop. Location is the little Chinatown quarter downtown. To become really comfortable this Comfort Inn needs a thorough facelift and cordiality in its reception staff. I can't recommend this one.

Connecticut Avenue Days Inn (4400 Connecticut Avenue NW; phone 202-244-5600): You're way north at this Days Inn, but within two blocks of the Metro. (Not that having your own car is a bad idea.) There are 155 clean-lined rooms, and continental breakfast is included in the rate, although there is no restaurant.

Days Inn Downtown (1201 K Street NW; phone 202-842-1020) is at once modern and convenient—especially so if you're a conventioneer; the Convention Center is two blocks distant, and the core of the city is within walking distance. Those of the 220 rooms I have inspected are good-sized and adequate. The restaurant-bar, though plain, is well priced, especially at breakfast when there's a bargain buffet. And the rooftop pool is a boon in summer. Friendly.

Georgetown Marbury Hotel (3000 M Street NW; phone 202-726-5000) welcomes with agreeable décor emulating the eighteenth century, offers 164 rooms and suites in a variety of shapes and sizes (one suite is duplex, with the bedroom up a flight), rooftop pool, and restaurant-bar. You're heart of Georgetown.

Highland Hotel (1914 Connecticut Avenue NW; phone 202-797-2000) is accurately named. Location is four blocks uphill from Dupont Circle Metro station—just opposite the Washington Hilton. This is a nicely updated house, with 140 rooms and suites, bar-lounge, and restaurant whose buffet breakfast is included in the room rate. Worth knowing about if you're a delegate to a big convention at the Hilton and can't get a room there.

Holiday Inn Georgetown (2101 Wisconsin Avenue NW; phone 202-338-4600) is among the nicer of the area's Holiday Inns. There are just under 300 brightly furnished suites and rooms, with floral-print spreads and draperies, typically good Holiday Inn baths, and a convenient café-restaurant. Location is the edge of Georgetown, beyond Dumbarton Oaks; there's no nearby Metro station.

Holiday Inn Thomas Circle (1155 14th Street NW; phone 202-737-1200) proved not easy to inspect—at least at first, what with near-hostile receptionists who did not welcome my interrupting their personal conversation. Eventually help came to show me about—the general manager, no less. She apologized for my reception and showed me several rooms, each pleasantly contemporary and with good baths albeit of differing sizes. The restaurant serves inexpensive buffets at breakfast, lunch, and dinner, with the first-mentioned a good buy.

Howard Johnson Hotel (2601 Virginia Avenue NW; phone 202-965-2700) is mod-look and unpretentious but with the advantage of a rooftop pool and the Kennedy Center but a block distant. There are 152 rooms and a convenient restaurant.

Ramada Inn Central (1430 Rhode Island Avenue NW; phone 202-462-7777) is considerably closer to Logan Circle (which does not have a Metro station) than Dupont Circle (which does). Still, you're reasonably well located, a 15–20 minute walk from the White House. There are 186 rooms and suites, restaurant, bar, and rooftop pool. A good deal.

Savoy Suites Hotel (2505 Wisconsin Avenue NW; phone 202-337-9700) is considerably northwest, with no nearby Metro station. Still, if you're with car, this can be a pleasant headquarters, especially in summer, what with its swimming pool. There are kitchens in 30 of the 150 rooms and suites, phones (and in some cases whirlpools) in baths, and a restaurant.

JUST OVER THE D.C. BORDER:
SELECTED MARYLAND, VIRGINIA,
AND AIRPORT HOTELS

Bethesda Marriott Hotel (5151 Pooks Hill Road, Bethesda, Maryland; phone 301-897-9400): Subdued tones of its traditional-style lobby create a welcoming atmosphere in the Bethesda Marriott, set amidst 18 green acres. There are just over 400 pastel-hued rooms, all with proper desks and two phones, plus a slew of snazzy suites. The swimming pool is indoor/outdoor with a fitness center adjoining and there are a pair of lighted tennis courts on the grounds. The hotel's restaurant, Bello Mondo, not surprisingly given its name, is Italian, but with Continental options. And there are both bar-lounge and coffee shop. Ideally, you have a car, although you're not all that far from a Metro station link to Washington. *Luxury.*

Crystal City Marriott Hotel (1999 Jefferson Davis Highway, Arlington, Virginia; phone 703-521-5500) could not be more convenient of access to Washington. It's plop atop Crystal City Metro station, and the plant-filled lobby is adjoined by Capriccio, with Italian specialties, and Chatfield's, the bar-lounge. There's a nifty indoor picture-windowed pool, with adjacent sauna. The 340 rooms have generous desk space, fine baths, and there's an Executive Level of premium-category, extra-amenity accommodations. You're close to the Pentagon and five minutes from National Airport. *Luxury.*

Days Inn Crystal City (2000 Jefferson Davis Highway, Arlington, Virginia; phone 703-920-8600) is clean-lined contemporary with 250 neat rooms, restaurant-bar, swimming pool, the Metro but two blocks distant, and a gratis shuttle to National Airport, less than a mile away. *Moderate.*

Holiday Inn National Airport (1489 Jefferson Davis Highway, Arlington, Virginia; phone 703-521-1600) is a neat high rise. There are 300 well-equipped rooms with good Inn baths, Fred's Place restaurant and its bar-lounge, and an outdoor pool that's a summer pleasure, not to mention proximity to the Metro (one block) and National Airport (one mile, via the hotel's complimentary to-and-from transportation). *Moderate.*

Holiday Inn Old Town (480 King Street, Alexandria, Virginia; phone 703-549-6080) is appropriately neo-Georgian, without and within, as an act of homage to its surroundings, heart of Alexandria's Old Town. Indeed, it is an exceptionally felicitous-looking link in a chain whose décor can be prosaic. The lobby mixes wing chairs, soft paper-pleated potter lamps, and brass chandeliers. Rooms—227 all told—follow the Georgian motif. There are a restaurant, a bar, and an indoor pool. You're wise to have a car, although a local bus will take you to the nearest Metro station, with central Washington then but minutes distant. *First Class.*

Hyatt Regency Bethesda Hotel (Bethesda Metro Center, Bethesda, Maryland; phone 301-657-1234) is based on a socko 12-story atrium. There's a choice of places to eat and drink, fitness center, indoor pool, and 380 rooms and suites, including a couple of floors with extra-fee Regency Club accommodations, which include complimentary hot breakfast and cocktails with canapés. Location is atop Bethesda Metro station, convenient to the city. *Luxury.*

Hyatt Regency Crystal City Hotel (2799 Jefferson Davis Highway, Arlington, Virginia; phone 703-486-1234) tempts first with location: Alexandria and the Pentagon are near neighbors and there's a complimentary shuttle to both National Airport and Crystal City Metro station, for a quick trip into Washington. The hotel is based on a five-story atrium enlivened by cascading water. It's big: close to 700 smart rooms and suites including a Regency Club section—premium-tab with extra amenities, including hot breakfast and cocktails with canapés. There are a pair of restaurants, an outdoor pool, and a fitness center. *Luxury.*

Hyatt Regency Dulles Hotel (2300 Dulles Boulevard, Herndon, Virginia; phone 703-834-1234) is worth knowing about, should you want to be near Dulles the night before an early-morning flight, or on the evening of a late arrival. This is a typically full-facility Hyatt Regency, with 317 well-designed rooms and suites, restaurants, bar-lounge, indoor pool, health club, and complimentary shuttle linking the hotel with the airport. *Luxury.*

Key Bridge Marriott Hotel (1401 Lee Highway, Arlington, Virginia; phone 703-524-6400)—just across the Potomac's Key Bridge from D.C.'s Georgetown—is closer to the center of the capital than you may realize. It's fun to walk over the bridge to Georgetown, or take the Metro—Rosslyn station is three blocks distant—if you prefer. This is an inviting 558-room-and-suite house, with fabulous D.C. views from many of its accommodations and from the aptly titled View Restaurant, topside, in full view of the Washington skyline; adjacent bar-lounge. There's more casual dining, too, and an indoor-outdoor pool and fitness center. *First Class.*

Marriott Suites Alexandria Hotel (901 North St. Asaph Street, Alexandria, Virginia; phone 703-836-4700): All 250 suites comprise three distinct rooms: living room, king-sized bedroom, and bath. Rooms offer a pair of televisions and a pair of phones, big desk, wet bar and fridge, and there are a full-service restaurant and a bar-lounge, an indoor pool, and a fitness center. Location is Old Town Alexandria, a short city bus ride from the Metro to Washington, should you be without a car. *First Class.*

Morrison House Hotel (116 South Alfred Street, Alexandria, Virginia; phone 703-838-8000) is Alexandria's *grande dame* with 45 no-two-alike guest rooms and suites, the lot of them late-eighteenth-century style and some with canopied beds. Equally atmospheric public spaces include a modish restaurant specializing in modern American fare, bar-lounge with entertainment, and a honey of a library that's richly paneled. Drop in for afternoon tea. *Luxury.*

Ramada Hotel Ballston Metro Center (950 North Stafford Street, Arlington, Virginia; phone 703-528-6000)—the only hotel with which I'm familiar that's named for a subway station—is a relatively recent tower adjacent to the Metro, with 209 up-to-date rooms, restaurant, bar-lounge, and fitness center that includes a lap pool and sauna. *Moderate.*

Ritz-Carlton Pentagon City Hotel (1250 South Hayes Street, Arlington, Virginia; phone 703-415-5000) is significant for three reasons: First is that it is, without question, one of the most beautiful hotels in the Washington area: its décor based, in typically Ritz-Carlton style, on paneled walls; English eighteenth-century-style furniture; crystal chandeliers and sconces; fine textiles employed as draperies, wall-coverings, upholstery, and spreads on beds; and an extraordinarily good collection of paintings and prints. Second reason is the surprising convenience of the location adjacent to Pentagon City Metro station, a quick hop from the Pentagon proper (if you've business there), and, just beyond, Downtown Washington. Third has to do with shops: the enormous Pentagon City Fashion Centre (chapter 6) is adjacent. There are a pair of dining rooms: the Restaurant (evaluated in chapter 5), with silk-paneled walls and Rosenthal china; and the casual Grill, based on a green-marble mantel over its fireplace that could be out of a French château. The lobby lounge serves afternoon tea but is especially noted for its early-evening martini hour; dry martini buffs may choose any of a dozen types, the range James Bond to Silver Bullet. Forty-one of the 345 guest rooms are suites. There are two floors of Club Levels—premium-tabbed with extra amenities, including continental breakfast and cocktails with canapés. And the fitness center includes lap pool, sauna, and massage room. *Luxury.*

5

Washington to Eat and Drink

DINING DIMENSIONS OF A WORLD-CLASS RESTAURANT CITY

Washington is climbing rapidly in the planetary restaurant sweepstakes. The seat of the American government, in the course of being more internationally attuned in recent decades than ever before, has become correspondingly sophisticated with respect to restaurants. Eateries in the burgeoning clutch of luxury hotels are among the best in the District of Columbia—invariably with chefs (often from abroad) of notable caliber. At the same time, the independent restaurant has made its mark. French cuisine—in part a consequence of the French-influenced diplomatic corps—remains even more popular than it is in other major U.S. cities like New York. The Italian restaurant, for long relatively inconsequential, now vies with the French in popularity, not to mention authenticity.

Restaurants of nationalities like Chinese, Japanese and Thai, Middle Eastern, Mexican and German are dotted about—and invariably creditable. And as you sample the scene, you come to a veritable network—unique in America—of Ethiopian restaurants operated by Ethiopian nationals. The cafeteria, in many cities virtually extinct except within company or factory premises and in museums, remains a Washington restaurant option, at its best in a host of museums and government buildings open to visitors intent on a rapid, inexpensive meal. Withal, it's the restaurants whose fare is what can best be called Creative American that is the all-Washington leader, as popular with locals as with visitors, both domestic and imported. Herewith, a selection employing the same price-range breakdown of all the books of my *World at Its Best* series—Luxury, First Class, Moderate—presented alphabetically by category, more than a score of categories all told. For better places, I suggest you reserve in advance by phone.

AFLOAT

The Dandy (departs from foot of Prince Street in Old Town Alexandria, Virginia; phone 703-683-6076) is a comfortable excursion vessel with a restaurant and upper observation deck that cruises the Potomac River, taking you past the Jefferson and Lincoln memorials, the Washington Monument, and the Kennedy Center, either at midday for lunch or for dinner and dancing in the evening. Three-course lunches are centered on entrées of chicken, fish, and quiche, opening with salad and ending with desserts that include carrot and cheese cakes. Dinner, more elaborate, runs to five courses based on entrées including prime rib and crab-stuffed shrimp. Full bar. *First Class.*

AFTERNOON TEA

As in other leading American cities, New York especially, the British custom of afternoon tea, generally served between 3 P.M. and 5 P.M., has caught on in Washington, as for example at these locales:

Fairfax Bar (Ritz-Carlton Hotel, 2100 Massachusetts Avenue NW; phone 202-293-2100) is properly English in look, with an open fire in winter and aged paintings. The set tea includes tiny sandwiches, also-small pastries, and scones, with a choice of teas. *First Class.*

Garden Terrace (Four Seasons Hotel, 2800 Pennsylvania Avenue NW; phone 202-342-0444), invariably buzzing, is the ideal setting for a mid-afternoon break. Choose either scones and tea, a traditional sandwich-pastries tea, or strawberry tea—with the berries buried under a strawberry coulis, dusted with powdered sugar accompanied by lemon curd and thick Devon-style cream. *First Class.*

John Hay Room (Hay-Adams Hotel, 800 16th Street NW; phone 202-638-6600): Setting is the principal restaurant of an opposite-the-White-House hotel, with the décor—paneled walls hung with tapestries and fine paintings—appropriate to the refreshments at hand. *First Class.*

Morrison House Hotel (116 South Alfred Street, Alexandria, Virginia; phone 703-838-8000) is indicated in the course of Old Town Alexandria exploration. Setting is a late-eighteenth-century-style inn. *First Class.*

AMERICAN

Adirondacks (Union Station, 50 Massachusetts Avenue NE; phone 202-682-1840): If you grew up in upstate New York, summering at a Boy Scout camp in the Adirondack Mountains to the north—as I did—your expectation of this restaurant, in advance of arrival, is an eatery in a rustic setting. You've only to enter to see that the name's a put-on. Adirondacks is nothing less than the palatial salon that had been used as the presidential reception room from the time of Union Station's turn-of-the-century opening through the presidency of Dwight Eisenhower in the mid-1950s, by which time the chief executive and his state visitors were arriving and departing more by air than by rail. The room fell into disuse until, with major refurbishment of the station, it opened as Adirondacks as the 80s became the 90s. The look—based on a motif of eagles with wall panels smartly papered, tables generously spaced—is sensational. But you want to be flush. This is a pricey place, especially at dinner—entirely à la carte—with what may be the costliest first courses in town, the range smoked salmon and oysters on the half-shell through ever-so-minuscule portions of the day's pasta, and beyond to inventive salads (as, for example, quail with onions, wild rice and avocado, corn and tomatoes) and soups. Entrées—like openers, tasty but tiny—run to grilled tarragon chicken with french fries, pork and veal specialties, lamb chops, and sirloin steak. Strawberry-rhubarb is a mix of those fruits in a pastry crust—and is among the top sweets, although Tin Roof sundae (surprise ingredient is peanuts) is a winner, too. Wines are for moneybags customers—*very* steeply priced—and you've no say in what you tip (fortunately, service by good-natured, scrubbed-up youngsters is generally okay): a service charge is added to the check. *Luxury.*

America (Union Station, 50 Massachusetts Avenue NE; phone 202-682-9555) is not unlike its New York counterpart—big, brassy, and fun. The look is Elderly America, perhaps best typified by chairs at tables that are dead ringers for those our teachers sat in at elementary school. The idea here is diversity at a reasonable price. You can't expect everything to be super, not with a choice of seventeen omelets, at least that many appetizers (grilled little-neck clams are good, ditto grilled brie), salads (some, I caution, based on iceberg lettuce), sandwiches (go for the American Dagwood), and entrées (Mom's meat loaf with mashed potatoes is deservedly popular). Super sweets include peach cobbler and peanut butter pie with vanilla ice cream. Lunch through latish dinner. *First Class.*

Ashby's (Washington Hilton Hotel, 1919 Connecticut Avenue NW; phone 202-483-3000) makes for a quiet respite at this always-busy convention hotel. Gold paneling picked out with white is the background for à la carte lunches that run to popular favorites—crab cocktail, onion soup, chicken salad, or lobster club sandwich—with hot entrées including sautéed rainbow trout and grilled chicken breast. Dinner is more formal, with backfin crab cake an indicated opener, roast rack of lamb or grilled pork chops justifiably favored entrées. Ask to see the wine list (it's a good one) and the pastry cart (it tempts). *First Class/ Luxury.*

Aux Beaux Champs (Four Seasons Hotel, 2800 Pennsylvania Avenue; phone 202-302-0444): My theory is that the secrets of Aux Beaux Champs's success are threefold. Setting, first: this is a big, pale-toned room, with plenty, but plenty, of space between tables. Staff, second: maitre d' and captains to buspersons, waiters, and bartenders most definitely included. Everyone is a pro, everyone smiles. And menu, third: Fare is at once American Creative albeit with French antecedents, but it is invariably sensible, never frivolous. Both dinner and lunch (with the latter less expensive) are à la carte. At dinner, appetizers are imaginative: duck and goose foie gras with mesclun salad, its sauce a passion-fruit-based vinaigrette; Parma ham with grilled eggplant and goat cheese fritters; blinis teamed with smoked salmon, caviar, quail eggs, and crème fraîche, chive-accented. Entrées are novel too: sea bass filet in a potato crust, winesauced; filet of beef with a pear-and-barley flan, appropriately sauced; sirloin steak with mushrooms, matchstick potatoes, and a Cabernet-thyme-butter sauce. Don't skip the vegetable casserole. And from the dessert cart, consider candied apples and cranberries in cider cream with cinnamon honey ice cream. Or, perhaps, Stilton cheese with apples and nuts in their shells. The wine list is one of the best in town. *Luxury.*

Bradshaw's (2319 18th Street NW; phone 202-462-8330): Contemporary in look (the color scheme is black and gray set off by orchids at tables) and cuisine, Bradshaw's may fill the bill if what you seek is a reasonably priced, inventive meal in the trendy Adams-Morgan part of town, with a basement disco as a bonus. The three-course dinner—choice of appetizers; breast of chicken, roast lamb or the day's fish; festive dessert—is an exceptional buy. Friendly. *First Class.*

Brighton Grill (Watergate Hotel, 2650 Virginia Avenue NW; phone 202-298-4455) is a good pre- or postperformance dinner choice in connection with a visit to the nearby Kennedy Center. Good-looking (it's on the lower level) and cordially staffed, the grill's best value is its prix-fixe dinner, opening with the day's soup or salad, a choice of such entrées as roast loin of pork or grilled swordfish, and pastry to conclude. There are à la carte

dinners and lunches (the latter including club and Reuben sandwiches and burgers). *Moderate/First Class.*

Celadon (J. W. Marriott Hotel, 1331 Pennsylvania Avenue NW;
phone 202-393-2000): It should go without saying that this
beautiful room's dominant color is the shade of green whose
name it takes, set off by a central floral display and pink linen on
tables. Dine in the evening, and you order from an à la carte that
includes a crabmeat-avocado appetizer, herbed rack of lamb, and,
perhaps, Grand Marnier soufflé. Go midday and there's a buffet
(hot entrées, salads, sweets) that's one of the best buys in town, as
indeed is the temptingly tabbed pretheater dinner. These *First
Class* specials excepted, Celadon is *Luxury.*

Coeur de Lion (Henley Park Hotel, 926 Massachusetts Avenue
NW; phone 202-638-5200) is a surprise package of a restaurant
in Downtown's surprise package of a hotel (above). Coeur de
Lion's principal space is a skylit atrium, handsome enough, to be
sure. But it's edged by alcoves so that you may take your meal in
the center or on the periphery. French name notwithstanding,
cuisine is Yank-international. Go at midday and if it's summer
you do well to open with as good a bowl of gazpacho—
Andalusia's classic cold soup—as you are likely to have in Spain.
Cognac-infused lobster bisque is special, too. Consider entrées
like medallions of veal, beef with mushrooms in shallot sauce,
imported Dutch Dover sole broiled to order, or grilled jumbo
shrimp teamed with spinach fettucini. Select one of the chocolate
desserts. And ask to see the wine list; it's impressive. So, indeed,
is service. *First Class/Luxury.*

Colonnade (Westin Washington Hotel, 24th and M streets NW;
phone 202-429-2400): Setting first: a greenhouse-cum-crystal
chandeliers and velvet banquettes, whose French doors give onto
a fountain-centered courtyard. Fare is contemporary. By that I
mean smoked medallions of lobster in poppy-seed-flecked tempura batter among appetizers; spinach with marinated shrimp
and fresh mozzarella among salads; mixed grill embracing beef
filet, lobster, and breast of chicken among entrées. Best buy is the

buffet at lunch—a spread of utterly delicious comestibles, coarse country pâté through superb sweets. The prix-fixe four-course-and-coffee dinner is well priced, too. Service is at once cordial and professional. *Luxury.*

Duke Zeibert's (up a flight in Washington Square Office Building, 1050 Connecticut Avenue NW; phone 202-466-3730) is a contemporary successor, in agreeable enough albeit unexceptional quarters, to a long-on-scene Washington restaurant that can be interesting midday, when clientele comprises a mix of business, the professions, and government. Duke's specialties include matzo ball soup, chicken in pot, roast beef hash, chopped liver and salami sandwiches. Otherwise, fare is standard, oysters and steaks through cheese and chocolate cakes. *First Class.*

English Grill (Hay-Adams Hotel, 800 16th Street NW; phone 202-638-6600): No question but that the main-floor John Hay Room is higher-ceilinged, tapestry-hung, and—from breakfast onward—populated with patrons of consequence. It could not be otherwise in this posh hotel, just across Lafayette Park from the White House. Withal, the basement English Grill, with its carved woodwork, is atmospheric, expertly staffed, and less expensive than its sister restaurant up a flight. Go for either lunch (when the crowd is talky) or quieter dinner, for selections from an à la carte with such standouts as smoked salmon or lobster bisque to begin, followed by entrées of swordfish or tuna steaks, grilled lamb chops, or super sirloins. Burgers are all-Washington rankers and hot pastrami on rye is an option. Fine wines. *First Class.*

Gadsby's Tavern (138 North Royal Street, in the Old Town quarter of Alexandria, Virginia; phone 703-548-1288) is the genuine eighteenth-century article (it opened in 1772), to the point where its upper floors are a museum, separately entered and inspected on guided tours (above). The tavern, whose ballroom hosted early presidents, Washington onward, was nearly razed in the 1920s but survived to be smartly restored for the 1976 Bicentennial. The look is Nostalgic Colonial, even to costumes of servers. There's a fair choice of appetizers and entrées (roast duck is a standout) at both lunch and dinner. Make sure that you sample Sally Lunn bread and—for dessert—trifle as the colonists remembered it from England. Traditionally, on Sunday and Monday evenings, there's a "publick table" at dinner, when customers are seated at a common table and served a special prix-fixe that includes a glass of port or Madeira. Gadsby's is fun. *First Class.*

Garden Terrace (Four Seasons Hotel, 2800 Pennsylvania Avenue NW; 202-342-0444) buzzes merrily at lunch. Proportions of this high-ceilinged, off-lobby, plant-filled space are generous, ambience agreeable. The midday à la carte might run to asparagus and endive vinaigrette, or duck terrine with corn relish and red cabbage compôte among openers; entrées include smoked salmon with Bermuda onions, capers, and pumpernickel pinwheels, the day's French baguette sandwich, and pizza with a filling of, say, spinach, goat cheese, and tomatoes. Chocolate mousse cake is a dessert winner, and if it's summer, note this beverage option: Garden Terrace is one of the few places I know—anywhere—offering freshly squeezed lemonade. *First Class.*

Georgetown Bar & Grill (Georgetown Inn, 1310 Wisconsin Avenue NW; phone 202-333-8900) is an engaging venue to savor the Georgetown scene, especially at lunch (less expensive than dinner), with appetizers like fried calamari, salads, cheeseburgers (French-imported boursin is among the cheeses), and stir-fried breast of chicken. At dinner, entrée choice is wider. Friendly. *Moderate/First Class.*

Jefferson Hotel Restaurant (16th and M streets NW; phone 202-347-2200) has been relatively recently—and stylishly—redecorated with individually lighted portraits of American Indians embellishing walls. Go for lunch and the à la carte yields corn blinis teamed with smoked salmon, caviar, and chive cream or smoked duck breast in wild rice broth among first courses; with a choice of lighter entrées (how about a grilled chicken breast and bacon club sandwich?) or more substantial grilled pork loin accented with pineapple salsa. Dinner is prix-fixe. The separate card for dessert offers tempters; consider ginger or Kahlua crème caramel, if your mood dictates eschewing the exuberant. Otherwise, go all the way with, say, grilled pineapple on ice cream, or macadamia coconut tart with white chocolate. American wines. *Luxury.*

Jockey Club (Ritz-Carlton Hotel, 2100 Massachusetts Avenue NW; phone 202-293-2100): When the Ritz-Carlton was treated to a major (and very tasteful) facelift a few seasons back, management wisely left the Jockey Club—beamed and with red-checked cloths on its tables—quite as it had been. The Jockey has for so long been a Washington gathering place—a definitive see-and-be-seen venue—that it needed no tampering with. You go as much for the customers as for the cooking. With the Willard's Willard Room and the Hay-Adams John Hay Room, the Jockey is distinguished for power breakfasts. (Think of me when you order the French toast.) But lunch and pricier dinner are special, too. The former meal's fitness menu (low-cholesterol, low-sodium, low-fat) is among the tastiest of its kind in town (try grilled veal paillard with citrus sauce, to see what I mean). But the à la carte stands out: beef carpaccio and lobster ravioli, beyond to crab cakes, chicken pie, grilled lamb chops, or broiled swordfish with basil butter sauce, at lunch; and appetizers including caviar on blinis and clams casino, as well as soups like crabmeat gumbo to precede entrées of lobster or lamb chops at dinner, when chocolate soufflé is an indicated dessert. Service is white-glove, by which I mean classy. *Luxury.*

Kennedy Center (foot of New Hampshire Avenue West, at the Potomac) offers several choices, all on the roof. Snazziest—*Roof Terrace* (202-833-8870)—is at its smartest in the evening (it's open postcurtain) but also serves lunch. The bar-lounge-café—*Hors d'Oeuverie*—is evenings only, while the *Cafeteria* is open early lunch through dinner, concluding at 8 P.M. *Moderate* through *Luxury.*

Martin's (1264 Wisconsin Avenue NW; phone 202-333-7370) is a casual, heart-of-Georgetown favorite. Potato skins topped with bacon and cheddar cheese with a side of sour cream lead among openers, but Caesar salad is good, too. Washington is a club sandwich city of consequence; they're good here, as are Reubens, Monte Cristos, and BLTs. Not to mention eggs benedict and broiled pork chops. At my last count, fourteen species of bottled beer were stocked. *Moderate.*

McPherson Grill (950 15th Street NW; phone 202-638-0950) is a generous contemporary space—walls are blond wood, lighting discreetly indirect, glassware black-stemmed—generously populated (especially at lunch) with a loquacious clientele intent on gossip. Not everything is successful; crabmeat salad can be boring and flavorless. On the other hand, summery gazpacho (Spain's ice-cold soup nicely spiced and topped with Parmesan croutons) is superlative. Crab cakes, T-bone steak, and bacon-cheeseburgers are other good lunch entrées. And chocolate espresso fudge cake buried under lemon sauce is an indicated sweet. *First Class.*

Melrose (Park Hyatt Hotel, 24th and M streets NW; phone 202-789-1234) attracts with good looks. Its two-story glass walls overlook a flower-lined outdoor café whose cascading fountain has become a landmark of Washington's West End. Cuisine is creative American. Midday, the à la carte comprises chicken soup with grilled mushrooms, horseradish-accented crab salad, and tortellini salad with olive and lemon dressing—among starters; memorably good poached salmon with dill sauce and Vidalia onion and medallions of pork among entrées; and—to be missed on no account if it's on the menu—blueberry crisp with vanilla ice cream. There's an especially good value prix-fixe at dinner. Wines—both American and French—come from an outstanding cellar. And the staff is caring. *Luxury.*

Metro Center Grille (Holiday Inn Crowne Plaza, 12th and H streets NW; phone 202-737-2200) is a worth-knowing-about source of sustenance near the Convention Center, Downtown. Bright and with a pert staff, it is à la carte at both lunch and dinner. The former is less expensive and offers such inventive appetizers as warm goat cheese with grilled asparagus and smoked tomato salad. There are entrées like smoked turkey club sandwich with roasted eggplant, peppers, and fontina cheese. Caramel bread pudding with bananas, rum-soaked raisins, and hazelnut sauce is delicious. Note that the adjacent bar-lounge offers a bargain-tabbed cocktail hour buffet for about the price of a drink, when purchased with a drink, as well as good-value *Moderate* lunch; otherwise, *First Class.*

Monocle (107 D Street NE; phone 202-546-4488) occupies a contiguous pair of early-nineteenth-century houses, between the Capitol and Union Station. Not surprisingly, this locale draws politicos. You'll see autographed photos of them on the white-washed brick walls, but don't be surprised to observe familiar faces at a table adjacent. Fare may not be adventuresome as at some of the competition, but it's competent. By that I mean oysters on the half-shell, smoked salmon or baked clams, seafood bisque or onion soup, steaks or rack of lamb. Lunch supplements hot entrées with sandwiches including crab cake. At both meals, the dessert to try is lemon sorbet served in an almond-studded basket of chocolate topped by a coulis of fresh berries. And I append a bravo for the staff, as alert as it is congenial. *First Class.*

Mount Vernon Inn (George Washington Parkway, just outside the gate to Mount Vernon, Mount Vernon, Virginia; phone 703-780-0011) is strategically situated for viewers of George Washington's country house ("Essential Washington," chapter 2, above). Salads, daily specials, and sandwiches are among choices at lunch, which is served, customarily, until 4:45 P.M. week-days, with candlelit dinner—the three-course prix-fixe is good value—beginning at 5 P.M. Attractive. *First Class.* (And with the casual Snack Bar—*Moderate*—as a Mount Vernon alternative.)

National Café (J. W. Marriott Hotel, 1331 Pennsylvania Avenue NW; phone 202-393-2000) takes its name from the next-door National Theater (chapter 4) and is convenient, if you've tickets to a performance, for a pretheater buffet dinner. There are buffets, as well as table service, at breakfast and lunch. Seafood and pasta are specialties, but the menu is wide-ranging. *Moderate.*

Nicholas (Mayflower Hotel, 1127 Connecticut Avenue NW; phone 202-347-8900) wins you over, upon entering, with its intimate scale and smashing good looks. Crystal chandeliers and complementary crystal sconces provide illumination. Tables are flanked by pale-gray-and-mauve-upholstered Louis XV–style chairs. There's an extensive à la carte lunch—duck terrine with foie gras and lobster minestrone with ravioli among starters; grilled quails and sautéed veal chops among entrées; cheesecake and crème brûlée on the dessert card. But the time to go is in the evening. Nicholas is quieter then, and presents an utterly delicious three-course prix-fixe that represents one of the city's best values and is beautifully served. Crabmeat-stuffed artichoke might be your best first course, sautéed noisettes of beef and veal teamed with spinach, mustard-sauced, your entrée, tiramisù spiked with espresso sauce your dessert. The wine list is first-rate, the staff is a pleasure. *Luxury.*

Occidental (1475 Pennsylvania Avenue NW; phone 202-783-1475) is a relatively recent successor to a restaurant that first opened in 1906. It comes in two parts. The Grill, on the main floor, offers an unchanging menu from 11:30 A.M. to 11:30 P.M. and is less expensive than the upstairs Dining Room, which has lunch and dinner menus of its own. In all cases, fare is à la carte. Which floor? My preference is the Grill, easily as good-looking as its up-a-flight counterpart. Grill décor is well-proportioned traditional, with contemporary touches. Good things to eat include not only burgers but the Occidental's grilled swordfish club sandwich, served on a toasted brioche with lemon-tartar sauce. As well as entrées such as full-pound T-bones and the day's catch, along with french fries that are among the city's crispest, and commendable creamed spinach. In no event omit dessert: pecan pie with chocolate sauce and whipped-cream-slathered peach crisp are both irresistible. And servers are super. *First Class/Luxury.*

Old Ebbitt Grill (675 15th Street NW; phone 202-347-4801), though not in the quarters where it opened in 1856, is appropriately Victorian and packed at lunch and at cocktails, when it's amusing, delicious, and professionally staffed. You order à la carte, opening perhaps with New England clam chowder, shrimp salad, or North Carolina clams on the half-shell. Burgers are good here, but you may opt for pasta or pork chops. Breakfast is something else again, at least in my experience, with staff skeletal and unsmiling, service plodding, the experience unpleasant. *First Class.*

Powerscourt (Phoenix Park Hotel, 520 North Capitol Street; phone 202-737-3776): Elegant in the style of the celebrated Irish country mansion for which it is named—and in a hotel called after a lovely Dublin park—Powerscourt tastes as good as it looks. It's animated at lunch, with the chatter of congressional types melded with that of hotel guests and others from the Capitol Hill neighborhood. A meal might embrace Irish smoked salmon, potato soup, or oysters Rockefeller as openers; mixed grill, broiled veal chop, or filet of sole among entrées. Bailey's Irish Cream mousse is the house's special sweet. And service is at once professional and cordial. *Luxury.*

Ritz-Carlton Hotel Pentagon City (1250 South Hayes Street, at Pentagon City Metro station, Arlington, Virginia; phone 703-415-5000): A meal—lunch perhaps—in the course of a tour of adjacent Pentagon City shopping mall (below), is a good way to take in the beauty of this relatively recent addition to the area's hotel scene (chapter 4). The Ritz-Carlton's main restaurant is high-ceilinged, chandeliered, and with tables widely spaced. At midday, commence with Maryland crab soup, following with one of several pastas or a chicken club sandwich, and, if you're splurging, raspberry crème brûlée to conclude. Dinner is more costly and more elaborate, with caviar and smoked salmon among openers, filet of beef and roast duck popular entrées—and fine wines. At lunch: *First Class.* At dinner: *Luxury.*

Rumors (1900 M Street NW; phone 202-466-7378) is good-looking; modified Victorian might describe the décor, with a packed-in-summer terrace edging the corner location at 19th and M. Sound-value prime-rib platters are among D.C.'s better buys. *Moderate.*

Seaport Inn (6 King Street, Alexandria, Virginia; phone 703-549-2341) has impeccable credentials. It went up in 1765, was purchased a few years later by George Washington's aide-de-camp, Colonel John Fitzgerald, and—according to management—knew President Washington as a guest on more than one occasion. It's not surprising that the Inn has held up well: walls of stone and oyster-shell mortar are 28 inches thick. This is a good spot for lunch in connection with a day of Alexandria exploration. Midday menu runs to chef's and Greek salads, burgers, crab-cake sandwiches, and omelets. Dinner—pricier—emphasizes seafood. *Moderate.*

1789 (36th and Prospect streets NW; phone 202-965-1789): This aged Georgetown house is more attractive from without (modernization of the interior has not been entirely felicitous), but it's agreeable enough, with a cheerful staff, and an okay (if not distinguished) kitchen that turns out such à la carte dishes as Smithfield ham and ratatouille, snails in Roquefort sauce and Virginia mozzarella-tomato-onion salad among first courses; and, as typical entrées, grilled tuna, roast rack of rosemary-scented lamb, and medallions of pork with green peppercorn sauce served with Italian-type polenta—this last rarely come upon in Washington. American wines. *First Class.*

Stephanie's (Dupont Plaza Hotel, 1500 New Hampshire Avenue NW; phone 202-483-6000): With its Dupont Circle location, this is a convenient venue for lunch. Sandwiches—French dip, California patty melt, Reuben, grilled chicken, burgers—are well priced and there are hot specials like grilled tuna, pan-fried trout, and the day's pasta. Dinner entrées, mostly steaks and seafood, are preceded by a first course for which there is no extra charge. Friendly. *Moderate/First Class.*

Top o' the Town (1414 North 14th Street, Arlington, Virginia; phone 703-525-9200) is at the summit of an Arlington apartment house. Ask, when you reserve, for a table by the window, so that your view is of the Iwo Jima statue and The Netherlands Carillon (chapter 2, "All around the Town") with the skyline of

Washington across the Potomac—Lincoln Memorial, Washington Monument, and Capitol dome especially dominant in the panoramic vista. Fare is adequate à la carte. Stick to basics like shrimp cocktail or oysters on the half-shell to start; grilled swordfish, steak, or lamb chops among entrées; concluding with, say, ice cream or cheesecake, bearing in mind that you go principally for the scenery. *First Class.*

Twenty-One Federal (1736 L Street NW; phone 202-331-9771) is named for the street address of the first Twenty-One Federal— on the lovely Massachusetts island of Nantucket. It's best summed up in two adjectives: smart and delicious. Black, white, and blond are the colors, beginning with marble borders fringing walls as you enter, black-and-white servers' uniforms, and massed flowers as a backdrop. The chef has a sure hand with inventive albeit familiar enough American dishes. Specials can be mighty good, as for example grilled tuna with olives, capers, and dried tomatoes teamed with soup or salad. (Otherwise everything is à la carte, with dinner costlier than lunch, which is nicely noisy.) A soup whose title gives it away, corn crab and chili chowder, is better than it sounds—which means tasty. So are Portuguese seafood stew, spit-roasted chicken, and pan-blackened beef. The Fed's potatoes—Anna potato cake, shoe-string fries—warrant consideration. As do sweets, two in particular: warm berry gratin and lime tart with blueberry sauce. You'll like the alert staff. *First Class/Luxury.*

Twigs (Capital Hilton Hotel, 1001 16th Street NW; phone 202-393-1000) attracts first with its catchy name, then with its good looks—Louis XVI–influenced chairs surrounding white-linen tables complementing white walls whose draperies match the chairs' upholstery. Lunch is well priced—the day's soup as an opener, grilled herb-accented flank steak in tandem with Bordelaise sauce. Dinner is more costly. At both, dessert specialties are based on strawberries—and worth experiencing. *First Class.*

Two Continents (Washington Hotel, 15th Street and Pennsylvania Avenue NW; phone 202-638-5900) is actually two restaurants.

All year round—for the first two meals of the day, breakfast and lunch—it's a high-ceilinged, mural-embellished, Corinthian-colonnaded space off the hotel's lobby. Dinner, too, is served in the street-level Two Continents between October and May. In summer, though, the evening meal moves to the roof, the better for smashing views, in a setting of crystal chandeliers and mid-nineteenth-century art. All three meals are good value and good-tasting. Breakfast represents the best value in any Downtown hotel's main restaurant. Lunch and dinner are à la carte, with salads and sandwiches featured midday, a more elaborate menu in the evening, the range escargots à la Bourguignonne as you remember them from France through rib-eye steak and broiled seafood platter to dessert, with fruit tarts indicated. Delightful service. *First Class.*

Willard Room (Willard Inter-Continental Hotel, 1401 Pennsylvania Avenue NW; phone 202-628-9100) has been a hit since the history-laden hotel of which it's a part reopened some years back after an extensive refurbishing. Intimate and good-looking, with tables beautifully appointed, it's popular for business breakfasts and again at midday. But the evening three-course-and-coffee prix-fixe is especially good value. And with a substantial choice of courses, as for example garlic-and-wine-sauced snails, crab-meat salad, and smoked salmon among appetizers; grilled sole, sirloin or lamb chops, and tuna filet among entrées; a trolley brimming with sweets, and coffee. The Willard cellar is a big one, in the tradition of Inter-Continental Hotels. I hope menu covers remain unchanged, what with a photo of the hotel snapped in 1904, and a reproduction of an 1854 menu on which the first dish listed is Boiled Bass, Egg Sauce. Another boiled specialty, Leg of Mutton, Caper Sauce, comes next and leads to Tapioca Pudding among desserts. Tastes in food happily change. *Luxury.*

BRUNCH

American visitors to the capital, like Washington residents, are more often than not brunch fans, appreciative of this modern-day New World creation that offers midday/afternoon Sunday (and sometimes Saturday) meals at relatively modest prices.

Foreigners beginning American exploration in Washington, for whom brunch is a novelty, invariably enjoy the experience.

Coeur de Lion (Henley Park Hotel, 926 Massachusetts Avenue NW; phone 202-638-5200) is an attractive locale near the Convention Center. Its prix-fixe opens with salad or the day's soup, continues with a conventional brunch entrée like eggs benedict, with the option of a meat or poultry and vegetables special, and dessert following, to the accompaniment throughout of all the champagne or beer you would like. Exceptional value. *First Class.*

Four Seasons Hotel (2800 Pennsylvania Avenue NW; phone 202-342-0444) is unusual among hotels in that it serves brunch in both its restaurants rather than just one. That at *Aux Beaux Champs,* the posh principal eatery on the lower level, is the costlier, with price of the entrée—chicken hash with grilled peppers, smoked potatoes, and onion crisps; lamb sausage with saffron risotto fritters and tomato-onion relish; bran pancakes or waffles with sausage or bacon—inclusive also of appetizer, dessert, and coffee. New Orleans jazz accompanies brunch in the lobby-level *Garden Terrace,* with the menu à la carte, featuring openers like oysters on the half-shell and Cajun seafood gumbo, entrées like omelets, spiced Gulf shrimp and smoked scallops, prime rib with a Cajun accent, and broiled chicken. If you've room for dessert, my vote is for sweet potato and pecan pie, blanketed with whipped cream. Both these restaurants' brunches are, more or less, *First Class.*

Martin's (1264 Wisconsin Avenue NW; phone 202-333-7370)— heart-of-Georgetown and popular with locals—serves brunch à la carte, with such main-dish favorites as Welsh rarebit, steak and eggs, lox and bagels, and French toast. But you may have a breakfast-type brunch of simply toast and coffee. *Moderate.*

Metro Center Grille (Holiday Inn Crown Plaza, 775 12th Street NW; phone 202-737-2200) is worth knowing about if you're a conventioneer in the neighborhood. (The Convention Center is a neighbor.) The deal here is a prix-fixe including appetizer, salad, and dessert choices galore, all from the buffet, plus a cooked-to-order entrée (fare is New American, but there are conventional dishes, too) and a glass of champagne. Smart setting. *Moderate.*

Mr. Smith's (3104 M Street NW; phone 202-333-3104) is as value-packed at brunch as later in the day and evening, and for that reason is rarely tranquil. Brunch is a Saturday–Sunday operation, with steak and eggs (served with home fries and toast), eggs benedict, and good old-fashioned bacon and eggs (you get three) the favorites. Fun. *Moderate.*

Tabard Inn (1739 N Street NW; phone 202-785-1277) is a small hotel (it's scruffy, not all rooms have baths, and I don't recommend it) as well as a good restaurant that really stands out with its Sunday brunch, especially on a fine late-spring or summer day when the humidity is low and the sun shining, so that you will enjoy a table under an umbrella in the garden. The à la carte is fairly extensive. A pepper vodka Bloody Mary makes for a good starter. Delicious entrées include polenta baked with mozzarella and served with sausage and mushrooms; baked eggs with prosciutto and garbanzo-bean salad, lemon-vanilla pancakes with blueberry compote, and cinnamon-orange French toast with honey-spice butter. If your entrée has been savory rather than sweet, bear in mind that deserts—cakes, strawberries with heavy cream, crème brùlée—are excellent. Friendly. *Moderate.*

Willard Room (Willard Inter-Continental Hotel, 1401 Pennsylvania Avenue NW; phone 202-628-9100): The à la carte brunch in this intimate, good-looking restaurant is at once substantial and satisfying. Openers are festive—champagne fizz or champagne cocktail, for example. Precede your main course with pan-seared quail eggs in a nest of leeks, veal and mushroom terrine served with ratatouille, or smoked salmon. Go on then to an entrée, the range lobster frittata and cinnamon-walnut buttermilk pancakes, truffle-topped eggs benedict accompanied by asparagus, and grilled salmon, with broiled lamb chops and sirloin steak also reliable options. Fine wines. *Luxury.*

CAFÉS, CAFETERIAS, AND COFFEE SHOPS

American Café (227 Massachusetts Avenue NE; 1211 Wisconsin Avenue NW; National Place at 14th and F streets NW; 1331 Pennsylvania Avenue NW; other locations) is a coffee-shop chain (fifteen at last count) that's okay for casual meals and snacks or simply rest pauses over coffee or a cold drink. *Moderate.*

Au Bon Pain (branches in National Place at 14th and F streets NW; L'Enfant Plaza underground shopping arcade; other locations) is a chain whose specialty is French breakfast pastries: croissants, brioches, pain au chocolat, with other snack-style food and beverages; good for quick breakfasts. *Moderate.*

Bistro (Westin Washington Hotel, 24th and M streets NW; phone 202-429-2400) is the No. 2 restaurant of a handsome hotel, centered on a marble-topped mahogany bar, with tile floors, etched-glass panels, and wallpaper designs of the turn-of-the-century Briton William Morris. It's ideal for breakfast, and lunchtime choices include favorites like clam chowder, fruit salad, burgers, and club sandwiches. Dinner, though, tends to be too Creative American; burgers and sandwiches of midday are, alas, missing, and your meal ends up being more elaborate and expensive than you may have anticipated. Friendly. *First Class.*

Bullfeathers (410 1st Street SE; phone 202-543-5005) might fill the bill at midday—or in the afternoon—in conjunction with exploration of the nearby Capitol. Excellent lobster bisque, club sandwiches; more substantial fare as well. *Moderate.*

Café Florentine (Ramada Renaissance Techworld Hotel, 999 9th Street NW; phone 202-898-9000) is called to the attention of delegates to meetings in the nearby D.C. Convention Center. This is an attractive restaurant in an attractive hotel, with buffet lunches and dinners the specialty and an interesting à la carte, the range baked brie and she-crab soup through baby back pork ribs and poached red snapper—as well as pizzas and burgers—not to mention banana splits among desserts. *Moderate.*

Café Promenade (Mayflower Hotel, 1127 Connecticut Avenue NW; phone 202-347-3000) is arguably the grandest hotel coffee shop in town, and with good reason: It was the Mayflower's main restaurant when the hotel opened more than half a century back. The look is of generous proportions, high ceilings, and great chandeliers. And friendly waitresses serve nice things to eat, including the Mayflower's version of the Senate Restaurant's bean soup, veal piccata and seafood stew, shrimp-salad-stuffed croissants, and omelets, with excellent pastries. Breakfast, too. *Moderate/First Class.*

Clyde's (3236 M Street NW; phone 202-333-9180) is a long-on-scene Georgetown institution. Go for a drink, a snack, or a meal. The menu, management avers, has not been changed for two decades. Soups (cream of asparagus, especially) and chili, sandwiches (roasted turkey breast, Reuben, crab cake) and burgers, wines by the glass in abundance and Clyde's own lager—all are good here. So is service. Early breakfast through very late—traditionally 2 A.M. *Moderate/First Class.*

Dubliner (Phoenix Park Hotel, 520 North Capitol Street NW; phone 202-638-6900) is a no-nonsense Irish pub in the shadow of the Capitol. Go midday and the place is packed with government types lunching on fish and chips, burgers, crab cakes, or roast beef sandwiches, concluding with sherry trifle as it's served across the Atlantic. There are daily specials like seafood chowder or corned beef and cabbage. Dinner is more substantial— T-bones and sirloins, Irish stew and shepherd's pie, broiled swordfish and salmon filet. And there's Gaelic entertainment nightly. Fun. *Moderate/First Class.*

Eastern Market (7th Street SE) has been operating continuously as a covered food market since the beginning of the nineteenth century; it moved into its present quarters in 1873. It's fun to go Saturdays when the indoor stalls have company: farmers in from the country with produce sold at outdoor booths along with crafts, and with any number of café stalls, including *Market Lunch,* where you want to order a fried oyster sandwich. *Moderate.*

Garden Terrace (J. W. Marriott Hotel, 1331 Pennsylvania Avenue NW; phone 202-393-2000—not to be confused with an also-commendable restaurant of the same name in the Four Seasons Hotel) is essentially a cocktail lounge but is herewith called to your attention because it serves a socko buffet lunch and still *another* socko buffet at cocktail time that's available when you purchase a drink. Both are such bargains that my category for these purposes is *Moderate.*

Grand Café (Grand Hyatt Hotel, 24th and M streets NW; phone 202-789-1234) is arguably the friendliest hotel coffee shop in town, with a super staff and marvelous things at breakfast. (How about a pancake sandwich, enclosing two eggs with bacon or sausage? Or eggs Maryland—two poached eggs served atop fresh crab with Hollandaise sauce?) Later in the day you may select warm duck salad, tortillas with guacamole and chili con queso, shrimp jambalaya, or veal scaloppini. With vanilla-sauced bread pudding the top dessert. *Moderate/First Class.*

Hot Shoppes Cafeteria (1750 Pennsylvania Avenue NW; phone 202-347-1927) takes the name J. W. Marriott gave to eateries that preceded the Marriott hotel chain. This Hot Shoppe is a Monday-through-Friday 12-hour-per-day operation (7 A.M.–7 P.M.) with inexpensively tabbed daily specials popular with regulars and including ham and sweets, spare ribs, and baked chicken. Breakfast, too. *Moderate.*

J. Paul's (3218 M Street NW; phone 202-333-3450) is a near neighbor to—and competitor of—Clyde's (above). You want to go at least for a drink at the antique bar, which was salvaged from an old saloon at the Chicago stockyards. But there are good things to eat—clams and crab dip, chicken and cobb salads, chili and club sandwiches. With burgers and substantial entrées as well. Nice. *First Class.*

Library of Congress (James Madison Building, Independence Avenue at First Street SE) offers a convenient Coffee Shop on the ground floor, but much more fun is the sixth-floor Cafeteria—

soups through sweets—glass-walled so that views of the city are fabulous. Both are *Moderate*.

Mr. Smith's (3104 M Street NW; phone 202-333-3104) is, arguably, Georgetown's most consistently packed restaurant, and with good reason: good grub and low tabs. Its menu is not only printed on newsprint, but the cover is a reproduction of *The Washington Post* for December 5, 1933, with the principal headline reading "U.S. Prohibition Ends Today Through Presidential Edict; Nation's Rum Flows at 3 P.M." The *Post* cost three cents in those days. Nothing at Mr. Smith's, contemporarily, is quite that inexpensive. But you're not going to find better-priced onion soup, spinach salad, steaks, chili, quiche, or burgers (in a dozen varieties, bacon through French with blue cheese, not to mention a thirteenth—the house's wineburger, served with a bottle of Château Lafitte Rothschild and priced, when last I checked, at $999). Mr. Smith claims he sells more than a ton of burgers each month. Desserts are rich (try hot pecan pie) and there are nine variations on the theme of coffee. The wineburger (above) excepted: *Moderate*.

Monique (Omni Shoreham Hotel, 2500 Calvert Street NW; phone 202-234-0700): If you've gone out to see the pandas at the nearby National Zoo and you're hungry, Monique—so much nicer than the zoo eateries—is a good choice for sustenance. The look is Modified French Brasserie, even to Gallic aperitifs (kir royal among them); beers, and more French wines than you might expect in a nonluxury restaurant. Fare is eclectic, though—French onion soup and Indian-style tandoori chicken-breast salad, vegetable lasagna and hot pastrami on rye, the day's pasta and the day's omelet. *Moderate/First Class.*

Scholl's Colonial Cafeteria (1990 K Street NW, in Esplanade Mall; phone 202-296-3065): The old-fashioned open-to-the-public cafeteria is, alas, almost extinct, the victim primarily of fast-food joints. There are, to be sure, plenty of self-service restaurants in factories and office complexes, but counterparts of the Washington institution called Scholl's are relatively rare. This old-reliable

is perhaps best noted for desserts—pies especially, but dough-
nuts and custards too. Still, it's a source of sustenance breakfast
through dinner (with closed-breaks between meals and final
Monday-through-Saturday shuttering traditionally at 8 P.M.,
albeit never on Sunday). *Moderate.*

Sherrill's Bakery (233 Pennsylvania Avenue SE; phone 202-544-
2480): You may have seen Sherrill's in the movies; it was the
subject of a 1990 documentary nominated for an Oscar. Point
about this Capitol Hill bakery is that it's a kind of café as well as a
retail shop. Stop in for breakfast. *Moderate.*

Sky Terrace (Washington Hotel, 515 15th Street NW; phone
202-638-5900): Chances are good that most of your fellow
customers at this rooftop spot—open only from May to October—will be Washingtonians, often with out-of-town guests
whom they've brought for something to eat or drink and for
spectacular views of the White House and the Mall. The menu
is sensibly minimal: soups and salads; roast beef, tuna- and
chicken-salad sandwiches; burgers and quiches; with cake and
ice cream to conclude and full bar service. Not to be missed.
Moderate.

Supreme Court Cafeteria and Snack Bar (United States Supreme
Court, Maryland Avenue and 1st Street NE; phone 202-479-
3000)—opposite each other on the main floor—are convenient
snack or lunch stops in connection with a Court visit, or when
you're otherwise exploring Capitol Hill. The cafeteria, with a
somewhat more extensive menu than the snack bar, opens for
early breakfast through mid-morning, customarily closing for
an hour at 10:30 A.M., before reopening for lunch. The snack bar
operates straight through—10:30 A.M. to 3:30 P.M., with soups,
salads, burgers, desserts, weak coffee, and a sign admonishing
visitors that "Court Employees Are Served First." Both are
Moderate.

The Tombs (1226 36th Street NW; phone 202-337-6668)—a
casual café in the basement of the eighteenth-century house

that's the site of the more formal 1789 Restaurant (above) is enjoyable at lunch—order a club sandwich and don't skip dessert—but remains open for dinner. Good soups and a mean lasagna—daily specials as well. The staff is youthful and thoughtful. *Moderate.*

Union Station Lower Level Restaurants (60 Massachusetts Avenue NE)—in contrast to the substantial main-floor restaurants that are evaluated in this chapter under their own names—are mostly, if not entirely, fast-food and worth knowing about if you're hungry en route to or from a train. Most substantial of the lot— it's a proper eatery—is *Georgetown Seafood Grill*, outpost of a Georgetown establishment, and where I've enjoyed oysters on the half-shell and crab-cake sandwiches. Others include *Bernie's BBQ, Dogs Plus* (frankfurters), *Flame's* (burgers), *Lee's Ice Cream, Mama Ilardo's Pizzeria, Rain's Deli* (corned beef and pastrami sandwiches), and *Skyline Chili*. They all share a massive common seating area, and (except for the seafood spot, which is *First Class*) are *Moderate.*

U.S. Senate Restaurant (on the main floor of the Senate side of the Capitol and not to be confused, heaven forbid, with the Senators' Dining Room, open only to senators and their invited guests) is a coffee shop, whose prime pluses are a delightful serving staff, rock-bottom prices, and no D.C. sales tax. The Senate's celebrated bean soup is always available—it's watery and lacks flavor—but there's no cheaper half-pound New York strip minute steak in town; ditto omelets, burgers, and other sandwiches (including an excellent grilled cheese), salads (Senate ladies' chunky chicken salad with tropical fruits is a winner), and weeklong specials (like grilled breast of chicken on a roll with salad) that are bargains, as indeed are changed-daily entrées, rack of lamb through smoked shrimp platter. *Moderate.*

CAJUN

New Orleans Café (1790 Columbia Road NW; phone 202-234-5111) is an authentic transplant, of the cuisine of the city whose name it takes, to D.C.'s Adams-Morgan. Everyone who has been there likes the café, if not for the same reasons. Go for breakfast (8:30 A.M. is the traditional opening time) and there are beignets and egg specialties served with grits. Pop in for lunch and order a po' boy sandwich. Arrive in the evening for a feast of red bean soup, jambalaya, and whiskey-spiked bread pudding. Sunday brunch, too. Casual—very casual. *Moderate.*

CHINESE

China Inn (631 H Street NW; phone 202-842-0909) is a question of luck. You may or may not like the décor; you may or may not be served promptly; you may or may not like what you're served. Still, you can be very lucky indeed here. This long-on-scene Chinatown institution has never stopped drawing crowds for dishes that are mostly Cantonese, with shrimp, chicken, and pork specialties invariably the best bets. *Moderate.*

City Lights of China (1731 Connecticut Avenue NW; phone 202-265-6688) is small but special, an apt choice for dinner when you're in the neighborhood of Dupont Circle or at a convention in the Washington Hilton. Embracing but two hardly overlarge rooms, this spot is popular with good reason: You can rely on fried dumplings, noodle specialties, stir-fried favorites based on seafood and pork, and the most gala dish of the lot, Peking duck. *First Class.*

Hunan Chinatown (624 H Street NW; phone 202-783-5858) is essentially un-Oriental in look (it could be a high-grade coffee shop) except primarily for two giant temple lions guarding its dining room. Hot Szechuan and Hunan dishes are standouts— Hunan lamb, crispy prawns, and Kung Po beef among them— with more conventional choices, too: spring roll and fried dumplings as starters, orange beef, and a variety of duck and chicken preparations. Friendly. *First Class.*

Tony Cheng's Mongolian (619 H Street NW; phone 202-842-8669) is a Chinatown landmark with the Mongolian barbecue as its kicker; you select the makings from a counter—varied meats and vegetables—and turn them over to a chef who prepares them. Or make your meal yourself in tableside hot pots. Fun. *Moderate.*

DELIS

Jack's (Washington Square office building basement, 1050 Connecticut Avenue NW; phone 202-467-4440): Walls are white tile, bill of fare appears on blackboardlike displays beyond counters, and sandwiches are easily the equal of the legendary New York delis, a number of which (see *New York at Its Best*) are neither as attractive nor as friendly as Jack's. Zero in on multilayered hot pastrami, corned beef, salami, roast turkey, baked ham, rare roast beef, or tongue, opting for sides including potato salad and coleslaw. And if you're not up to an entire vast sandwich, you may order a half. Kosher hot dogs, too, with bagels and cream cheese at breakfast. *Moderate.*

Loeb's New York Deli (832 15th Street NW; phone 202-737-2071) is big and chrome-accented. There are specialties like chicken salad and a smoked whitefish platter, but the big news here is the corned beef on rye. Unless you prefer hot pastrami. *Moderate.*

Zephyr Deli (Grand Hyatt Hotel, 1000 H Street NW; phone 202-582-1234) is indicated if you find yourself bored with a meeting at the just-opposite Convention Center—and hungry. The drill is corned beef, pastrami, and other deli sandwiches, along with soups, salads, and good Hyatt desserts. Continental breakfast, too. *Moderate.*

DEPARTMENT STORES

Bloomingdale's (White Flint Shopping Mall, Kensington, Maryland; phone 301-984-4600): You've taken the Metro to the White Flint station for a bout of shopping (see chapter 6) and it's time for a break. The restaurant in this branch of New York–based

Bloomingdale's is not going to put you in mind of the trendy eateries in the mother house at 59th Street and Lexington Avenue, but it's a reliable coffee shop, stucco-walled with blond wood furnishings and chatty waitresses. Select from a menu offering quiche, the day's pasta, fried shrimp, Caesar and chef salads, or perhaps a steak sandwich. Pastries are reliable. And there are wines by the carafe or glass. *Moderate.*

Macy's (Pentagon City Fashion Centre, Arlington, Virginia; phone 703-418-4488) lacks a proper restaurant, oddly enough for so big an outlet of this major chain, but does offer limited sustenance in its smallish third-floor *Marketplace Café*, adjacent to housewares. Soup of the day, chili, sandwiches, and salads, not to mention ice-cream sodas. *Moderate.*

Nordstrom (Pentagon City Fashion Centre, Arlington, Virginia; phone 703-415-1121)—Pentagon City's outlet of the Seattle-based department-store chain—has a pair of eateries. *Espresso Bar,* on the main floor, serves a dozen variations of espresso either single or double strength, regular or decaffeinated, with a dollop of whipped cream at an extra charge. But there are other beverages, and Italian pastries for dunking in your espresso. *Café Nordstrom,* up the escalator on 3, is semi-self-service, by which I mean you place your order at the counter and it's taken to your table by a server. Full breakfast—including scrambled eggs and bacon—is served early and you've an impressive choice for lunch, from a soup-and-salad bargain special through a dozen substantial salad entrées, at least as many sandwiches, French dip and hot pastrami through club and tuna-plus. Desserts are super. And there's beer and wine. Nice. *Moderate.*

Woodward & Lothrop (11th and F streets NW; phone 202-347-5300) offers two choices. Preferred is the *Terrace* on the seventh floor, with a temptingly tabbed buffet offering salads, hot entrées, fresh fruit, cheeses, and desserts; as well as à la carte specialties, chicken pie through crab cakes. Wine and beer, too. *Café Sbarro,* down in the basement—dubbed Down Under by Woodies—is a so-so self-service pizzeria. Both are *Moderate.*

ETHIOPIAN

Meskerem (2434 18th Street NW; phone 202-462-4100): Washington has many attributes, among them eminence—Addis Ababa of course excepted—as the Ethiopian-restaurant capital of the world. Ethiopian immigrants have achieved stunning success with their restaurants—the first such featuring a cuisine of black Africa in any U.S. city. Meskerem, arguably the most luxe of the group (clustered mainly in the Adams-Morgan quarter of town) offers conventional seating in a main dining room, as well as Ethiopian-style furnishings upstairs—where stools replace chairs and tables are embellished with traditional straw in Ethiopian motifs. Key dish, *injera*, is not only a food but serves as the implement with which you eat the rest of your dinner—using it as a kind of funnel, or scoop—and made from the ancient grain called millet. You might start your meal with fingers of beef in a zesty sauce, continuing perhaps with entrées including chicken (in a variety of sauces, as you select), the house's beef-chicken-vegetable platter, or a vegetarian entrée. Salads, too, more or less conventionally dressed. Dinner only. *Moderate.*

FRENCH

La Bergerie (218 North Lee Street, Alexandria, Virginia; phone 703-683-1007), with its Old Town location, is a sensible lunch choice in the course of a day devoted to Alexandria. Which is hardly to counsel against dining there, when clientele can be at least as interesting. Ambience is provincial French—brick walls punctuated by nicely draped windows, crystal chandeliers, tables set in pink linen surrounded by royal-blue upholstered chairs. The owning Campagne brothers hail from the Basque country and turn out an exemplary meal. Consider selecting from the à la carte an opener of crab-and-shrimp-stuffed artichoke hearts preparatory to an entrée of, say, rosemary-scented saddle of lamb, breast of duck, or dill-sauced broiled salmon. Made-on-premises desserts are a Bergerie requisite; you dare not leave without having tried the pastry, French-style coupe or sundae, or a soufflé, raspberry most especially. *First Class.*

Bistro Français (3128 M Street NW; phone 202-338-3830) could
not be more aptly named. The look is French bistro, the fare is
French bistro, and though there are some American wines,
enough vintages are French to compensate. Study both the à la
carte and the daily specials before you order dinner—an animated, amusing time at the Bistro. The chef's country pâté is
coarse and flavorful, and he makes rillettes—usually a coarse
pork pâté—of duck instead. Fish and onion soups are reliable,
and entrecôte marchand du vin or entrecôte au poivre are no
better in France. Satisfying, too: traditional gigot d'agneau (roast
lamb), filet de porc roti (roast pork), côte de veau aux champig-
nons (veal chop with mushrooms in a cream sauce), and deliciously prepared tuna steak. Desserts are limited but satisfactory. There's a well-priced prix-fixe lunch. And service is swift
and sincere. Un bon choix. *First Class.*

La Brasserie (239 Massachusetts Avenue NW; phone 202-546-
6066)—on Capitol Hill—is precisely what its name implies: a
no-nonsense brasserie in the best French sense, operated by
chef-propriétaire Gaby Aubouin, with a concern more for the
authenticity of his cuisine than for an elaborate look to the place.
Gaby writes out his menus each day. His soups—classic gratinée
à l'oignon, chilled cucumber, spinach—are among the tastiest in
town. At lunch he offers quiches and omelets, Hollandaise-
sauced grilled trout or breast of chicken in a basil-tomato coulis.
Dinner is pricier: smoked-in-house Norwegian salmon and also
house-made pâté among openers; grilled lobster, imported
Dover sole, traditional daube de boeuf, and tournedos sauce
Béarnaise among entrées. Desserts are smashing and include
the first chilled (as distinct from warm) crème brûlée I've come
across. If the day is fine, reserve a table on the terrace. *First Class.*

La Colline (400 North Capitol Street NW; phone 202-737-0400)
takes its name (*colline* means hill in the French language) from its
Capitol Hill location. It's big, high-ceilinged, and ordinary with
respect to appearance: blond wood walls hung with paintings
that have for-sale tabs on them, green-upholstered banquettes. I
suspect that if you're a Hill regular, you're warmly greeted. The
accueil, otherwise, is polite but quite distant. The à la carte is

extensive enough at lunch—the bubbly, busy time—with the range imported-from-France cavaillon melon and seafood terrine, beyond to swordfish steak and hardly-Gallic Hungarian goulash. At dinner, choices are wider and costlier. Unless—and this is a major *unless*—you select the bargain-tabbed prix-fixe served only in the evening (undistinguished at best, in my experience) with such openers as baked mussels, leek and potato soup, and stuffed avocado; the restaurant's version of Provence's bouillabaisse or a beef special as entrées. Withal, your reason for coming is end-of-meal. Although not a passionate chocoholic—I enjoy chocolate in moderation—I have nowhere else, in France or America, tasted such superb chocolate desserts. When the *chariot* is rolled over, implore the waiter for tastes of as many of the chocolate sweets as are on the trolley, the marquise au chocolat especially. *First Class.*

Dominique's (Pennsylvania Avenue at 20th Street NW; phone 202-452-1126) is in the category of French restaurants only because it calls itself French. Actually, it's mixed-bag with respect to cuisine, offering exotics like buffalo sausage and imported Swedish herring, crabmeat ravioli, and rattlesnake salad. There is, to be sure, some French fare—the classic beef dish châteaubriand, tournedos Rossini, and truite au bleu among them. Preparation is competent and service is correct, but Dominique's—its two-story-high walls lined with photos of luminaries who have been customers—represents a Washington of yore, and unless you're a longtime regular among clients, it is without contemporary appeal—at least to me. *First Class.*

La Fourchette (2429 18th Street NW; phone 202-332-3077) is a good choice if you hanker after a meal in multiethnic Adams-Morgan. Its brick walls hung with blown-up photos, this is a bistro-style spot with competent traditional dishes ordered from an à la carte, the range Burgundy-style snails, onion soup, or onion tart among openers; steak or chicken breast, a D.C. version of bouillabaisse, or only so-so mussels à la marinière among entrées. The outdoor café is pleasant in good weather. *First Class.*

Le Gaulois (1106 King Street, Alexandria, Virginia; phone 703-739-9494) gained fame as one of the best-buy (and tastiest) restaurants in D.C. while it occupied a now-razed house on upper Pennsylvania Avenue. The house it occupies in Old Town Alexandria is not as cramped as the old Washington location, but the grub is quite as good—and as inexpensive. French bread is coarse and chewy; you won't find much better in the region. Select from an à la carte such openers as duck pâté with pistachios, crab soup, or utterly delicious mussels, Burgundy-style; chicken fricassee, blanquette of veal, sautéed mignonettes of beef in green peppercorn with cream and brandy sauce, and pot au feu—France's boiled beef—are among entrées. Desserts are unpretentious—crème caramel or apple tart, for example—but satisfying. *Moderate.*

Jean-Louis (Watergate Hotel, 2650 Virginia Avenue NW; phone 202-298-4488) is the only Luxury-category restaurant—anywhere, at least in my experience—that offers guests no à la carte as an option for customers not wanting either of its extremely costly prix-fixe dinners and that does not open for lunch (cheaper, in most restaurants, than dinner). Dinner begins at 5:30 P.M. Between that hour and 6:30 P.M. it offers a four-course pretheater menu that would be considered expensive in most restaurants but is Jean-Louis's bargain repast. After 6:30, there's a choice of two *really* expensive menus, one of five courses costing about twice as much as the pretheater meal and the other of six courses (more than most people want to eat) well over twice as much as the pretheater dinner. Priciest dinners offer no choice for any of the half-dozen courses; with the other menus, there are certain options, particularly with the No. 2 in cost. Cuisine is nouvelle-influenced, in my experience ranging from competent to good, with the usual nouvelle combinations of rarely paired ingredients the rule, but excitement—with respect to flavor—can be clacking. The pretheater menu might open with watercress soup afloat with quenelles—forcemeat dumplings—of crab and vegetables, continue with swordfish filet teamed with eggplant purée as well as fried eggplant, tarragon-sauced, or curried tuna served with collard greens. Main course might be roast capon and fava beans or duck confit and new potatoes.

There is but one dessert on this menu, perhaps sauced, sliced-apple-topped ice cream. Coffee is extra, and wines, from a well-selected list, are—not surprisingly—expensive. The room is small, its walls oddly surfaced with pale, solid-color silk squares that overlap. Service is professional, as well it might be considering the tabs. If there were an à la carte, so that diners could select, say, an appetizer and main course in combination with a glass of wine, or if there were a relatively unexorbitant prix-fixe lunch, I would have fewer objections to Jean-Louis. As it is, post–6:30 P.M. prices are so steep that I cannot recommend it. *Luxury.*

Jean-Pierre (1835 K Street NW; phone 202-466-2022) is attractive—the look is sleek and clean-lined, and you're made to feel comfortable immediately upon arrival—with an extensive à la carte that is less expensive at midday, when the ambience is brisk with the talk of gossipy execs. Lobster bisque, the house's reliable terrine, or tomato-and-garlic-accented mussels are satisfactory openers. Jean-Pierre sautés fresh grouper with basil and tomatoes and successfully embellishes prime rib with shallot sauce but serves a classic veal scaloppini with only a squeeze of lemon. Hot apple tart is a favored dessert, but note that the ice cream is made in-house. Kindly service. *Luxury.*

Le Lion d'Or (1150 Connecticut Avenue NW; phone 202-296-7972): You wonder, as you make your first approach to this restaurant—a subterranean space in a Downtown office block—if Madame, the well-dressed, well-coiffed Frenchwoman who greets you, reserves warmer salutations for regular customers. And, after being seated, as you watch others arrive who no doubt *are* steady patrons, you assume your appraisal to have been correct. Withal, the environment pleases: brass chandeliers hang from a silk tentlike ceiling, to illuminate a big room whose walls are hung with pottery and paintings. Louis XVI–style chairs encircle tables; banquettes are of black leather, and floral arrangements are extravagant. A French captain appears, wishes Monsieur a "bon soir," you reply in his language, and rapport develops—with the mostly French serving staff, as well. The bill of fare is extensive and unilingual—in French only, with willing waiters standing by to translate when necessary. Appetizers run a wide gamut: lobster soufflé, sautéed scallops, foie gras, pastry-encased quail or caviar, oyster-stuffed crêpes, smoked salmon, or quenelles de brochet superbly sauced—quite as you remember them from France. Fish comes in a dozen variations, with the catch of the day grilled and mustard-sauced. And meat entrées are classic, from poulet rôti a l'estragon—an entire roast chicken, tarragon-flavored, is brought to table to be carved—through veal filet and roast lamb to tournedos and port-sauced kidneys. Pommes dauphiné are no better in the mother country's Alpine resorts, and épinards au gratin constitute a spinach masterwork. Apricot crêpes want to be ordered at the start of the meal, but even simpler desserts satisfy. Ditto wines from an extensive French list. This is one of Washington's don't-miss restaurants. *Luxury.*

Maison Blanche (1725 F Street NW; phone 202-842-0070) translates from the French as White House—the Executive Mansion is a near neighbor. Look is stiffly, heavily formal—bulky draperies backing oversized black banquettes, with crystal chandeliers unsuccessful in detracting from the gracelessness of a big, pretentious room. Proximity to the seat of government brings a variety of government servants, especially at lunch, but dinner clientele can be as unprepossessing as much of what I have sampled from the menu. Service can be very slow and very indifferent—pricey lobster bisque, which should arrive piping hot, arrives cold. Duck terrine lacks flavor, rack of lamb is not pink as ordered, Bordelaise sauce with the filet of beef is lackluster. Both wine and food prices, except for the prix-fixe or very early pretheater dinner, are very steep indeed. Maison Blanche appears not to have changed from the time it opened, several presidencies back, when a fancy French restaurant was considered a big deal in the federal capital. It has too much superior competition contemporarily to be recommended, at least by me. *Luxury.*

Le Pavillon (1050 Connecticut Avenue NW; phone 202-833-3846)—unless you are either very well-heeled or very extravagant—is to be visited midday. Like Jean-Louis (above) it is prix-fixe only, but it *is* open for lunches that are half the price of dinners, with the latter considerably less expensive than the evening-only meals at Jean-Louis. Indeed, the cheaper of Le Pavillon's two lunches—consisting of appetizer and entrée—is not all that hard on the pocketbook and might include lobster-and-leek salad, coriander flavored; foie-gras-and-eggplant salad; roast lobster or lobster-and-tomato-flecked risotto among openers. (You will have detected by now that the style of cuisine is nouvelle.) Saddle of rabbit in rosemary cream sauce with turnips, rack of lamb with green bean purée, and lobster stew are among entrées. Desserts can be delicious, albeit costly. Ditto wines. Staff is cordial. *Luxury.*

Le Rivage (1000 Water Street SW; phone 202-488-8111) is indicated when you would enjoy dinner on the waterfront, with views north to the Mall and west to Washington Channel. If it's an agreeable evening, book a table on the terrace, ordering à la carte from a menu featuring such specialties as Burgundy-style snails or mussels in garlic butter to start, followed by pepper steak or the house's sauté de boeuf, with profiteroles au chocolat an ideal dessert. There's a well-priced pretheater menu, convenient if you've tickets for the nearby Arena Stage. *First Class.*

GERMAN/AUSTRIAN

Washington places more emphasis on German and Austrian cuisine than any other Eastern Seaboard city.

Café Berlin (322 Massachusetts Avenue NE; phone 202-543-7656): This unpretentious townhouse near the Capitol is at its best in summer, when service is extended to tables out front. Favorite dishes, not all of them actually German or Austrian, include Hungarian-origin goulash and strudel, chilled fruit soups, German sausage salad, the classic German beef dish of sauerbraten, the veal favorite, wienerschnitzel, and the popular pork-based kassler rippchen. *First Class.*

Old Europe (2434 Wisconsin Avenue NW; phone 202-333-7600): Call the cuckoo clock and beer steins corny if you will, but consider the authenticity of the German fare. If the potato pancakes with apple sauce are served immediately after they're made, they'll be delicious as an opener. Entrées can satisfy, too: the Wiener paprika and other schnitzels, sauerbraten in tandem with red cabbage and potato dumplings, and grilled bratwurst with sauerkraut. Rich desserts. *First Class.*

HUNGARIAN

Csikos (3601 Connecticut Avenue NW; phone 202-362-5624): It was a knowledgeable doorman at the Four Seasons Hotel who brought Csikos to my attention. It is, as far as I can determine, D.C.'s only Hungarian restaurant. And—decorated with folk art from the mother country, its servers in national dress—it comes off as authentic, as indeed does its cuisine. Hungarians are such great soup makers that you do well to start off with a bowl—cold fruit soup in summer, goulash soup in cool weather. If you've opened with goulash soup, select chicken paprikash or stuffed cabbage as an entrée; if not, zero in on beef or lamb goulash. And hope that strudel will be among desserts on the occasion of your visit. *First Class.*

INDIAN

Bombay Place (1835 K Street NW; phone 202-331-0111) is, to start, snazzy. The look—more stylish and traditional Western than the usual elaborate Indian décor of most Indian restaurants, especially those abroad—is engaging, and the rattan-furnished bar is inviting. Not surprisingly, tandoors—roasts from Indian ovens—appeal; choose chicken or lamb, as well as a special seafood tandoor. But other Indian favorites, curries especially, are satisfactory; so are breads, of which I can never have enough, like nan and puri. Lunch is cheaper than dinner, and there's a good-value Sunday brunch. Sprightly staff. *First Class.*

ITALIAN

Café Petitto (1724 Connecticut Avenue NW; phone 202-462-8771) is offputting from the moment of entry. The down-at-heels look cries out for a major refurbishing. The house specialty—fried pizza—is easily the least appealing Italian dish I can remember having, and I speak as an avowed Italophile (see *Italy at Its Best*). The redeeming feature here is an antipasto table—lovely things to help yourself to (alas, you're limited to one trip). Otherwise, Petitto has little to recommend it. *Moderate.*

Cantina d'Italia (1214 18th Street NW; phone 202-659-1830) opened nearly a quarter-century back, when Italian restaurants were a Washington novelty. They are no longer, and there is no need, today, to have to trek down to this graceless, low-ceilinged, hardly comfortable or inviting basement space. And it's not as though you put up with the unattractive setting for a bargain. The Cantina is expensive, pastas through scaloppine, not to mention wines. And service may or may not be cordial. With any number of really good Italian restaurants dotted about. I can't recommend this one. *Luxury.*

Charing Cross (3027 M Street NW; phone 202-338-2141)—the name of a London railway station—seems odd as the title of an Italian eatery. But there you are. This Georgetown spot packs in crowds, principally because the price is right, the service okay, and the grub good. Tabs are rock-bottom on the à la carte lunch menu—with a dozen-plus pastas including lasagna, cannelloni, and spaghetti sauced four different ways. Dinner is pricier but still a buy. At both meals, salad as well as Italian bread and butter are served with entrées, and again, at both meals, you may opt for burgers, with additional sandwiches at lunch. Well-priced Italian wines. Fun. *Moderate.*

Donatello (2514 L Street NW; phone 202-333-1485) is a stunner to look upon—two brick and stucco-walled stories, with inset stained glass in abstract designs. Dinner is engaging here. The Kennedy Center is not far distant, West End hotels are a hop and a skip, the crowd is lively, and the food is A-okay. There are not-often-encountered appetizers like fried squid and bresaola—dried Italian beef, wafer-thin. I had always thought stracciatella—chicken broth with beaten egg drops—Roman, but

Donatello, by adding spinach to the beaten egg, dubs it Florentine, which is fair enough. Pasta is fabulous: linguine in red or white clam sauce, and penne with bacon, onion, and tomato. Chicken breast and veal entrées stand out. Zabaglione, served for no fewer than two persons, is the ideal dessert. Italian wines, Italian waiters. *First Class.*

Galileo (1110 21st Street NW; phone 202-293-7191): Though it's less expensive at lunch, chances are good Galileo will be more fun and more festive at dinner, full of neighborhood—and all-Washington—regulars, come for an invariably satisfying meal, for reasons having to do with ambience: most especially charming watercolors on the walls, quick-as-a-wink service from congenial waiters, and of course the cuisine. Appetizers can be memorable: bresaola (paper-thin sliced dried beef served with lemon and olive oil dressing), marinated mussels, and Galileo's own bean soup. Or start with pasta: rigatoni with gorgonzola and pistachio sauce is unusual and delicious; ditto ravioli di vitello—the pockets are stuffed with veal, sage, and veal stock. And this is one of the few places is Washington that serves authentic gnocchi—potato dumplings that substitute for pasta. *First Class.*

I Matti (2436 18th Street NW; phone 202-462-8844): Brick-walled I Matti proudly flies the colors of Italy as its principal interior embellishment. A mainstay of the trendy Adams-Morgan district, it fulfills its mission—good Italian fare at good prices and with good service—admirably. Not unlike its sister restaurant, Galileo (above), it does well with openers. The platter of mixed antipasto—nibble-sized portions of hors d'oeuvres: anchovies and peppers through salami and, say, white beans—is a pleasure. As is bruschetta alla marinara—grilled bread rubbed with garlic and topped with diced tomatoes, basil, and olive oil. There are a dozen types of pizza and a substantial choice of pastas with spaghettini ai quattro formaggi (thin spaghetti with a sauce embracing four cheeses) a leader. Entrées are special, too; salsiccia alla griglia con polenta grigliata—grilled sausage with grilled polenta—is quite as delicious as you may remember it from Italy. *Moderate/First Class.*

Obelisk (2029 P Street NW; phone 202-872-1180) is small and smart: a study in white, walls through linen, with framed prints as decorative embellishment and subdued indirect lighting. Contemporary caned armchairs surround tables served with skill and good will by a trio of waiters. The American owner-chef turns out smashing specialties as part of a limited-choice prix-fixe dinner. You open with, say, roasted peppers and anchovies, or mushroom-topped crostini, follow with noodle soup combining both Liguria-origin pesto sauce and potatoes, or choose a more conventional crab soup. Main course might be grilled trout with tarragon, a sage-seasoned veal chop, or chicken with morels, thyme-seasoned. Choose either cheese or one of the house-made desserts (lemon tart buried under fresh blackberries is satisfying, but the chocolate cake is delicious, and so is a glass of vino santo with biscuits provided for dipping). Lovely. *First Class.*

Paolo's (1305 Wisconsin Avenue NW; phone 202-333-7353) is a Georgetown hangout, at once good-natured and good-tasting, of no special aesthetic distinction; it is big, long, and mirrored, with flowers on tables. Servers are cordial, and fare delicious. Mussels marinara and minestrone are stick-to-the-ribs openers, herbed mozzarella-topped pizza is excellent, but so are pastas like penne bolognese or duck-sausage lasagna. Broiled shrimp scampi are good, and you could do worse than settle for grilled sausages served with sautéed peppers over linguini. Enjoyable. *Moderate/ First Class.*

Primi Piatti (2013 Eye [I] Street NW; phone 202-223-3600), appealing Art Deco and spacious, packs in loquacious crowds at lunch—understandable, given its good looks, good food, and good prices. Five selections from the antipasto *carrello* make for a tasty opener, as might grilled radicchio in tandem with gorgonzola sauce, tomato-sauced mussels topping grilled Italian bread, or tomato-bread soup, garlic-and-basil-seasoned. Pastas are made in-house, and those I have sampled are delicious—square-shaped quadrucci with spinach sauce and ear-shaped orecchiette with broccoli, especially. The pizza oven turns out pies with a variety of fillings; the cheese and prosciutto is a favorite. Italy's veal-shank specialty, osso bucco, is a wise choice; ditto grilled red snapper. The lunch menu is valid into the evening, when daily dinner specials are appended. Friendly. *First Class.*

I Ricchi (1220 19th Street NW; phone 202-835-0459) exudes excitement: big space, big crowds, big serving staff, talky clients on rush-seated chairs surrounding a maze of tables flanked by textile-surfaced walls. And it houses an open kitchen half a block long, from which emanate Florence-influenced comestibles. The only Italian in residence—by his own admission—is the owner-chef, Francesco Ricchi. But his sous-chefs have learned well from the master. Open with acqua cotta—a Tuscan onion-bean-spinach soup served over a giant garlic-scented crouton. Or select pasta to start—rigatoni, say—or the day's risotto. As a main course, evoke memories of the Tuscan capital with bistecca alla Fiorentina, prepared as you direct. Other entrées tempt—grilled veal steak, sausage-stuffed quail, the chef's own grigliata mista (a distinctly Italian mixed grill). If you're up to it, conclude with a glass of vino santo, or holy wine, into which you dunk the hazelnut-and-almond cookies accompanying it. *First Class/ Luxury.*

Sfuzzi (Union Station, 50 Massachusetts Avenue NE; phone 202-842-4141): Familiar with—and a fan of—its New York counterpart, the name Sfuzzi (hardly unforgettable) struck me in the course of a stroll through Union Station. And I stayed to sample it. It's even bigger than the New York Sfuzzi, and very contemporary—with black wrought iron a major element of the décor. Waiters scurry about, invariably pleasing clients with the likes of arugula and radicchio salad, grilled mushrooms, or the day's hearty soup among appetizers; a range of pizzas (sausage, peppers, and cheese is a good choice) and what I most enjoy at Sfuzzi: pasta—fettucini pomodoro with sautéed shrimp and clam-sauced linguini in particular. Substantial entrées too; you do well with red snapper or—novel, this—grilled chicken salad with green beans and an unusual rosemary-honey-mustard dressing. *First Class.*

Uno (Union Station, 50 Massachusetts Avenue NE; phone 202-842-0438)—an outlet of a Chicago-based chain for deep-dish pizza—is convenient for quick, inexpensive meals or snacks when you're in or near the station. Uno's deep-dish pizza comes in close to a dozen guises, that dubbed "Chicago's famous" perhaps the most popular; it's filled with sausage, two types of cheese, and tomato. But there are other options, soups and salads through burgers and cheesecake. Well-priced wines, too—mostly Italian. *Moderate.*

Veneziano (2305 18th Street NW; phone 202-483-9300) is a sprightly Adams-Morgan source of solid Italian fare. Look is bright, customers invariably appear pleased with selections, and service is pleasant. If it's summer you do well to open with the classy chilled tuna-veal appetizer, vitello tonnato—as good as you'll find in Milan or Rome. Mixed antipasto is another good appetizer. Pastas please at Veneziano; spaghetti alle vongole is counseled; risotto, too. Fish is properly grilled here. And the house wine is indicated. *Moderate/First Class.*

Vincenzo (1606 20th Street NW; phone 202-667-0047): Italian restaurants with frigid, unsmiling service are rare indeed, either in Italy or abroad, but Vincenzo has come through to me in that manner, more's the pity. Its bare-white, virtually unadorned basement setting may encourage this kind of staff, both at the door upon arrival and in the case of waiters. Combined with steepish tabs and acceptable but hardly exciting fare—the menu ranges from antipasto misto (disappointing, in my experience) through a range of pastas and quite as many meat and fish options—this is not a place I can recommend. The whole idea of an Italian restaurant, aside from fare, is to reflect the ebullient Italian personality. When that is so noticeably absent, what's the point of a visit, when, in a city like Washington, there are so many truly enjoyable *and* delicious Italian restaurants? I can't recommend this one. *First Class.*

JAPANESE

Appetizer Plus (117B North 19th Street, Rosslyn, Virginia; phone 703-525-3171) is worth the trip across the Potomac if you're a sushi nut who can't get enough of the stuff. Its kicker is an evening buffet—all you can eat not only of sushi but of teriyaki, tempura, and other tasty dishes as well. For the buffet: *Moderate.*

Sushi-Ko (2309 Wisconsin Avenue NW; phone 202-333-1487) is No. 1 for not a few sushi buffs, and not only residents of Georgetown where it's located. The look is typical, with lots of bamboo. Proportions are compact. Menu offers regular, deluxe, and extra-large sushi assortments and multicourse dinners. And there are other Japanese dishes as well, most significantly sashimi, tempura, teriyaki, and one of my favorites, udonski—a jumbo bowl of noodle soup to which has been added a mix of seafood and chicken. *First Class.*

MEXICAN

Enriqueta's (2811 M Street NW; phone 202-338-7772) is a crowd-pleaser. By that I mean everyone complains about the uncomfortable chairs of this Georgetown magnet, but they pack the place anyway, for the likes of stuffed chilis and enchiladas, tortillas, tamales, and chicken smothered with the chocolaty mole sauce that I have liked ever since it was served with an order of turkey, on a long-ago visit to Veracruz. Oh, and frozen margaritas. They're super at Enriqueta's. *Moderate/First Class.*

MUSEUMS

National Air and Space Museum (Independence Avenue at 6th Street SW; entered also from the Mall at Jefferson Drive and 6th Street NW; phone 202-357-2700)—what with some ten million customers per year in its old cafeteria—wisely appended a striking-looking addition several stories in height, glass-walled and -roofed, its frame white wrought iron. This restaurant wing houses two eateries. The main floor's catchily titled *The Flight Line* is the less pricey of the pair, self-service, and with a wide-ranging choice. There are sandwiches galore—the ham, turkey, and Swiss on toast with fries and fruit garnish is a winner—as well as hot standbys like pizza, ribs, and fried chicken, along with salads and sweets. Take a table, if you can, with a view of the Capitol dome. Up a flight, *The Wright Place* offers table service and a somewhat costlier menu with such specialties as crab cakes, pastas, and daily hot specials. Nice. *Moderate.*

National Gallery of Art (West Building—the original building—is at Constitution Avenue at 6th Street NW with an entrance also on Madison Drive, while the newer East Building is at 4th Street between Constitution Avenue and Madison Drive): The two buildings are linked by an underground concourse, which is the site of two restaurants: enormous *Buffet*, a cafeteria with separate counters for each type of food, which makes selection relatively speedy even with crowds—which are the rule midday. There are good things to eat, especially roast beef from the carvery section, as well as a range of hot entrées, chicken, tuna, and ham salads, and fresh-fruit desserts, not to mention irresistible brownies. The concourse's smaller *Café*—with table service—offers luncheon plates and, later in the afternoon, desserts and salads. The West Building's lower-level restaurant is the attractive *Garden Café*. Generally the least crowded of the lot—because it's highest up and not as frequently passed by—is the East Building's top-floor *Terrace Café*, with table service and good prix-fixe options. Level of cooking and presentation throughout is relatively high for mass museum feeding, and prices are *Moderate.*

National Museum of American History (Constitution Avenue between 12th and 14th streets NW, with an entrance also on Madison Drive; phone 202-357-2700) has two restaurants—a prosaic *Cafeteria* a steep flight down to the basement from the main floor, with okay selections of sandwiches, salads, hot entrées, and desserts; and the class act of the duo—the *Ice Cream Parlor* on the main floor—easily the most inventive and amusing of Mall eateries, and reached through the museum's Palm Court, a white-wicker-furnished lounge where visitors may rest and relax in the course of exploration. Adjacent are reconstructions of an early Horn and Hardart Automat (these were the first self-service restaurants to open in the U.S. in 1902) and a mock-up of Stohlmann's Confectionery, a long-ago source of ice cream, cake, and candy. With soda fountains now virtually extinct in Ameri-

can pharmacies, and restaurants specializing in ice-cream con-
fections almost as rare, you zero in, at the Ice Cream Parlor, on
ice-cream sodas (there are eight soda flavors, including sar-
saparilla), milk shakes, malts, banana splits, gooey sundaes
(chocolate and vanilla ice cream with hot fudge, whipped cream,
and sliced almonds is sublime), birch-beer floats, and fudge cake
topped with vanilla ice cream and hot fudge. And you may
substitute frozen yogurt for ice cream. There are soups, sandwiches (with names like Washington Monument and Senate
Lunch), chef salad, wine by the glass, and beer. And lovely
service. *Moderate.*

National Museum of Natural History (Constitution Avenue at
10th Street NW, with an entrance also on Madison Drive; phone
202-357-2700) calls its cafeteria *Public Carousel,* which indeed it
is: a constantly revolving counter, from which you pick sandwiches and hot entrées and desserts, with beverages adjacent to
the cashiers. *Moderate.*

National Museum of Women in the Arts (1250 New York Avenue
NW; phone 202-783-5000) has a restaurant, *Palette Café,* on the
mezzanine. Soups, salads, sandwiches, and sweets. *Moderate.*

National Portrait Gallery/National Museum of American Art share
the historic old Patent Office Building (8th and F through G
streets NW; phone 202-357-2700) and a restaurant—the most
frivolously named of the Smithsonian eateries, *Patent Pending.* It is
small but charming, with tables spilling into the courtyard in
warm weather. Sandwiches, salads, desserts. *Moderate.*

Phillips Collections (1600 21st Street NW; phone 202-387-2151)
Café at the Phillips has a homemade touch with salads, sandwiches, daily specials, and super sweets. Lunch traditionally
starts at 10:45 A.M. and extends to 4:15 P.M. except on Sunday,
when the meal of the day is afternoon tea, from 2 P.M.,
with buttery croissants, currant scones, rum-walnut tarte, and
chocolate-almond cake among available tempters. Nice. *Moderate.*

SEAFOOD

Aux Fruits de Mer (1334 Wisconsin Avenue; phone 202-333-2333) is an unpretentious Georgetown choice for cioppino and lobster bisque, smoked salmon and clams casino, fish chowder and lobster thermidor, scallops and shrimp, and the day's catch prepared as you direct. Friendly. *First Class.*

Center Café and Union Station Oyster Bar (Union Station, 50 Massachusetts Avenue NE; phone 202-682-0143) offers bivalves at the bar, and such other seafood specialties as clam chowder, crabmeat salad, croissant sandwiches, tuna Niçoise salad, and lobster-stuffed ravioli. Lively. *Moderate/First Class.*

Georgetown Seafood Grill (3063 M Street NW; phone 202-333-7038—with a branch in Union Station basement, 50 Massachusetts Avenue NE) is busy and bustling with an extensive and generally tasty seafood menu, including clam chowder, not-often-encountered barbecued scallops, stuffed shrimps, oysters and clams on the half-shell, broiled lump crab cakes, even fish and chips. Everything I've had is fresh and tasty. *First Class.*

Jonah's Oyster Bar (Hyatt Regency Washington Hotel, 400 New Jersey Avenue NW; phone 202-737-1234) will serve you any of five types of oyster (James Point, Chincoteagues, Bay Point, Pine Island, and Florida) by the oyster or by the dozen, on the half-shell. Consider also oysters Rockefeller, oyster stew, chilled poached salmon, or the day's catch prepared as you prefer. *First Class.*

Sea Catch (Canal Square, 1054 31st Street NW; phone 202-337-8855): The trick here is to select a fine day for your meal, warm enough—but not too humid—to book a table on the covered terrace that overlooks the placid, tree-lined Chesapeake and Ohio Canal (which constitutes a national historic park). Not that the fare here is unimportant. Open with oysters, clams, smoked trout, shrimp in varied guises, French-style mussels or snails, or a bracing chowder. If lobster is your choice, trot over to the tank and select it. Mixed seafood grill is satisfying and any of the day's fresh fish will be cooked as you indicate, with or without a sauce. Friendly. *First Class.*

SOUL

Florida Avenue Grill (1100 Florida Avenue NW; phone 202-265-1586) is more old-style diner than grill of the title, with framed photos on walls of civil-rights and other leaders who have been customers over the decades. You do not depart hungry, nor with a seriously depleted wallet. Order soul standbys like chitterlings and ham hocks, collard greens and grits, considering chicken, pork, and beef entrées as well, not to mention breakfasts that can be hearty enough to hold you through early dinner. *Moderate.*

STEAKS AND ROAST BEEF

Gary's (1800 M Street NW; phone 202-463-6470) is, to be sure, spacious, with tables widely separated, and it draws considerable lunchtime—if not dinnertime—clientele. My experience has been unhappy—dry and flavorless steak, dry and overbaked potato, generally blah fare devoid of any spark—and service to match. With so many engaging sources of deliciously prepared beef in Washington, there is no point in my recommending this place. *First Class.*

Hugo's (Hyatt Regency Washington Hotel, 400 New Jersey Avenue NW; phone 202-737-1234): Up you go to the roof of the Hyatt Regency, first perhaps for a drink in the accurately named Capitol View Lounge, then for New York strip, prime rib, or extra-thick lamb chops, preceded by, say, shrimp or crabmeat cocktail, oysters Chesapeake, or chicken consommé afloat with angel-hair pasta. Good spuds, too, especially baked or scalloped. And creamed spinach is a winner. *Luxury.*

Joe and Moe's (1211 Connecticut Avenue NW, down a flight; phone 202-659-1211) is a magnet for politicos and steak aficionados come to observe politicos in action—or at least have a look at photos of them surfacing walls. Go with a meal comprising, say, shrimp cocktail, clams on the half-shell, or seafood soup, beyond to an entrée of sirloin or porterhouse, grilled veal chop, or boiled whole lobster. Busy at breakfast, too. *Luxury.*

Morton's (3251 Prospect Street NW; phone 202-342-6258) draws residents and visitors alike to see and be seen and, equally important, to tuck into Morton's sirloin, prime ribs, or lamb chops. Open with a salad or one of the standard appetizers, and order a side of potatoes if not creamed spinach as well. I doubt you'll be up to it, but soufflés prepared to advance order are the indicated dessert. *Caveat:* You may reserve for dinner only between 5:30 and 6:45 P.M. After that, expect slow-moving queues and/or waits at the bar. *Luxury.*

Prime Rib (2020 K Street NW; phone 202-466-8811): Steak and beef restaurants are often exuberant and attractive, not to mention delicious—but they're rarely elegant. Prime Rib is an exception: paneled walls, pleated silk shades on wall sconces and table lamps, contemporary paintings, a massive central floral display. The maitre d' can be smilingly arrogant, but waiters are polite. Clientele runs to navy-blue-suited gents, with women correspondingly dressy. You order à la carte—smoked salmon served with honey-mustard sauce or smoked trout, oysters Rockefeller, or clams casino among starters (unless you're a lobbyist with a *really* big budget, in which case you go for caviar). There is a wide choice of seafood entrées, lobster of course among these. But this is essentially a red-meat restaurant: prime rib and filet mignon, New York strip and steak au poivre; with extra-thick grilled pork chops, rack of lamb, and center-cut veal chops as well. Mashed potatoes are billed as "old-fashioned lump" and they're good; ditto potato skins (they come in baskets), string beans sautéed with tomatoes and onions, and fresh asparagus. There's a separate dessert card (made-in-house pecan and key lime pies are popular). The wine list is impressive. And so is the card brought with dessert—for digestifs, calvados and armagnac through Courvoisier and Rémy Martin, with an irresistible choice of eaux-de-vie—including poire William, framboise, and mirabelle. Lunch is less expensive than dinner. *Luxury.*

Ruth's Chris (1801 Connecticut Avenue NW; phone 202-797-0033) first came to my attention in Honolulu, where it has an excellent branch. Washington's is up to snuff too. This is a worth-knowing-about dinner stop, especially if you're a conventioneer at the nearby Washington Hilton. Sirloins and strip porterhouses I've sampled are no better in New York, reputedly the U.S. steak capital. And everything accompanying, most especially creamed spinach, is delicious, too. *First Class.*

Sam and Harry's (1200 19th Street NW; phone 202-296-4333): As good-looking (richly paneled, traditionally furnished, and art-accented) as it is good-tasting, Sam and Harry's concentrates on carefully cooked New York strips and porterhouses, prime ribs, and generous-sized and really good veal and lamb chops. Lobster and other seafood are options, and the obligatory shrimp cocktail and smoked salmon are reliable openers. Lunch is built around a less expensive menu than dinner. Professional service. *Luxury.*

THAI

Ploy (2218 Wisconsin Avenue NW; phone 202-337-2324) pleases with its unpretentious contemporary look and welcoming waiters. Not to mention its skill with the cuisine of Thailand; a range of curries, super seafood (try the assorted platter), sliced beef as only Thais sauce it, and Thai variations on the theme of satays—skewered chunks of meat, variously sauced—which are a Southeast Asian mainstay, especially popular in Indonesia. *Moderate/First Class.*

6

Washington to Buy

THE CAPITAL AS SHOPPING CENTER

Recent decades have seen Washington and surrounding Maryland and Virginia areas become shopping territory of consequence—geographically spread out, to be sure (Downtown Washington is but a single mercantile neighborhood), but the site of major department stores, innovative shopping malls, and a considerable diversity of appealing smaller emporia. By and large (there are exceptions of course, in every type of store—the heavy-traffic, child-filled museum shops, especially) service is cordial and knowledgeable, frequently smiling, and very often you are thanked for your purchases.

PRINCIPAL SHOPPING AREAS

Downtown Washington: More than a smallish concentrated sector, Downtown embraces the territory extending from north of the museum-fringed Mall to south of Dupont Circle. F Street, principal Downtown street closest to the Mall (in whose museums the shops—bigger than you might imagine—are invariably packed), is the core of an area of department stores and smaller shops, extending west on the east–west (letters of the alphabet) streets and north on the perpendicular numbered streets, including the important area north of K Street, cut through by Connecticut Avenue.

Dupont Circle: This area, to Downtown's north, might be called smart Washington in a single dose: Embassy-lined Massachusetts Avenue takes a northwest turn from the circle; New Hampshire Avenue, also a diplomatic enclave, heads northwest from it, with Connecticut Avenue and its shops due north. All about, amid oft-excellent restaurants and gossipy cafés, are smaller stores, book shops especially, but a diversity of others as well.

Georgetown: Noted for side streets with eighteenth- and early-nineteenth-century townhouses, for the university bearing its name, for restaurants and after-dark lures, Georgetown is, as well, a shopping district. M Street is the main drag, as filled with shops as eateries; and Wisconsin Avenue, which intersects it, is significant, too.

Adams-Morgan: This oddly named northerly neighborhood is a colorful mix of cultures—African and Hispanic, European and Yankee—with Columbia Road, leading from the area of Connecticut Avenue dominated by the Washington Hilton, its main thoroughfare, and Kalorama Park, due north, its terminus. Shops represent the diverse cultures of the neighborhood. Browseworthy.

Capitol Hill has, to understate, attributes other than shops. Still, the hundred boutiques in Union Station are of consequence, and Eastern Market, C and 7th streets, SE—called to your attention for its cafés (chapter 5)—is an absorbing place to check out the capital's most impressive sources of fresh produce.

SHOPPING MALLS ACCESSIBLE BY METRO

Residents of the District and its suburbs shop extensively at malls—as well they might. In this book I concentrate on a representative group of malls in town and/or accessible by Metro. Representative shops within the malls are called to your attention on later pages of this chapter, wherein stores are divided by category.

Georgetown Park (3200 M Street NW)is the in-town leader, hands down: an unlikely albeit successful meld of Federal and Victorian motifs, completely enclosed, with dramatic spaces on four levels. This one's good-looking enough to warrant a stroll, even if you're a positively adamant nonshopper.

Shops at National Place/National Press Club (F Street NW, between 13th and 14th streets): A loyal member of the National Press Club, in whose building this mall is anchored, I must confess that there are no irresistible boutiques in this cluster. The lure is convenience—including a number of places for an on-the-run breakfast, lunch, or pick-me-up—with 80-plus outlets all told on two attractive levels, heart of Downtown.

Union Station (50 Massachusetts Avenue NE), splendidly restored (chapter 2, "All around the Town," above) doubles as a mall—with 100 mostly good-quality shops.

Old Post Office (Pennsylvania Avenue NW at 11th Street): We must be—and I am, certainly—grateful that this exceptional turn-of-the-century Richardson Romanesque building, with one of Washington's memorable towers, has not only been saved but restored. The pity is that neither its shops nor its fast-food joints are in any way distinguished. But you do want to stop in for a look and, if it's a hot day, a cold drink. A pity that standards were not higher in the selection process.

Mazza Gallerie (Wisconsin at Western Avenue NW) is, to be sure, considerably northwest of the center, near the Maryland border. Its saving grace is location: at Friendship Heights Metro station. There's distinguished shopping here, with Nieman Marcus perhaps the best-known store.

White Flint (Kensington, Maryland) is reached by the same Metro route—the Red Line—as Mazza Gallerie, above. (It's not a bad idea to combine them on a single day's outing, lunching at one or the other.) White Flint—a few Metro stops beyond Mazza—is just over the state border in Maryland and has standout stores, Bloomingdale's, Lord & Taylor, and I. Magnin among them. Note, though, that it's not adjacent to the Metro. Take the escalator to the street upon arrival and you'll see a sign indicating the stop for a White Flint shuttle bus, for which, inappropriately I believe, there's an irritating small fare, when there should be none for passengers, who are, after all, customers or would-be customers.

Fashion Centre at Pentagon City (Pentagon City, between 15th Street and Army-Navy Drive, Arlington, Virginia) is a case of saving best for last. This, in my view at least, is the handsomest of the D.C.-area malls. Escalators lead directly from Pentagon City Metro station (Blue and Yellow lines) to the mall, and you're adjacent, as well, to the Ritz-Carlton Pentagon City, one of the region's standout hotels—and a nice spot for lunch. Two major department stores, New York–origin Macy's and Seattle-based Nordstrom, anchor this 130-shop cluster, among whose features are a dozen-plus restaurants and a six-screen Loews cinema.

PROFILING THE DEPARTMENT STORES

Although one of the major Washington-origin department stores, Garfinckel's, closed in the early 1990s, stores from other regions of the country—Seattle's classy Nordstrom, New York's increasingly upscale Macy's, trendy Bloomingdale's, and reliable Lord & Taylor, for example—have supplemented Washington's Big Two: Woodward & Lothrop and Hecht's. Service in the department stores, in town and beyond, is, in my experience, very good indeed. Here they are, alphabetically, as indeed are store categories that follow.

Bloomingdale's (White Flint Shopping Mall, Kensington, Maryland) is among the pioneer out-of-town department stores in the region. Although much of the merchandise is similar to that on sale in the original New York store, you must not expect the ambience of 59th Street and Lexington Avenue in Manhattan. This is by no means the handsomest of the department stores in the area, but quality is good. Children's clothing, linens, gourmet food, and a bakery are among main-floor departments, women's clothing and accessories are on 2, with men's clothing and men's and women's shoes on 3, and the restaurant (chapter 5), housewares, carpets, and luggage on 4.

Hecht's (12th and G Street NW, and branches in Maryland and Virginia) is one of the Washington-founded Big Two. Its main store (called Metro Center after the subway station beneath it, with which there's a direct connection) is a modern building and nicely staffed. Women's and men's accessories (Hecht's has super neckties) are on main, men's clothing on 2, women's clothing on 3 and 4, with kids' clothing also on 4. Housewares, including china and crystal, are in the basement, as is the store's convenient snack bar, Metro Fare (*Moderate*), which you pass by en route to or from the subway.

Lord & Taylor (White Flint shopping mall, Kensington, Maryland)—one of a number of branches of the Fifth Avenue-based store in the region—occupies two good-looking levels at White Flint, with cosmetics, accessories, and the like on main, as well as women's clothing, which extends to the second floor, sharing space with menswear, china, crystal, and gifts.

Macy's (Fashion Centre at Pentagon City, Arlington, Virginia) is as impressive from without—the main entrance is boldly arched—as within. This is a big Macy's. Its excellent men's store occupies fully half of main, with separate young men's and Ralph Lauren/Polo departments. On this same level are women's shoes, bags, and cosmetics, with additional women's clothing extending throughout the second floor. On 3, you find the fancy-food Marketplace (with a café—chapter 5), as well as housewares, home furnishings, and a big kids' section. Special services include a gift-consultant staff whose members will take you around the store to coordinate purchases; corporate gift service and a bridal registry.

Nordstrom (Fashion Center at Pentagon City, Arlington, Virginia) is co-anchor department store with Macy's (above) at Pentagon

City. It is, at least to this observer, the most imaginatively operated department store in the area, with its merchandise as high-
quality as its décor is smart and its sales staff razor-sharp, quick,
and cordial. Look for women's accessories and shoes on main,
additional women's wear on 2 along with an outstanding men's
clothing department, children's and infants' departments and
one of two restaurants (chapter 5) on 3. This store represents, in
my view, the most outstanding advance in retailing that the
Washington area has seen in recent years.

Woodward & Lothrop (11th and F streets NW, with a dozen and a
half branches in Maryland and Virginia): The old Garfinckel's
was, in its final years, more conservative, and the thriving Hecht's
is strongly competitive. Still, it is surely safe to term Woodie's No.
1 of the Washington-origin department stores. On its main
floor—one of the standout Art Deco interiors in town—are
cosmetics, women's accessories, and the like. The top-rank men's
and young men's departments occupy 2, while the 3rd and 4th
floors are devoted to women's clothing. Excellent china and
crystal sections are on 5, furniture on 6, housewares and the
more substantial of two restaurants (chapter 5) on 7. Woodie's
has a team of personal shoppers who will take you around the
store, a worth-knowing-about alteration service (on 9) that will
make repairs to your own clothing as well as alter newly purchased garments, shoe and shaver repair Down Under (the
basement), passport photo service on 5, bridal and gift registry
and travel agency on 7, hairdresser and barber shop, Ticketron service for theater, concerts, and sporting events on 2. Still
other services include Quixsearch, a computerized house- and
apartment-finding office for newcomers to the area.

SELECTED SHOPS BY CATEGORY

Antiques: Cherishables (1608 20th Street NW) sells eighteenth-
and nineteenth-century specialties including American furniture, accessories, and paintings; *David N. Friedman* (1319 Wisconsin Avenue NW)—furniture and other pieces, eighteenth- and
nineteenth-century; *Georgetown Antiques Center* (2918 M Street

NW) includes a number of shops with accessories, furniture, and paintings from the two preceding centuries, American and continental European; *Miller & Arney* (1737 Wisconsin Avenue NW) offers French eighteenth- and nineteenth-century furniture and accessories, including screens; *Peter Mack Brown* (1742 Wisconsin Avenue NW) stocks European and Oriental furniture and accessories.

Appliances: *Radio Shack* (1150 Connecticut Avenue NW; 1100 15th Street NW, Georgetown Park; other locations) is a good source of TVs, VCRs, stereos, and computers.

Art Galleries: *Anne O'Brien* (2114 R Street NW) specializes in contemporary sculpture created from varied materials, American and imported; *Adams-Davidson* (3233 P Street NW) is heavy on American work of the nineteenth century; *Franz Bader* (1701 Pennsylvania Avenue NW) draws on local talent; *Gallery K* (2010 R Street NW) leans toward art by contemporary Americans; *Guarisco* (2828 Pennsylvania Avenue NW) runs a gamut, with work from both sides of the Atlantic; *Harmattan* (228 7th Street SE) is a leading source of the arts of black Africa; *Mickelson* (707 G Street NW) shows both American and European paintings; *Old Print Gallery* (1220 31st Street NW) is well named—elderly and antique prints are its stock in trade; *Oskar Gallery* (2715 M Street NW) concentrates on art of Eastern Europe and the USSR. Last, watch newspapers for notices of art exhibitions in embassies, which often bring to the capital work by talented citizens of their countries.

Books: *B. Dalton* (1776 K Street NW, 50 Massachusetts Avenue NE, as well as shops at National Place, Mazza Gallerie, and White Flint shopping malls) is a national chain you no doubt know from home; *Bridge Street Books* (2814 Pennsylvania Avenue NW) has politics and philosophy among specialties; *Crown Books* has five Super Crowns outside D.C. (including White Flint Plaza, the largest, in Kensington, Maryland), as well as several Classic Crowns within the city limits; *Kramerbooks & Afterwords* (1517

Connecticut Avenue NW) is at once a source of literature—and of coffee and accompaniments in its adjacent café, an open-late (including all night Friday and Saturday) landmark of the Dupont Circle area; *Brentano's*—one of the historic names in U.S. bookstores—is located at Pentagon City Fashion Centre; linguists will find *Modern Language Bookstore* (3160 O Street NW) absorbing, with titles in French, German, and Spanish, and foreign-language dictionaries among specialties; *Nature Co.* (1323 Wisconsin Avenue NW and Fashion Centre at Pentagon City) sells not only books about nature but seeds and birdhouses, compasses and Eskimo soapstone sculptures; *Olsson's* (1307 19th Street NW, 1239 Wisconsin Avenue NW, 1900 L Street NW for records only, and other locations) stocks tens of thousands of titles on an extraordinary range of subjects, fiction and nonfiction as well as LPs, compact discs, and cassettes, both classical and popular—Wisconsin Avenue and Dupont Circle branches are open seven days; *Travel Books Unlimited* (4931 Cordell Avenue, Bethesda, Maryland), relatively recently doubled in size—not surprising, given its success—is one of the world's great sources of books on travel, atlases, maps, language cassettes, and foreign-language dictionaries and phrase books, with an astute lady named Rochelle Jaffe its guiding light—ask to speak with her if you've special requests, and ask for their catalog; *Waldenbooks*, the popular chain, has links at 1700 Pennsylvania Avenue NW, Georgetown Park shopping mall, and other regional points.

Cameras: Check out *Ritz Camera* (423 12th Street NW, 1029 Connecticut Avenue NW, 1239 Wisconsin Avenue NW, as well as White Flint and Fashion Centre at Pentagon City shopping malls, and other regional locations; *Camera One* (1101 14th Street NW) is another source.

Children's Clothes: The department stores (above) of course, but consider also *Gap Kids* (Fashion Centre at Pentagon City), *Kid's Closet* (1226 Connecticut Avenue NW and 1990 K Street NW)—and with toys, too; *Laura Ashley Mother & Child* (White Flint shopping mall); and *Little Sprout* (Georgetown Park shopping center).

China, Ceramics, Glass: There are choice selections in department stores, but be aware as well of *Ceramica Mia* (Willard Collection, 1455 Pennsylvania Avenue NW), which makes a specialty of hand-painted Italian ceramics that are charming; *Crate & Barrel* (Fashion Centre at Pentagon City), a Chicago-origin firm with nifty dinnerware, glassware, and kitchenware; *Martin's* (1304 Wisconsin Avenue NW) with big names in porcelain—Britain's Spode, France's Haviland, and Italy's Richard Ginori among them—as well as brands of crystal including France's Baccarat and Christofle silver flatware, among much else; and *Villeroy & Boch* (Fashion Centre at Pentagon City) with fine china imported from its factories in Luxembourg and Germany.

Chocolates: The department stores have tempting candy counters (try to pass by the fudge at *Woodward & Lothrop*). *Nieman-Marcus* (Mazza Gallerie shopping mall) sells boxed chocolates with its own label that are scrumptious; *Godiva* and *Schoof's* are both Belgian and have outlets at Georgetown Park shopping mall.

Crafts: *Appalachian Spring* (Union Station and 1415 Wisconsin Avenue NW) is a source of wares quite as lovely as its catchy name. It's all American and handmade, the range blankets through jewelry, glass through rugs. Expensive. *Artifactory* (641 Indiana Avenue NW) deals in West African sculpture, masks, jewelry, and textiles, including costly Kente cloth—each bedspread-sized cloth a composite of handwoven squares of heavy silk, worn as ceremonial cloaks by men in Ghana, in whose Ashanti province they are created. *Indian Craft Shop* (U.S. Department of the Interior Building, 1800 C Street NW, with a branch at 1050 Wisconsin Avenue NW) specializes in baskets, pottery, and other American Indian crafts. *Santa Fe Collection* (Union Station) brings Indian artisanship of the Southwest to Washington: silver, blankets, pottery, and other lovely objects.

Cutlery: *Hoffritz* (Union Station, as well as Fashion Centre at Pentagon City and White Flint shopping malls) are links of a chain dealing primarily in kitchen knives (many German imports of excellent quality), scissors, and manicure kits.

Dog Supplies: Bone Jour (2818 M Street NW) takes the cake—dog biscuit, rather—for being the most cleverly named store in town. Bravo, B.J.!

Drugstores/Pharmacies: People's Drug (7 Dupont Circle, NW) is open all night every night and is but one of scores of People's Drug outlets all over D.C. and surrounding territory; other Washington addresses include 1009 Connecticut Avenue NW, 2125 E Street NW, 1536 North Capitol Street NW, and 3601 12th Street NW).

Flowers: Georgetown Park Flowers (Georgetown Park shopping mall) is a reliable all-purpose florist. *Greenworks* (Willard Collection, 1455 Pennsylvania Avenue NW) is worth knowing about when you want a floral arrangement that will impress your host.

Furs: Rosendorf Evans (1750 K Street NW) is nothing if not diverse with regard to skins—beaver, fox, lynx, mink, sable—as with designers, including Anne Klein and Arnold Scaasi.

Gas Stations, all-night, that is, include *Exxon,* 22nd and M streets NW; *Chevron,* 22nd and P streets NW; and *Georgetown Texaco* (which tows), 1576 Wisconsin Avenue NW.

Hairdressers and Barbers: include *Woodward & Lothrop* department store (11th and F streets NW, second floor—for men as well as women), and these hairdressers, often unisex: *Bruno Dessange* (1523 Wisconsin Avenue NW), a French chain that's also in New York; *Ilo* (1637 Wisconsin Avenue NW); *Okyo* (1519 Wisconsin Avenue NW), and *Robin Weir* (2134 P Street NW, Georgetown Park shopping mall, and Westin Hotel, 1401 M Street NW). Note, too, *Elizabeth Arden* (1147 Connecticut Avenue NW, and 5225

Wisconsin Avenue NW) and the widespread *Hair Cutters* chain, blanketing the region with D.C. outlets at 1645 Connecticut Avenue NW, 1342 G Street NW, and 3209 M Street NW—among others.

Jewelry: Black, Starr & Frost (5300 Wisconsin Avenue NW; Fashion Centre at Pentagon City) originated in New York; fine diamonds, gold, and watches. *J. E. Caldwell Co.* (1140 Connecticut Avenue NW and White Flint shopping mall) dates to 1839; pearls are a specialty, along with diamonds, gold, and watches. *Cartier* (1127 Connecticut Avenue NW, in the Mayflower Hotel) is the 1847-founded French-oriented firm, now with considerable branches. *Charles Schwartz & Son* (Willard Collection, 1455 Pennsylvania Avenue NW) is still another old house—founded in Washington in 1888—with Rolex among its watch brands and fine jewelry. *Galt & Bro.* (Metropolitan Square, 15th and G streets NW) bills itself as both America's oldest jeweler and Washington's oldest business; year of founding: 1802. China and crystal as well as jewelry and silver. *Time Flies* (Union Station) presents an interesting, at times amusing, selection of watches.

Kitchen Equipment: *Williams Sonoma* (White Flint shopping mall) has expanded east from San Francisco; glassware and tableware. *Kitchen Bazaar* (Fashion Centre at Pentagon City) is among the more imaginative such shops in the region. *B. Gallerie* (Union Station) is worth investigating with wares not only for the kitchen but for the dining room as well.

Luggage: *MCM* (Willard Collection, 1455 Pennsylvania Avenue NW) is an Italian firm that's also in New York; very snazzy print-design trademark pieces, brass- and leather-accented. *T. Anthony* (1201 Rhode Island Avenue NW) is an outlet of a posh New York store; everything is top quality and costly.

Men's Clothing: *Alexander Julian* (1242 Wisconsin Avenue NW) is a retail outlet for clothing—suits, sports jackets, shirts, ties—

designed by the chap whose name it takes. *Britches* is a ranking men's shop—adept at style, selection, and service—whose main store is at 1247 Wisconsin Avenue NW, but which has many branches, including one at Fashion Centre, Pentagon City; a group of Britches Great Outdoors shops (sportswear) and Great Outdoors for Women's Shops as well. *Brooks Brothers* (1840 L Street NW and 5500 Wisconsin Avenue in Chevy Chase, Maryland) is the formerly exclusive Madison Avenue, New York, store that has become a massive chain. Still, it continues to stock its long-famous conservative line (including the button-down-collar shirts it claims to have created). *Custom Shop* (Georgetown Mall, Fashion Centre at Pentagon City, White Flint shopping mall, and 1033 Connecticut Avenue NW) is a New York firm whose specialty is made-to-measure shirts at relatively reasonable tabs, as such things go; ties, too. *The Gap* (Wisconsin Avenue at N Street NW, 1217 Connecticut Avenue NW) is a burgeoning chain with mid-category prices for nicely styled and tailored sportswear, often for women and kids as well as gents. *Hugo Boss* (1517 Wisconsin Avenue NW and 1201 Connecticut Avenue NW) hails from Germany, where I was told in the course of researching *Germany at Its Best* that "Hugo" is actually three guys, not one. Very nice sense of style. *Joseph A. Bank* (1118 19th Street NW and Fashion Centre at Pentagon City) came to the neighborhood by way of Baltimore, from whose headquarters it established a successful mail-order business; neckties are a principal reason, but Bank has a complete clothing line, mid-category to expensive. *Linea Pitti* (Georgetown Park shopping mall) features pricey European couturiers like Gianni Versace, Claude Montana, and Gianfranco Ferre. *Polo Ralph Lauren* (1220 Connecticut Avenue NW) presents new designs each season, but the clothes and accessories are essentially classic-style and grow ever more costly. *Raleighs* (1133 Connecticut Avenue NW) is, not unlike the Wallachs chain in New York, a retail outlet of the Hart Schaffner & Marx clothing manufacturers, with HSM and other labels including Austin Reed, Christian Dior, and the premium-tab Burberrys and Hickey-Freeman. And with a women's department. *Tommy Hilfiger* (Georgetown Park shopping mall) is a snappy young designer with a chain of shops in which his wares are retailed. Hilfiger is inventive but never way out. Mid-category to expensive.

Men's and Women's Clothing: *Abercrombie & Fitch* (Georgetown Park shopping mall): New Yorkers around at the time still have not accepted the razing of the long-on-scene Abercrombie & Fitch store on Madison Avenue. Abercrombie's resumed business eventually, and though it's not the Abercrombie's of yore, it's nice—with stylish mid-category duds, dressy and sporty both, for dad, mom, and the kids. *Burberrys* (1155 Connecticut Avenue NW): Downtown Washington north of, say, K Street has so few instantly recognizable landmarks that the red-brick, turn-of-the-century building-cum-corner tower that houses Burberrys is welcome in the neighborhood. Of course you know the plaid that lines its trenchcoats and serves as the pattern for its scarves. But this London-origin chain sells a complete line of men's and women's clothing and accessories, the lot of it expensive. *Saks Fifth Avenue* (5555 Wisconsin Avenue NW, Chevy Chase, Maryland) is a hop and skip from Mazza Gallerie shopping mall. Pricey but classy men's and women's clothing and accessories.

Museum and Government-Building Shops: Rare is the building in Washington admitting spectators that does not have a shop—or sell *something*. Even the White House vends postcards of its interiors in addition to the illustrated book long on sale about the mansion (invariably opening with a welcome from the first lady in residence). There's a shop in the *Capitol*, too, unexceptional though it may be. Of others in public buildings, the best, in my view, are those of the *Library of Congress* (1st Street and Independence Avenue NE) and the *Supreme Court of the United States* (East Capitol and 1st streets NE). Virtually every museum has a shop of some sort. Smaller—but okay—shops include those of the *Corcoran Gallery* (17th Street and New York Avenue NW) and of the *National Portrait Gallery* and *National Museum of American Art* (sharing the same building at G and 8th streets NW).

But the important museum shops are those of the *National Gallery of Art* (Constitution Avenue, 4th to 6th streets NW, in the long passage linking East and West Buildings on the Mall), with huge stocks of art books, reproductions, and posters—framed, if you prefer—and postcards of paintings in the collection; *National Museum of African Art* (950 Independence Avenue SW), with virtually all of its stock imported from Africa, including handwoven silk Kente cloths from Ghana and good-quality masks; *National Museum of American History* (Constitution Avenue, 12th to 14th streets NW), down a couple of flights but worth the trek, with a fascinating cache of books on our nation's history and imaginative wares, all U.S.-made, with objects of china, glass, tin, and textiles; *National Museum of Natural History* (Constitution Avenue at 10th Street NW), with minerals, to be sure, but other theme-related wares, books included, the lot adored by kids who pour in to have a look; *Arthur M. Sackler Gallery* (1050 Independence Avenue SW), relatively small but with choice Oriental imports, as for example Chinese cinnabar lacquerware; and—although it is not actually a museum even if under the aegis of the Smithsonian Institution—*National Zoo* (3000 Connecticut Avenue NW), a huge and amusing shop, the most fun of the lot, with animals in every form save live, and as popular with adults as with children; and *National Air and Space Museum* (Independence Avenue at 6th Street NW), brimming with books, games, and all manner of assorted doodads based on the themes of space and aviation, invariably customer-packed.

Opticians: *Lugène* (Georgetown Park shopping mall) is a reliable shop that's a branch of a New York–founded company. *L'Image* (White Flint shopping mall) provides prompt service.

Pens: *Washington Pen Co.* (Union Station), imported and domestic, reasonably priced and costly. A big selection.

Records and Tapes: *Record World* (Georgetown Park, Fashion Centre at Pentagon City, White Flint shopping malls); *Sam Goody* (Union Station and 3111 M Street NW), New York–born, with diverse stocks.

Shoes: The department stores (Bloomingdale's, Hecht's, Lord & Taylor, Macy's, Nordstrom, for example) and specialty shops (like I. Magnin, Saks Fifth Avenue, and Nieman Marcus) are shoe-territory par excellence. But consider also *Bally of Switzer-*

land (1020 Connecticut Avenue NW); *G. H. Bass* (Fashion Centre at Pentagon City), whose loafers are justifiably esteemed; *Florsheim* (1218 Connecticut Avenue NW and 5300 Wisconsin Avenue NW), arguably the best-known of the American men's chains; links of the *Hahn* chain (including those at 1776 K Street NW and 14th and G street NW); the *Hess* chain (Georgetown Park and White Flint shopping malls, as well as 1820 L Street NW, 20th Street and Pennsylvania Avenue NW, and 3222 M Street NW); and *Johnston and Murphy* (1718 G Street NW and 1814 M Street NW), a quality men's chain.

Shoe Repair: *Fortuna's* (in the Washington Square Office Building, 1050 Connecticut Avenue NW) and *Woodward & Lothrop* (11th and F streets NW). At both: while you wait.

Stationery: *Dempsey & Carroll* (Georgetown Park), a branch of a store long established in New York, is a source of engraved stationery and invitations to your wedding. Classy.

Toys: *F.A.O. Schwartz* (Georgetown Mall and White Flint shopping mall), a veritable Fifth Avenue institution in New York (you wait in line to get in, at Christmas) is particularly celebrated for stuffed animals, some of them veritable giants.

Women's Clothing: *Ann Taylor* (Georgetown Park, Fashion Centre at Pentagon City, and White Flint shopping mall): Links of a national chain popular for its mid-category, classic-style but classy designs; *Benetton* (1350 Connecticut Avenue NW, 2001 M Street NW, Mazza Gallerie, and White Flint shopping malls, other locations) is of Italian origin, and has spread throughout the United States because its style is tailored but catchy and its mid-category prices affordable; *Chanel* (Willard Collection, 1455 Pennsylvania Avenue NW) is the genuine Paris article; suits and costume jewelry, accessories and cosmetics—with men's ties, if you want to buy a bauble for us, ladies; *Forgotten Woman* (Mazza Gallerie shopping mall) is a branch of a successful New York shop specializing in larger sizes; *I. Magnin* (White Flint shopping mall) is a second-level magnet at White Flint; women who know or know of the West Coast original pop in—clothing, accessories, shoes; *Jaeger* (1202 Connecticut Avenue NW and 3251 Prospect Street NW in Georgetown Court) are branches in the Colonies of a highly esteemed London firm, with smartly tailored clothing and accessories for women; *Lane Bryant* (932 F Street NW and Fashion Centre at Pentagon City) is known nationally for good-looking duds in larger sizes at mid-category tabs; *Laura Ashley* (3213 M Street NW, Fashion Centre at Pentagon City, and White Flint shopping mall) are links of the international chain founded by a Welshwoman a couple of decades back, with small-pattern designs of fabrics and smart albeit classic style the trademark; *Liberty of London* (Georgetown Park shopping mall) is London-based albeit internationally celebrated for its textiles, neckties, and, in the case of this outlet, women's accessories—conservative and tasteful; *Rodier Plus* (Fashion Centre at Pentagon City) is a distinguished French firm, noted for tailored separates and accessories, at mid- to high-category tabs; *Saks Fifth Avenue* (5555 Wisconsin Avenue, Chevy Chase, Maryland) is a branch of the New York original, with modish fashions, accessories like bags and gloves included, and expensive; *Saks Jandel* (5510 Wisconsin Avenue, Chevy Chase, Maryland), though no relation to Saks Fifth Avenue, its neighbor in Chevy Chase, is a specialty shop with name couturiers—Karl Lagerfeld, for example—the basis of its stock; *Talbots* (4801 Massachusetts Avenue NW; Georgetown Park, Fashion Centre at Pentagon City, White Flint shopping mall, and other locations) made its reputation on contemporary variations on the theme of classical—with the prices right; *The Limited* (Georgetown Park and Fashion Centre at Pentagon City shopping mall), a West Coast chain that is succeeding on the Atlantic Seabord; mid- to upper-category tabs.

Acknowledgments

The final research trip for this book—an in-depth exploration of the nation's capital that was the culmination of shorter bouts of discovery undertaken over many years, has been principally aided and abetted by the Washingtonian par excellence—Thomas G. Murphy, tourism promotion manager of the Washington Convention and Visitors Association, supportive of this project from the start, and the man who virtually singlehandedly represents Washington, with few facets of which he is unfamiliar, to the nation's travel press. I am most appreciative of Tom's help, and I want, as well, to express sincere thanks to these friends and colleagues, alphabetically, for their personal kindness and professional cooperation:

Phyliss Allen, Cathy Arbert, Jane L. G. Barton, Diane Bechtol, Deborah M. Bernstein, Bettye Bradley, Rev. Winthrop Brainerd, Anita Claybrook, Cheryl Crispen, Bill Comstock, L. Paige Dagurt, John Dawson, Vivian A. Deuschl, Joyce de Guerin, Mary Jane Enterkin, June Farrell, John Feather.

Also Heather Freeman, David W. Giger, John S. Gleiber, Sheila J. Greenwald, Linda C. Gwinn, Marisa M. Hanscum, Christopher W. Hart, Mary Hassell, Jean Hayes, James S. Henderson, Alan J. Hermesch, Matt Hessburg, Mary Johnson, Diana T. Kaiser, Brian Kelleher, Patricia Duricka Kelly, Jeanne Kendig, David Kidd, Carolyn Killian, Earl Kittleman.

Also Kristin Krathwohl, Sandy Lavery, Mort Lawrence, Hulda Lawrence, Patsy Lee, Paul Limbert, Tammi Long, Beth Lucca, Ann McCracken, Michelle McFaul, Paula Mohr, Meredith Pillon, Carol Poister, Abraham Pokrassa, Thomas F. Puccio, Rita Rehman, Paula B. Rothenberg, Karen Rugen.

Also Linda St. Thomas, Gayle Serfaty, Stefanie L. Sferra, Anne Smith, George F. Söderberg II, Renée Kluger Subrin, Richard Swain, Heidi Swanson, Anne Sweeney, H. A. Tanakorn, Sharyn Thomas, Judy Turner-Meyer, Michael Van Deven, John P. Washko, Dianne M. Welch, Dashiel Wham, Rod White, William Maxwell Wood, and J. J. Zarza.

Appreciation, too, to Max Drechsler, the research editor for my *World at Its Best* series; my agent, Anita Diamant; and last but hardly least, my editor, Michael Ross, editorial director of Passport Books.

—R.S.K.

Index

ABOUT THE AUTHOR

Robert S. Kane's initial writing stint came about when, as an Eagle Scout, he was editor of the [Boy Scout] *Troop Two Bugle* in his native Albany, New York. After graduation from Syracuse University's noted journalism school, he did graduate work at England's Southampton University, first making notes as he explored in the course of class field trips through the Hampshire countryside. Back in the U.S., he worked, successively, for the *Great Bend* (Kansas) *Daily Tribune, Staten Island Advance, New York Herald Tribune,* and *New York World-Telegram & Sun* before becoming travel editor of, first, *Playbill,* and later *Cue* and *50 Plus.* His byline has appeared in such leading magazines as *Travel & Leisure, Vogue, House & Garden, Atlantic, Harper's Bazaar, Family Circle, New York, Saturday Review,* and *Modern Bride;* and such newspapers as the *Newark Star-Ledger, New York Post, New York Daily News, New York Times, Los Angeles Times, Chicago Sun-Times, Boston Globe, San Diego Union, Dallas Morning News, San Francisco Examiner,* and *Toronto Globe & Mail.* And he guests frequently, with the subject travel, on TV and radio talk shows.

Africa A to Z, the first U.S.-published guide to largely independent, post–World War II Africa, was the progenitor of his acclaimed 14-book *A to Z* series, other pioneering volumes of which were *Eastern Europe A to Z,* the first guide to the USSR and the Soviet Bloc countries as seen through the eyes of a candid American author, and *Canada A to Z,* the first modern-day, province-by-province guide to the world's second-largest country. His current *World at Its Best* series includes two volumes *(Britain at Its Best* and *France at Its Best),* tapped by a pair of major book clubs, and a third *(Germany at Its Best)* that's a prize-winner.

Kane, the only American authoring an entire multivolume travel series, has the distinction of having served as president of both the Society of American Travel Writers and the New York Travel Writers' Association, and is a member, as well, of the National Press Club (Washington), P.E.N., Authors Guild, Society of Professional Journalists/Sigma Delta Chi, and American Society of Journalists and Authors. He makes his home on the Upper East Side of Manhattan.